WRITING ON THE MOVE

PITTSBURGH SERIES IN COMPOSITION, LITERACY, AND CULTURE

David Bartholomae and Jean Ferguson Carr, Editors

WRITING ON THE MOVE

Migrant Women and the Value of Literacy

REBECCA LORIMER LEONARD

University of Pittsburgh Press

Published by the University of Pittsburgh Press, Pittsburgh, Pa., 15260
Copyright © 2017, University of Pittsburgh Press
All rights reserved
Manufactured in the United States of America
Printed on acid-free paper
10 9 8 7 6 5 4 3 2 1

Cataloging-in-Publication data is available from the Library of Congress

ISBN 13: 978-0-8229-6505-3
ISBN 10: 0-8229-6505-4

Cover art: Sculpture by Nora Valdez
Cover design by Melissa Dias-Mandoly

For the three Idas

CONTENTS

Acknowledgments   ix

PREFACE: Traveling Literacies   xi

INTRODUCTION: Why Writing Matters   3

CHAPTER 1. Studying Writing on the Move   18

CHAPTER 2. Fluidity: When Writing Moves   32

CHAPTER 3. Fixity: When Writing Stalls   66

CHAPTER 4. Friction: When Writing Stalls in Motion   92

CHAPTER 5. Deep Contradictions in the Value of Literacy   123

Appendixes   135

Notes   143

Bibliography   157

Index   177

ACKNOWLEDGMENTS

I have been fortunate to encounter smart, challenging people throughout the course of this research project, and each of them has left a mark on this book. I am grateful first and foremost to the women whose voices give this book life. There would be no book if not for their generosity and wisdom about multilingual lives. I wish I could spend much more time talking with them about language and writing, their students and their children, their work and their communities.

My University of Massachusetts–Amherst colleagues—Rebecca Dingo, David Fleming, Anne Herrington, Haivan Hoang, Donna LeCourt, and Janine Solberg—have modeled how to be balanced, human academics, and I am thankful for their example. The graduate and undergraduate students I've been fortunate to work with at UMass, especially in the Writing Center, shaped the book's conception of literacy's consequences. The book especially has benefited immensely from the sharp eyes and brain of my research assistant, Jenny Krichevsky.

I am grateful to the community of University of Wisconsin–Madison colleagues who support each other in pursuit of ambitious ideas and curiosity-driven research. In particular, I appreciate the feedback and virtual writing accountability provided by Rebecca Nowacek, Tim Laquintano, and Annette Vee. My dissertation committee—Morris Young, Michael Bernard-Donals, Jane Zeungler, and Christa Olson—provided early feedback on this project that pushed me to take the project seriously. I am immensely grateful to Deborah Brandt, who once asked a roomful of graduate students what we felt responsible for, which helped me to understand both that I should figure that out and that I had entered a profession where that mattered.

The ideas in this book developed over the course of many years and formative encounters with groups of scholars. The conversations that covered the walls of our (very cold) room at the 2013 UMass Transnational Literacy Seminar honed my understanding of what transnational literacy could be and might not be. The Rhetoric Society of America (RSA) Summer Institute workshops and seminars on the rhetoric of multilingual writing, translingual rhetorics, comparative rhetorics, and transnational rhetorical research influenced my thinking in ways that shape the book's introduction and first chapter especially. I am indebted to the generous scholars who ran these RSA gatherings and gave participants feedback: Suresh Canagarajah, Maria Jerskey, Xiaoye You, LuMing Mao, Arabella Lyon, Rebecca Dingo, and Sara McKinnon. The Watson seminar on Mobility Work in Composition took place as I was completing revisions on this book, and the conversations with seminar scholars and students beneficially impacted how I articulate the consequences of this research. I am especially grateful to Eli Goldblatt, Anis Bawarshi, and Bruce Horner for their close and careful comments on my work there. Participating in Roger Waldinger's National Endowment for the Humanities (NEH) seminar on The Cross-border Connection updated my reading in migration studies and pushed me to frame the exigence and meaning of my research for audiences beyond my field. My fellow participants' wide-ranging questions especially impacted chapter 3 of this book. I am grateful for the continued existence of organizations like the NEH and for their continued support of research in the humanities.

I continue to marvel at the generosity of my field and its scholars. Feedback on early versions of chapter 4 from Ellen Cushman encouraged me to think harder about the phenomena of immobility in literacy. Christina Haas's feedback on my article in *Written Communication* shaped the ways I present my methods in this book. Conference conversations with Gail Shuck, Min-Zhan Lu, Steve Alvarez, Sara Alvarez, Amy Wan, Susan Meyers, Deirdre Vinyard, and Shanti Bruce have been essential to keeping me on my theoretical and practical toes. Most of all, I am so thankful for the always insightful, always generous reading relationships I've been fortunate to develop with Kate Vieira and Angela Rounsaville. They slow me down when I need to think harder and speed me up when my motivation lags.

Finally, I am thankful for the dinner table conversation of my parents, Jon and Kathy, who modeled teacher talk early on and taught me what it means to critique and care about educational systems. I am deeply and immensely grateful to Ben Leonard, whose support of my work is superhuman. I am uniquely thankful for my sister, Christina, who I've been conversing with since before she could talk and with whom I have shared the most important and intellectual conversations of my life.

PREFACE
TRAVELING LITERACIES

Writing on the Move: Migrant Women and the Value of Literacy originated in a community writing center where I worked with several migrant women on their writing. Every Saturday afternoon, I worked with whoever walked in the door on whatever writing project they brought with them. Library materials are by definition intended to be circulated; literacy in the library likewise was handed off, passed around, exchanged. In the library's single large room, language and literacy moved through people's hands and mouths, in and out the door.

As I worked side-by-side with these writers, I was often caught off guard by their language and literacy repertoires—reading strategies based in three or four languages, or writing habits informed by previous teaching, nursing, or communications jobs. I wasn't surprised by their knowledge per se, since my previous ESL teaching experience taught me long ago that adult literacy and language learners bring far more knowledge, skills, and life experience to the table than many curricula and textbooks acknowledge. Instead, I was surprised by how their literate repertoires didn't seem to serve them in their lives in the United States, even as their repertoires were clearly supporting them in our interactions in the community writing center. I was surprised by the conviction, good humor, and control with which many of them passed literacies to me. The vast literate resources they called upon to conduct our exchanges led me to wonder about the histories of their multilingual literacy practices. I was curious about why their repertoires did or did not move with them from their home countries to the United States. How did migration to the United States alter or affect their writing? Among which languages had these literacy practices traveled before ending up in English? How were these writers propelled into migration or held back by their literacy? This curiosity led me to conduct a pilot study with one Azerbaijani woman with whom I worked at the center. That small case study led to this book.

In the years since I worked at the library, the world has witnessed several intense regional migrations caused by civil wars, religious persecution, environmental change, and gang violence that forced traditional and new receiving countries to respond (or not respond) to human movement in unprecedented ways. The historical long view shows this migration is not entirely new. Scholars point to evidence that late nineteenth-century global migration was more extensive than late twentieth, and to claims that the invention of the passport created regulation of what was formerly an "extraordinarily free-moving world" (Favell 394).[1] Scholars critique claims that increasing human movement has resulted in increasingly complex diversity, saying this is a matter of Eurocentric perception rather than actual social change.[2] Still others historicize mobility by conceiving of illegal migrants not as those who cross borders without documentation, but as laborers doing what they've always done for work, continuing their migratory work practices as administrative categories, policies, and paperwork shift around them (Karakayali and Rigo 124).

However, scholars admit that even given the historical precedent of human mobility, a qualitative shift is taking place in which the circulation of people and products are "of a different order": restructured global capital and technological change and the "massification" of movement after the early nineteenth century have made transnational links more dense, bureaucratized, and of a higher frequency and velocity.[3] Held et al. list a number of "unprecedented phenomena" brought about by globalization, including the institutionalization of worldwide organizational infrastructures and the reflexivity that comes with globalization being named: a worldwide "consciousness of global interconnectedness" and "self-conscious . . . visions of world order" (430). Thus, although transnational movement is an ordinary rather than exceptional human experience, movement remains a vibrant conceptual framework, shedding light on connections or processes previously overlooked. So perhaps with an eye toward history, I might still productively ask questions about how movement affects what multilingual writers can do with their literacies.

In fact, as international migrant numbers increase, rising from 154 million in 1990 to 232 million in 2013, teachers, employers, and the public at large find themselves among increasingly linguistically diverse students, coworkers, and neighbors. Much of this contemporary migration involves international migrants in a great deal of transnational communicative activity, producing and being subjected to a broad writing landscape of applications, forms, transcribed interviews, online communication, personal messages, and papered files, in addition to the work, school, and home writing occurring before and after migration. This writing activity is shot through with belonging and disorientation, state status and illegality, imagined futures and survival—all deeply felt or ambivalently tolerated in the everyday literacy experiences of migrants.

Writing on the Move seeks to understand the struggles of multilingual migrant writers for repertoire recognition. It aims to understand the socioeconomic tensions that allow or disallow repertoire mobility, asking how social and economic values regulate repertoires moving into and across them. I believed at the beginning of this project, and still believe, that the stakes of such studies are quite high, not only as university populations diversify but also as the discourse around neoliberalism and globalization continues to make and break promises about how language and literacy shape the geographic, social, and economic mobility of migrants.

WRITING ON THE MOVE

INTRODUCTION
WHY WRITING MATTERS

I ask Tashi how she thinks her life might be different if she didn't know how to write. She responds that without writing she wouldn't have made it to the United States or into her university nursing program. Everything involves writing, she says, "immigration procedures, interviewing, everything." Tashi's nursing program accepted her "all through the writing straight," and her immigration application required more written than oral communication. Being able to write to her husband in English, e-mailing him from India while he was a student in the United States, was essential to their relationship. Lack of a Tibetan keyboard demanded communication be in English. Tashi says, "So I was like, yeah, that's how writing saves."

As we talk in a study room in the campus nursing building, Tashi's hands constantly move, in the air and on the table we sit around. I can hear that movement on the interview recording. Her hands loop as she describes the karmic repercussions of not thanking sponsors who funded her early education. Her pointer fingers draw connected rings when she explains the "concentric" science curriculum she taught in India. Her palms skim circles on the table to demonstrate how she reads to understand "how the words go around" in writing. Around and around Tashi's hands go as she tells me how writing has moved in her life and how it has moved her. Since she was little, Tashi has written among Kannada, Hindi, Tibetan, and English. She has moved her self-taught literacies from home to school and back home to teach her parents. She wrote her way into college, graduate school, a teaching job, and another college in the United States. "So it all matters," she says. "Writing matters."

Tashi's belief that writing matters, and that it saves, is not hyperbolic; it is simply lived reality. Because she has learned, taught, and lived as a multilingual migrant in India and in the United States, Tashi understands writing in mundane and sophisticated ways. She connects writing to every kind of movement in her life. She reads not only for pleasure or content but to understand "how it works." She treats revision as hard essential work. She expresses surprise at the casual approach to writing of her U.S. college peers. When I wonder aloud if the immigration process was hard for her, she shrugs that "it wasn't too much" for her and she has been helping others with the writing it requires. Tashi is highly literate. She has a deep understanding of the writing process, of how to use her languages for rhetorical effect, of how to pass on these practices to other writers. But as a nursing student in the United States, she often has struggled to earn the grades or respect that might come easily to someone so experienced in writing in English and other languages. Although Tashi has identified as a highly literate person nearly her entire life, she also has found her literacies devalued in the United States, often to the detriment of the literate development that would grant the social and personal goals she imagined migrating for in the first place.

Like the migrant women featured throughout this book, Tashi experiences the perplexing contradictions of multilingual writing every day.[1] At work, at school, and with family, Tashi often finds herself at the complex intersection of simultaneously valued and devalued communication. The movement of migrants, and the language and literacy traditions they bring along, sometimes challenges the literate power structures they meet along the way. They encounter discrimination against accented or multilingual communication in contexts that maintain prestige-based (sometimes invisible) language standards. These are the tensions this book explores. Why are migrants' literate repertoires so unevenly valued? How do migrants maintain multilingual identities while writing against the pressures of assimilation, language change, and identity shifts in a new place? What does tracing writing on the move reveal about how literacy is valued?

Writing on the Move: Migrant Women and the Value of Literacy responds to these questions by showing how social and economic values affect what multilingual writers can do.[2] Throughout the book I explore how social and economic values in school, workplaces, and governments (held by teachers, colleagues, border agents, relatives, and the writers themselves) shape how literate repertoires come to be recognized or ignored. The book's structure, however, turns this equation inside out: I look at moving literacies to see how values work. Each chapter features a different kind of literate movement—fluid, fixed, frictive—to show how valuation differently enables writers to move their literacies. Writers move fluidly when their values agree with those of others; writers' movement is fixed when their and others' values are mismatched; and writers experience friction when their values simultaneously do and don't correspond to those of others. In three turns, fluidity, fixity, and friction prove to be different examples of the same phenomenon: multilingual migrants writing with and against the currents of socioeconomic values. Step by step, the book builds a process of literate valuation, supporting the main argument: literacies are revalued because they move.

This book is based on my qualitative study of twenty-five multilingual migrant women in the United States, which is described in detail in chapter 1. I initially set out to challenge narratives of downwardly mobile migrant women by exploring how multilingual women used their literacies to get what they needed or do what they wanted after migration. But as I met more and more writers, eventually creating a participant group from seventeen countries, cumulatively speaking twenty-two languages, my interest turned away from simple upward or downward social mobility and toward the phenomenon of mobile literacy itself. Beyond asking if literacies do or do not move among languages and the places these women have lived in the world, I focused instead on the how and why of movement: the ways in which literacies move, the agents of that movement, and the fluctuating values that mediate it. Throughout this study and the writing of this book, I have found that literate lives are not simply mobile or immobile, free or fixed, successful or failed, but are instead lived at a nexus of prestige, prejudice, and power that creates multiple mobilities, simultaneous struggle and success.

The argument that literacies and lives are subject to changing values is likely an obvious statement to many. But the commonsense quality of this claim should ring slightly false against the backdrop of contemporary conversations around migration and multilingualism in and outside academia.[3] Academic understandings of multilingual writing are in process. Researchers and teachers continue to debate the merits of teaching language standards, or encouraging students to use multiple languages in writing, or treating classrooms as experimental spaces while acknowledging that other spaces privilege dominant codes.[4] Rarely do scholars consider how the values that literacy meets as it moves affect these debates.[5] Questions remain about the communication preferences of increasingly globalized workplaces, the access that may or may not result from fluency in prestige codes, the cognitive and empathetic benefits of multilingual literacies, and the importance for humans of actualizing more than one cultural and linguistic background. In academia we continue, rightly, to worry about who should be giving or withholding which literate resources to whom.

Furthermore, widely held notions of literacy and language beyond academia are basic enough to cause real problems for multilingual migrants. Legislation that keeps literacy education monolingual in a dominant language, implicit or explicit policy that withholds language assistance in public services, everyday linguistic discrimination around accents, unconventional forms, or nondominant languages used in public—these are all official, institutionalized results of common misunderstandings about language acquisition and use. They are also the result of racism, ethnocentrism, and fear of the unknown. The coming together of these elements, particularly in a period of intensified migration, creates an especially fraught set of attitudes toward multilingualism, accent, and writing practices associated with difference. These attitudes stem from short-term memory of immigrant origins, bootstrap beliefs in meritocratic success, and cyclical xenophobia rooted in English monolingual, border-based, majority-white national assumptions. Literate success and struggle are assumed to be regulated by neutral literacy skills rather than by powerful social beliefs. Reading and writing in a dominant language continues to be treated as a miracle method for migrant assimilation, and a lack of dominant language literacy becomes evidence of migrants' unsuitability for citizenship. Such logic permeates debates about education policy, detention or deportation, and such public services as health care and welfare. It also makes the values that regulate languages and writers invisible.

In other words, the claim that literacies and lives are subject to changing values is not so obvious as to be recognized by those who make decisions about migrant literacies and lives. We have yet to decide who is responsible for literacy or who is in charge of developing and sharing literate resources. We have yet to fully consider how literacy materials of migration (passports, tests, keyboards, visas) and literacy contexts at the crossroads of mobility (immigration interview rooms, lines at the border, ESL classrooms, and refugee camps) are saturated with values. *Writing on the Move* assumes that there is work to be done in understanding the relationship of literacy, mobility, and values. The book extends transnational literacy studies and research on multilingual writing by accounting for the way social and economic values regulate the relative worth of migrants' literacies. As a result, the book offers a theory of literacy that complicates metaphors of mobility, transfer, and translation used in research on writing, showing how social and economic values have real consequences for multilingual migrant lives, including their felt ability to write and communicate. Writing matters not just for who multilingual migrant writers are and what skills they have, but also for what they can do in and understand about the world.

IN TERMS OF LITERACY

Writing on the Move relies on several key terms that are used in a variety of ways in research on multilingual writing. To put these terms in the context of literacy, and to use them with care, I explain what I mean by "literate repertoires and resources," "literate movement," and "literate valuation." In my use of "literate" I follow Prior's "literate activity," which indicates "situated, mediated, and dispersed" activity "strongly motivated and mediated by texts" (138). In this way, "literate" does not mean the opposite of "illiterate," or simply the ability to read and write, but rather all communicative activity that create literacy and language experiences with paper, books, screens, keyboards, pens and pencils, or any other compositional materials. By using "literate" as an adjective for resources, repertoires, movement, valuation, and life, I look at these phenomena specifically in the everyday activities of readers, writers, speakers, and listeners.

Literate Repertoires and Resources

"Literate repertoires" are the complex cluster of reading, writing, listening, and speaking strategies and experiences that multilingual migrants call on to write. I use "repertoire" to describe dynamic sets of literate practices learned in specific, lived social contexts. In this understanding, repertoires are not static containers of competence or skills but are instead "biographically organized complexes of resources" that reflect the both formal and ephemeral literate experiences gathered across the "rhythms of actual human lives" (Blommaert and Backus 8). Over time, repertoires include metalinguistic understandings and language ideologies.[6] Thus what may appear to be an incomplete repertoire is actually a lived repertoire in process.[7]

My use of repertoire also is influenced by terms or theories that emphasize what a repertoire *has* rather than what it *lacks*. Hornberger's continua of biliteracy and Valdés's L1/L2 user continuum, for example, emphasize the assets of bilinguality, which nevertheless fluctuate depending on communication topic, domain, or situation (Valdés, "Bilingualism" 414). The assumption underlying these continua, which I adopt throughout the book, is that fragmented learning opportunities do not limit users' skills but instead shape existing strengths in different ways. Brandt's theory of "accumulating literacy" emphasizes the impact of life experience on a repertoire, showing how "family histories and autobiographical constructions" condition literacy practices "piece[d] together" in response to "rapid social change" ("Accumulating" 651, 666). Moll et al.'s much-cited "funds of knowledge" approach recognizes students' rich cultural and cognitive resources and assumes that "people are competent, they have knowledge, and their life experiences have given them that knowledge" (González, Moll, and Amanti ix–x). Although these theories don't use repertoire explicitly, they contribute important additive approaches to the repertoires writers use to compose. In this book, repertoires include the literate strategies developed across the lifespan and around the world, as well as users' metalinguistic understandings and language ideologies that condition what they do with these practices in communicative situations.

When I call literate repertoires fluid, fixed, or frictive, I mean that participants have described materials or practices that do or do not move smoothly among languages, writers, or readers. Literate resources are slippery and elusive as writers grasp for them. This understanding of movement is informed by

Appadurai's theories of "scapes"—ethnoscapes, mediascapes, technoscapes, financescapes, and ideoscapes—that highlight "the fluid, irregular shapes" of a mobile global culture (33). Treating a repertoire as the *landscape* of a writer's literate life acknowledges the geography across which it was developed, the uneven or "irregular" nature of its resources, and the influence of global pressures migrants encounter.

If repertoires are a complex of resources, then resources likewise are created over the course of a literate life. But much scholarly work uses "resources" to mean skills or knowledge that writers call on to compose—strategies that are assumed to be durable, solid, or there for writers when they need them. Well-intentioned scholarship claims that writers use their resources to compose with intention, with language varieties they already possess rather than standard varieties they lack.[8] Scholars aim to foreground literate amplitude and challenge deficit models of literacy. But occasionally their claims treat literacy and language as stable tool-like resources that writers access from durable toolkit-like repertoires. Resources are said to be brought to classrooms, drawn on actively, and maintained at a writer's disposal. But it is not clear what these resources are made of or where they come from. How do writers' lives impact what resources are worth? Lu's notion of "discursive resources" as the "complex and sometimes conflicting templates of languages, Englishes, discourses, senses of self, visions of life, and notions of one's relations with others and the world" begins to account for the lived conflict that shapes resources ("Fast Capitalism" 28). But much use of "resource" lacks this consideration of inequality. Looking more closely at what literate resources are made of—literacy, language, and identity—suggests why resources might be wide open to constantly shifting valuation.

For example, literacy scholars have long noted that literacy is too volatile to guarantee any social or economic outcome.[9] Following Foucault and Bourdieu, Luke has argued that the value of literacy is not defined by literate competence that is "acquired in the school and fully credentialed through grades or degrees," but rather it is mediated through power structures within particular institutional and discursive domains ("Genres" 327). If one cannot access these domains because of accent, lack of documentation, or financial status, one cannot put their existing resources to use and these resources may remain inaccessible or invisible. In other words, whether existing literacy resources can be converted into further material or symbolic gain is contingent upon the relations of power that grant or withhold value. No matter the extent of one's literate repertoire or the deft wielding of one's literacy and language resources, literacy cannot guarantee social or economic mobility without access to these powerful relations. Therefore, according to Luke, the value of literacy has no "intrinsic power of the skill, text, competency or genre acquired" but instead depends on (1) any given market's valuing of that resource and (2) access to institutions, social networks, or powerful individuals who can convert those resources into further social purchase ("Genres" 329). If one is already at risk of discrimination within certain institutions like schools, as subjects are oftentimes immigrants, refugees, or dialect speakers, the value of one's literacy can be volatile indeed.

Furthermore, scholars have long demonstrated that languages are too dependent on social use and conditions to guarantee economic betterment. Because languages are "not fixed codes by themselves [but] are fluid codes framed within social practices" (García, *Bilingual* 32), language resources can easily lose their value from users' real or perceived accent, race, or gender.[10] So while Jacquemet claims that learning English, Chinese, or French in Albania is "the best—and sometimes the only—opportunity currently available to many bright people . . . for social and geographical mobility" (267), and Crawford notes that developing language resources in Vietnam can "secure a job with a foreign company that pays significantly more" (82), Brandt finds uneven literacy sponsorship—family support but not economic profit—behind the "unstable currency" of Spanish-English bilingualism in the United States (*Literacy* 179–80), and Prendergast finds that "no amount of English fluency" can "completely transcend" the stereotypical designations the global economy assigns Slovakian English users (4). The language resources gathered together in a repertoire certainly can be dependably utilized for social and personal betterment, but they also can be, in some contexts, less than dependable.

Finally, the identities of multilingual migrant writers are as shifting and in-process as they are for all, but they also are comprised of specific kinds of multiplicity—multiple languages, multiple cultures, and multiple globally minded epistemologies.[11] Writers might stand "on both shores at once" (Anzaldúa 100), or "be at once 'here' and 'there'" (Suárez-Orozco, "Everything" 73). Their language-based identity might be especially "the incarnation of the in-between, of the multiple intersections produced by the languages and cultures s/he has encountered" (Cronin 134). As applied linguist Jun Liu explains, multilingual identity and writing practices are mutually constitutive: "It is the establishment of my own L2 identity that makes me a good L2 writer. Likewise, it is the constant practice in L2 writing that helps me establish my L2 identity" (130). And Anzaldúa reminds us that "ethnic identity is twin skin to linguistic identity," vividly showing how multilingual identities are represented in bodies, emotions, and often painful life experiences. She famously provokes those who would separate language from identity, writing, "if you want to really hurt me, talk badly about my language" (Anzaldúa 81). In other words, literate identity is more than language heritage or affiliation. What writers can or can't do with their language resources has as much to do with the skills or strategies they've acquired as with the lives they've lived. Whether lived experiences are described by writers as positive or negative, they leave impressions and abrasions on writers, on their tongues and in their ears, on their emotions, self-perceptions, or imagined goals for the future. Literate resources inform not only writers' repertoires but also who they can or want to be.

Literate resources are informed by these volatile components of literacy, language, and identity. Made of this discursive matter, resources are fickle, as are the repertoires they comprise. Heller notes that it is hard to "abstract away" from the values "attached to linguistic forms and practices" ("Commodification" 102). But the abstract use of resources is still common in scholarship, opening up a terminological vacuum into which expectations and beliefs are loaded. One of these expectations is that literate resources are durable—unchanging, always on call, economically fungible—as writers carry them into new writing or communicative contexts. But the value of literate resources is always in flux. Although scholars emphasize literate resources in order to argue for what writers *have* rather than what they *lack*, an abstract discourse of resources can leave multilingual writers feeling less rather than more empowered. Literate repertoires and the resources are in process before, during, and after migration. They are continually produced in practice, making them subject to a process of literate valuation shaped by an assemblage of economic and social values.

Literate Mobility

Studies of mobility have considered all kinds of geographic, affective, embodied, literate, social, and economic mobilities in empirical, qualitative, and metaphorical ways. Mobility has been described as physical, as bodies traveling through space; intellectual, as minds are "'moved' . . . to see from a different point of view" (Reynolds, *Geographies* 2); and political, as protests slowly or suddenly make cultural change. Some scholars suggest that any consideration of human liberty is premised on the freedom to move, where mobility is not just a state-defined "human right" but definitive of the human capacity to "creatively transform our objective circumstances" (De Genova, "Deportation" 39). These forms of mobility often are related. Consider how the Great Migration shows African Americans enacting a social movement by physically moving north. I define mobility in terms of inequality: Having the choice to move or stay put, to mobilize oneself or one's literacies, is a form of economically and socially advantageous control.[12] Put another way, I define mobility in terms of the tensions—the oppositional energy between things moving and stalled—that this book seeks to pull apart. Fluidity, fixity, and friction are all *kinds* of mobility that differently reveal how literacy is valued. In three turns, I show how fluid, fixed, and frictive movement is dynamically related in the lived experience of everyday writers.

Mobility often has been understood as a product of globalization or transnationalism.[13] In many cases it has been framed as a phenomenon of fluidity—flexible and flowing, across ever-loosening borders and boundaries. A "mobilities paradigm" has deemed many kinds of movement (walking, subway-riding, electronic transmission) and many movers (from travelers and tourists to nomads and refugees) as participating in "an uninterrupted 'flow'" of global movement with "no single origin and no simple end" (Suárez-Orozco, "Everything" 73; Papastergiadis 4).[14] But in the context of globalization, mobility is not always experienced as free-flowing movement. The condition of late capitalism affects the trajectories of people moving within or against these flows: "some people are more in charge of it than others; some initiate flows and movement, others don't; some are more on the receiving-end of it than others; some are effectively imprisoned by it" (Massey 149).[15] Migration scholars suggest that forced movement like deportation maintains inequality, keeps workers available for exploitation, and seriously challenges claims about a free-flowing world.[16]

I take up this complexity by considering how a range of mobility is experienced by migrants. Specifically, I turn toward literate repertoires and resources, exploring how repertoires on the move perform different kinds of literate mobility. By "literate mobility," I mean the cross-border travel of literate practices and materials with migrants, the movement among languages in writing, and the persistence of literate identities in new contexts.[17] But the term "mobile" does not mean only fluid, productive movement. Following the above definition of mobility, I treat "literate mobility" as a complex phenomenon that includes fixed and frictive movements. This differentiated treatment has some precedent in literacy and language studies.

On the one hand, literacy and language have been treated as fluid phenomena. Literacy has been shown to "travel from informal school settings to more formal classroom ones" (Richardson Bruna 234); multilingual writers are said to enact "transcultural repositioning" to foster a literate "consciousness that travels well" and "move[s] back and forth more productively between and among different languages and dialects" (Guerra, "Putting Literacy" 32–33). Languages are defined not as "fixed codes" but as "fluid codes framed within social practices" (García, *Bilingual* 32).[18] Fluidity among practices, locations, or languages is especially emphasized by "trans" prefixes for -national, -lingual, or -languaging. For example, Pennycook characterizes a linguistic "fluidity of relations across global contexts" as one way "to think and be trans" (*Global Englishes* 36, 44). But these terms are often deployed precisely to emphasize innovation or creativity and thus can highlight fluidity to the sacrifice of a full examination of relations of movement.[19] For this reason scholars have argued for a more critical accounting of literate movement. For example, Reynolds argues that concepts of "dwelling" must account for "unequal access to modes of travel" (*Geographies* 40); Jacquemet notes that "transidiomatic practices" manifest not through free-flowing patterns one might expect under globalization, but against the "ideological hardening of social boundaries" of local social contexts (263).[20] Vieira's sociomaterial theory of literacy reminds us that migrants' control over their papers and practices is only "as strong as the strongest make them" ("Social Consequences").

I follow the critical approach. Sometimes in enthusiasm for supporting multilingual writers, scholars miss the fixity inherent in any literate movement. In this oversight, "trans" approaches can overlook the complicating factor of lost or stuck literacy attempts, fixed language identifications for purposes of cultural survival, and material conditions that mediate gained or lost languages. Furthermore, differentiated mobility has important explanatory power. A mobile analytic that includes fluidity, fixity, and friction highlights the social, political, and institutional boundaries that literacies cross and the powerful forces that move language around. It explains why literacy has the potential to simultaneously empower and disempower writers. By looking at literacy practices moving into and across contexts, we can see how migrants press up against socioeconomic values that regulate these contexts through tests, classroom-based routines, or implicit workplace policies. We see how appeals to efficiency or clarity in writing fit into claims about streamlined work demands and how social values carry economic worth and weight as they are put into practice. In effect, tracing literacies as they move reveals *how* they gain or lose meaning as they pick up traction or lose speed.

Literate Valuation

I argue that literacy is revalued because it moves. Literate valuation is one way to conceptualize this process. It shows not only what kinds of values are applied to literacy but how literacies are valued. Institutions such as schools place high or low value on resources; writers promote certain values through their routines and traditions; teachers or employers make implicit values official through practice. Each chapter explores how social values (family, community, and personal designations of importance or respect) meet up with economic assignments of value (the use or profitability of literate commodities) in multilingual migrant literacies.[21] This book shows how multilingual migrants regularly experience the effects—entrance to schools, citizenship gained, jobs won and lost—of economic or social forces that revalue their literate resources.

While actors—both writers and institutions—are distinct in what they value, they are similar in how they value, using both social and economic processes to deem some literacies and languages more worthy than others. This commonality shows literate valuation to be a fundamental experience of multilingual migrant literacy, one that shows how movement can change what literacies are worth. The book shows how the process of literate valuation is carried out and highlights the literate values woven through the everyday activity of this study's multilingual migrants. Literate valuation is especially shaped through the commodification of language.[22] The literate resources that power a globalizing economy differ from primary (metals, food) or industrialized (electronics, processed food) resources in that they trade in information and services (Heller and Duchene 9). That these resources are useful for economic goals turns language users into language workers who move literate information and materials around the world. This movement occurs across globalization's "territories of value" (Heyman) and linguistic markets (Bourdieu, "Economics") that drive the value of literate resources up and down and change their meaning. While scholars have argued that languages have shifted from markers of identity to identity-free items for exchange, others find that identity and commodity meet in language.[23] The social marginalization of certain groups thus impacts the economic valuation of these groups' literate repertoires.

In fact, literate valuation shows how tightly bound economic and social values are. Heller has argued that language-as-identity, too, is for sale (i.e., "authentic" language performances for tourism) ("Commodification"). But in this book literate valuation especially considers how values of social worth are put into lived practice in families, communities, work, and school. Based on several iterations of coded participant accounts (see Appendix D, "Detailed Coding Procedures"), Tables 1 and 2 elaborate the economic and social values that were salient in participants' literate experiences. Table 1 details the social and economic sources of literate valuation, their cultural, community, and family-based origins. Table 2 elaborates the actual features of these values, as described by participants. These tables are the result of analysis, rather than organizational schemes that guided analytic processes. Both tables show a generalized representation of values based on participants' insights rather than an exhaustive list of values that could exist in all literate lives.

In Table 1 the social values assigned to literate resources are driven by family, community, and cultural notions about important, beneficial, or respectful uses of literacy and language—principled notions for how literate resources merit respect or appreciation. Economic value is driven by the desire to support oneself and one's family. In order to find work, participants often converted multilingual practices they deemed "natural" or unremark-

TABLE 1. Where Participants' Literate Values Come From

Economic value	Work and school	Price of literacy-mediated access to visas, programs, spaces, organizations
		Price of classes, books, materials
		Pay for formal teaching
		Pay for formal translation/interpretation
	Communities	"Help" for neighbors or acquaintances
		Informal translation/interpretation
		Informal teaching
Social value	Families	Cultural traits judged to be important
		Community or individual activities deemed beneficial
		Family or community involvement that merits respect
		Language and literacy practices that are worth caring about
		Principles of appreciation for traditions, routines, habits

Source: Author.

able outside of the United States into literate assets in the United States. Their literate resources picked up economic value and produced beneficial material consequences in terms of pay, at professional levels not experienced before migration. But participants also assigned economic value to the informal labor exchanged among community members. As migrants offer their literate resources to basic literacy programs, social service organizations, or to acquaintances they just met, their literate resources become valuable in a different sense. Multilingual migrants aid each other's English language acquisition, serve as spur-of-the-moment interpreters, or participate in nonpaid language labor in order to support an informal community economy. In other words, their literate resources are valuable to them and their communities even when resources are not exchanged for pay.

Table 2 shows what the process of literate valuation produces for the migrant writers in this study—what, for them, literate values are. Across the top, the table lists the practices and language use participants described most frequently. Down the left side, the table lists the audiences and domains the participants used to contextualize descriptions of values. The boxes themselves are generalizations of the values participants frequently described. Again, the table is not meant to be exhaustive of all literate values. These are the beliefs

TABLE 2. What Participants' Literate Values Are

Audience and domain	Writing	Reading	English	Multilingualism
Parent as audience—at home or in community	Indicator of class, act of rebellion, communication to connect (notes, letters, texts)	Indicator of class, act of rebellion, necessary to live	Aspirational, indicator of class	Unremarkable norm
Child or sibling as audience—at home or in community	For play, for self-education	For bonding, for tradition	Necessary to live, indicator of class	Essential element of identity, unremarkable norm
Self as audience—at home or in community	To keep secrets, to express, for creativity	To keep company with self	To move beyond family	Expression, essential element of identity
Employer as audience—work in the United States	Necessary, constant, overwhelming	Assumed, rarely described	Unstated requirement, unstated policy	Reason for employment, profitable, unstated violation of norms and policy
Teachers as audience—in the United States	Informal, structured, to express a strong opinion	For comprehension, for content	Assumed norm, choppy, clear, short, discriminatory	Beneficial resources to showcase, resources to keep out of schoolwork
Teachers as audience—beyond the United States	To show content mastery, for testing, formal	Assumed, rarely described	Rule-based, colonial, monetized, profitable	Unremarkable norm
State as audience—in or beyond United States	Communication for bureaucratic demand, procedural, to produce paper trail		For proof of belonging, display assimilation	Outsider status (depending on racial appearance—if white, then could be marker of education)

Source: Author.

and designations of worth that participants in this study described and that support the chapters' analyses. The table shows the social and economic values that multilingual migrants hold and those that they meet as they move.

Table 2 previews what the chapters elaborate: personal and institutional values sometimes do and sometimes do not match. When writers' and institutional values are a good match (Zelizer), writers' repertoires often are more economically viable, but when they aren't, literate repertoires become economically and socially devalued.[24] Participants' accounts of literate movement especially show the benefit of matching values. Fluid movement of literate repertoires tends to promote literacy innovation and productivity because writers' values line up with institutional ones. In a way these writers know how to play the literacy game, and they benefit from this knowledge.[25] But as is clear in the tables, values can be contradictory or confusing. In these cases, writers don't know how to play the game and can't recognize how their own values aren't meeting institutional ones. They experience fixed literate movement that inhibits the realization of literate identities. In fact, the frictive movement of literate repertoires shows that writers' values can simultaneously match and not match institutional values. Writers experience friction when they know how to play the literacy game, matching their values to those of institutions, but the game keeps changing.

Thus multilingual migrants' repertoires come to be valued through the fortune of well-matched values, by "contingencies which arise in the cultural and social field" that literate practices on the move encounter continually (Luke, "Material" 330). In a way, multilingual migrants are always playing the literacy game: guessing what their resources are worth, hoping that new teachers, classmates, or bosses think their resources are as worthy as they do. The ones who succeed are the ones who can adapt as the game changes. Those who hold on tight or resist flexibility seem to lose. This does not mean that migrants alone are responsible for adapting or losing—powerful individuals and institutions also are implicated in these outcomes; they are responsible for creating conditions that support migrants who may or may not want to adapt. Nevertheless, the value of literacy seems to be much more about games and matches, the synergy of writers and institutional actors valuing and revaluing literacy in determined unity. The literacy game can be absurd (as the accounts in this book occasionally show), but it can also be very serious. Grades, jobs, raises, program progress, and family and emotional well-being are all at stake. These stakes are high for migrants with visa designations tied to good grades, kept jobs, and program progress. Thus the question becomes not why some literacies move with their writers while others are lost, but how writers on the move navigate the social and economic values that define literacy through constant contradictions.

Writing on the Move pulls apart the process of literate valuation in order to rebuild an understanding of how multilingual literacy is valued. After chapter 1's description of the study that informs this book, chapters 2, 3, and 4 focus on a different kind of literate movement. Migrant writers describe creating, adapting, and losing writing practices in motion, carrying around highly charged experiences and beliefs that influence the ways in which they are or are not able to write. Each chapter analyzes the everyday experiences of multilingual migrant writers in order to show with sharp specificity the complicated reality of multilingual literacy. In the end, tracing writing on the move reveals deep and sometimes debilitating contradictions in the way multilingual migrants' literate repertoires are valued.

CHAPTER 1
STUDYING WRITING ON THE MOVE

Researching literate lives is a visceral experience. I interviewed women in their homes, sitting on their couches or at kitchen tables, sharing prepared meals, pausing interviews when a kid would swoop in to sit on a lap. I interviewed participants in early morning cafes, in midday libraries with their children running circles around us, in their classrooms after their students had gone home, in my own TA office late after work shifts. My digital recorder picked up busy café sounds, husbands' yelled responses to my questions from other rooms, the occasional sniffles of participants and my worried tones when this happened. To experience research with these women is to experience, briefly, the vicissitudes of daily immigrant life in the U.S. Midwest.

The multilingual immigrant women I spoke with are a diverse group with widely varied class, ethnic, family, and professional backgrounds. Interviewing them sometimes induced research whiplash—I would move among participant workplaces or homes so different that it was easy to forget that I was interviewing people who shared anything in common. For example, in late spring in 2014, I conducted follow-up interviews with two participants in one day. In the morning I visited a participant in the new condo she shared with her husband, and in the afternoon I met with a participant in the older apartment she shared as a single mom with her school-age daughter. In the morning I found myself at a polished wooden table on the top story of a downtown condo building; in the afternoon I sat on a much-loved couch in a living room on the outskirts of town. The morning interview was conducted in silent privacy until the participant's husband came back from the condo building's gym. The afternoon interview was punctuated by a blender's whir as the participant's daughter made herself a smoothie. The participant and I shouted over the blending and the daughter's frequent admonishments to the pet rabbit hopping around the room.

Both of these women identify as highly literate and communicate in multiple languages; they are both teachers with advanced degrees; they both immigrated to the United States from upper-middle-class families; they both immigrated on their own to pursue further schooling in the United States;

they both met and married husbands in the United States. But five to six years after arriving in the United States, the two lives I walked into in one day could not have been more different. The different homes were supported by different jobs, which were earned through different schooling experiences, which were affected by differently arranged immediate and extended families. The immigrant experience in the United States is intensely differentiated, for many more reasons than the clear ones I suggest here. And the condition of multilingualism for immigrants can be intensely contradictory. In fact, the contrast in the vignette above points to the heart of this book: How can similar literate backgrounds produce such different literate lives? This chapter tells the story of how I found my way to this question.

I did not set out to speak only to amazing migrant women, but it turns out that the twenty-six I spoke with just are. I started this study with the hope that any multilingual migrant writer might be willing to talk with me. I wanted to understand how literacy moves with writers, so I sought out people who had moved across geographic locations but also move among multiple languages and literacies as a matter of their everyday lives. I used snowball sampling to expand a participant pool from an initial pilot participant to twenty-five women (see Appendix A. "Participants"). At the end of every interview, I asked, "Can you think of other friends or acquaintances who also might be reading and writing among multiple languages?" Over the course of three years, one participant referred me to friends and colleagues who referred me to neighbors, fellow churchgoers, and more friends and colleagues.

Along the way, for a variety of reasons, I decided to collect data only from women. First, women tended to refer me only to other women, which seemed partly to do with cultural norms for appropriate gendered behavior (many interviews felt intimate). Second, when men were present during interviews—I once interviewed a married couple together, for example—the men often talked over the women or answered questions I asked of the women. This made it hard to know what the women really thought, so I began interviewing them on their own. Finally, in the early stages of this study, my reading in two areas—migration studies and educational policy—presented narratives of migrant women that were challenged by what I was hearing from early participants. Research in these areas offered up narratives of migrant women experiencing inevitable downward mobility, describing them as professional prior to migration but less so afterward, ending up in low-paying jobs characterized by "the five Cs": "cleaning, catering, clerical, cashiering, and caring" (Cuban, "Examining" 188).[1] Interestingly, this narrative was simultaneously reinforced and complicated by the women I was speaking to. Their accounts suggested that professional and educational backgrounds, while sometimes lost, were also refigured after migration. Many participants happily returned to school, switched careers, or rerouted their existing skills and leveraged some new ones—newfound bilingual status, translation experiences—into different social and professional positions. This clash of narratives—between my participants and the research literature—motivated me to turn completely toward women for this study.

The study's participants are all multilingual and primarily professional. They are teachers and students, nurses and journalists, architects and lawyers, salespeople and social service providers. That participants almost always referred me to their colleagues was an unexpected pattern. The characteristics they share clearly are influenced by my snowball sample and collection method—I moved through professional peer groups; participants knew interviews would require a certain amount of English proficiency—and also by the time and place where the study took place. However, participants varied widely in class, educational, national, and linguistic background. For example, the nurses referred me to other nurses, but this group of seven nurses represented working-class to middle-class family backgrounds, high school to graduate degrees, six countries of origin, and ten languages.

Participants migrated to the United States from seventeen different countries, speaking twenty-two different languages among them—44 percent from Asia, 24 percent from Latin America, 16 percent from the Middle East, 8 percent from Eastern Europe, with singular individuals from Asia Minor and Africa. Of the twenty-six participants, seventeen immigrated to the United States with existing tertiary education—thirteen with undergraduate degrees and four with graduate degrees. Four participants immigrated at a young age and were in college programs, and two immigrated specifically to attend university in the United States and stayed. Fourteen held professional positions previous to immigration—five were teachers, three worked in communications, and the rest spanned such professions as architecture, law, environmental planning, and medicine. The majority of the migrants in this study are indeed educated, professional, "underemployed," and, importantly, multilingual with fluency in English prior to migration. In other words, the picture of literacy presented throughout this book is shaped by the women who described their literacy to me.

TIME AND PLACE

Though not intentional, this group of participants cohered for the most part with the demographic data of the study's research site for the three years I gathered data (2010–13). Demographic data from several sources—the 2009 and 2010 U.S. Census, the 2010 American Community Survey, and a 2009 Brookings Institution report (Hall et al.)—help describe the location and time in which the study took place. These data reveal two important shifts for migration that are exhibited by the participants: (1) migration to the United States, and especially to my research site, was shifting toward highly skilled migrants; and (2) like men, women were increasingly migrating (or perhaps they always have been without being studied) for purposes of labor and education, not just for family reunification.

A shift from low-skilled to high-skilled migration was occurring during this time, especially in the midsize Midwestern university town in which this study took place. According to data from the UN and the World Bank analyzed by the Pew Research Center, the United States remained the main destination country for international migrants from 1990 to 2013, and during this time the United States increased its share of the world's migrants who are increasingly from middle-income to higher-income countries (Connor, Cohn, and Gonzalez-Barrera). The Great Recession of 2008 in particular was not indiscriminate as demand for middle- and low-skilled employment fell away, while high-skilled "preferences" remained steady.[2] While the recession "slowed migration worldwide and abruptly curtailed foreign arrivals to the United States," the country is paradoxically experiencing "historically high levels" of immigration, with 38.5 million immigrants in the United States in 2009 and "extraordinary growth" in its foreign-born population (Hall et al. 2, 17). The percentage of the U.S. population that is foreign-born, 12.5 percent, is nearing percentages that occurred during the industrial era (Hall et al. 2). In other words, while immigration, by percentage of the total U.S. population, was higher in the late nineteenth century, the total number of immigrants is rising to unprecedented levels.

This shift appears to be historically distinct in that immigrants in the United States who have a bachelor's degree now outnumber those without a high school diploma, and almost half of those with BAs are overqualified for their jobs (Hall et al. 1–2). This is not to say that the United States is experiencing a wholesale shift away from low-skilled immigration, but that the high-skilled population is becoming more predominant, just as an economic squeeze is making low-skilled immigration more transient and temporary (Hall et al. 22). Hall et al.'s 2009 report, *The Geography of Migrant Skills*, identifies this shift in the overall trajectory of global mobility. The coauthors claim that the contemporary United States was experiencing a demographic transformation that is historic but also geographically specific in that it is being felt most noticeably in the country's metro and urban areas. In fact, the report points to this book's research site as a case study of this historic shift.

The metro area in which this study took place is designated a low-immigration metro, with modest inflows of migrants and a small "foreign-born" population that is highly skilled and educationally prepared. The metro area maintains a "high-skill level ratio," meaning it has double the high-skilled migrant population for every one hundred low-skilled migrants, a ratio attributed to the metro's large research university. In other words, although the migrant population in this midsize metro area is small, it is highly skilled. Recent census data from the area also shows this to be true: This area is 6.3 percent foreign-born, with a newer migrant population (63.7 percent without citizenship and 42.9 percent having entered after 2000) predominantly from Asia (43.2 percent) and Latin America (34.4 percent).[3]

Research in literacy studies and applied linguistics also has captured this migration shift over the past two decades, showing that multilingual migrants move with a host of unrecognized skills and experience. Their studies reveal a growing population of highly skilled migrants working in the United States in jobs for which they are overqualified: the women subjects in Norton's study of migrant literacy were college-educated professionals in their home countries but hadn't found jobs in their professions years after immigrating; the women in Cuban's research had "educational qualifications, academic resources, and sophisticated language and literacy practices (educational capital) [that were] missed or viewed deficiently" ("Home/work" 83); and the "new migrants" in Suárez-Orozco's work include "highly educated, highly skilled individuals . . . more likely to have advanced degrees than the native-born population . . . [and] are among the best educated and most skilled folk in the United States" ("Right Moves" 14).

The demographic backgrounds of the participants in my study generally correspond to these patterns. The study seems to have captured a contemporary migrant context experiencing fundamental shifts. Another migrant shift captured is the increasing, or increasingly studied, phenomenon of women migrating independently for work. This "feminization of migration" is both a corrective to the predominantly male focus of migration research of the past few decades—since women have long been migrating as economic actors—as well as an actual shift in gathered data showing women migrating for professional reasons rather than to follow or join husbands.[4] Research across the social sciences from the past few decades has shown that migrant women have a unique migration experience in that they are disproportionately subject to de-skilling as well as being overburdened with shifting cultural expectations after migration.[5] They struggle when government, employment, and educational institutions in their new countries do not recognize their existing professional and education credentials. School and workplaces also expect them to gain even further credentialing, including English language classes, to fulfill bureaucratic processes in a new country.[6]

As noted, this latter shift was simultaneously reinforced and complicated by participants in this study. For example, some participants did follow their husbands to the United States, challenging this supposed trend. But my analysis shows the complexity of such broad conclusions: although women may migrate to follow their husbands, this may be more due to cultural pressures or the kinds of jobs recruited by U.S. work visas (male-dominated sectors in engineering and tech) than the lack of desire or motivation on the part of women to professionalize in the United States. More likely, and as is shown to be true with this study's participants, women migrate according to tensions shaped by shifting gender roles and racial positions, socioeconomic status, and idiosyncratic family expectations—all of which cohere in a cluster of barriers and motivations that makes them simultaneously empowered and marginalized subjects after migration.

Therefore, the study's participants and research site prove to be both exemplary of and challenging to shifts in contemporary migration contexts. For example, the Brookings report attributes migrant underemployment partially to "lack of English language proficiency," but twenty-three of the twenty-five participants in this study spoke English with high proficiency. Ten were bilingual, eleven communicated among three languages, and four communicated among four or more languages. Yet many of them experienced the de-skilling reported in research and policy data. They often found themselves overqualified for their jobs or returning to school to start entirely new careers. This challenge to the Brookings claim indicates that these highly skilled migrants are not experiencing de-skilling in the United States simply because they lack English. Clearly something more complicated is occurring as migrants enter the United States with professional and educational experience *and* deeply developed literate repertoires.

My research questions pursued this complication. I wanted to know how literacy practices moved with writers and how that movement affected literacy itself. Specifically, I asked:

1. How do multilingual immigrant writers use literacy practices learned in one geographical location to write in another?

2. How do multilingual immigrant writers use literacy practices learned in one language to write in another or in many?

3. How does movement itself—among languages and locations—affect, change, or produce certain literacy practices?

These questions changed over time as I collected and analyzed data, focusing more on women migrants, for example, and considering the entirety of writers' repertoires beyond just their practices. I began to think differently about language as "one" or "another." However, because I originally wanted to know how writers were *using* their literacy, I was in pursuit of their practices.

COLLECTING AND ANALYZING LITERATE LIVES

In 2010 and 2011, I conducted semistructured literacy history interviews with twenty-six participants. In 2013, I carried out follow-up interviews with eight focal participants who were available and whose original interview insights proved particularly important for my evolving analysis. (Some participants had moved or had changed e-mails because they graduated or left their jobs). These follow-up interviews served as a form of member checking as I tested out my analytic claims with them, hoping they would complicate or confirm what I had seen in their original interview transcripts. Many did, and the follow-up interviews contributed essential nuance to this book.[7] Over the course of these three years, I wrote observation notes and reflections on completed interviews. I e-mailed back and forth with several focal participants. Four focal participants offered me school essays, journal excerpts, and textbooks that they had described in their interviews. I used these data to enrich my understanding of participants' literate lives. Observation notes especially triangulated well with my research memos and participant insights. But it was participants' interview responses that offered the most in-depth understandings of my research questions. While all the data inform my descriptions of participants' family, work, school, and community contexts, this book is driven by participants' own words.[8]

In interviews I treated "writing" as anything involving script or text. Participants often assumed I meant either handwriting or creative writing, and it usually took a portion of the interview to open up a definition that described writing as expansively as I did: lists and around-the-home jotting; texting, e-mailing, and social media conversations; letter writing; immigration, work, and school-based bureaucratic correspondence like applications and cover letters; journals and diaries; school notes, assignments, and texts; and so on. When participants and I began to share an understanding of writing as both mundane and essential, they understood why I was calling them writers. In some interviews these terms weren't shared until the end. In one interview, for example, it took almost an hour for a participant to remember that she had written at all as a child. In response to my questions about her early literacy activities, she insisted that she only read during her childhood, never wrote. During the interview she sat for long spells of silence, seemingly racking her brain for memories of writing. But while describing her own children's writing play, she suddenly remembered that, indeed, as a young girl she had no fewer than seventeen pen pals. She was writing with other girls from all over the world.

This example shows the promise of the semistructured interview. This participant and I talked for long enough that we rediscovered her literate past together. Interviews allow participants into the meaning-making process and treat them as authorities on their own lived experience.[9] My participants were aware of this fact, with seven of them remarking on how they and I together created the experience of the interview:

HANEEN: You're really bringing on some memories! Oh no!
SHIRIN: Oh that's something which I thought about right now when you say it.
TASHI: It's interesting I feel now. You are asking the questions and I am just learning it while I am feeling it.
FARIDAH: It's really nice to talk to you about our dreams.
KHADROMA: I don't know if I'm confusing you or if I'm just confusing myself. [laughing]
YOLANDA: I think I haven't even noticed until now that you are asking me. You are just making me think about things I never think of.
DEFNE: It's really interesting now that I'm talking with you, I'm like, I kind of thought about it, but not really deeply.
DEFNE: That's a very good question and I think about that a lot.

These moments of meta-awareness show participants pausing to look back in on what the interview was doing for them as well as for me. They reflected on the interview's potential to create insight for both of us. Furthermore, interviews draw out participants' own insights shaped by years of experience. Such participants as Nimet, Renan, and Sabohi took the upper hand throughout our interviews, drawing me maps and diagrams, approaching the conversation as an opportunity to teach me about certain languages and regions of the world. This open interview format offered flexibility and adaptability, allowing me to "respond to the situation at hand [and] to the emerging worldview of the respondent" (Merriam 74). Yielding research authority was particularly important in light of the power differential inherent in the research/participant relationship. It felt nice to mostly just listen. This dynamic was essential for giving participants room to clarify if I assumed too much (several responses to my follow-up questions started with "No" or "That's not what I mean") and for inviting participants to interpret and analyze phenomena from their own point of view.

Finally, interviews were the method that best supported my research questions. I hoped to understand how multilingual migrants moved their literacy practices, but I could not observe that phenomenon or find it in texts. As Barton and Hamilton have pointed out, literacy practices are not "observable units of behavior since they also involve values, attitudes, feelings, and social relationships" (7). I therefore used literacy history interviews to elicit recollections and interpretations of past literacy experiences in relation to current ones. Interviews drew out descriptions, memories, values, and interpretation of interaction with text. Because participants could not be observed as they migrated, nor asked questions along the way, literacy history interviews best revealed how writers understood their past and current practices to have moved among their languages and the places they had lived.

I designed interview questions to gather information about the shape and specificity of everyday multilingual reading, writing, and speaking, anticipating that these modes would connect and often overlap.[10] I hoped that asking about practices would show writers working in contexts, situating the micro-level of literate activity in relationship to macro-level forces pushing in on their everyday experience. I wanted to know how seemingly quotidian or random literacy events can become significant under the force of language ideologies. Therefore, asking participants about their remembered and current practices helped me probe beyond the observable use of language and text to their social meaning and use.[11] Although these questions were not explicitly framed in terms of movement, answers were often offered through mobility metaphors, as is clear in participant quotations included throughout the book.

In the end, this constructionist approach to data collection made the process importantly subjective. I was not an objective observer or analyzer of their experiences. No method could transparently replicate the participants' experiences without interpretation. While methods like surveys and ethnographic observation could certainly have deepened my understanding of participants' practices, their interview responses provided the initial insights I hoped for into the lived experience of multilingual literacy. This somewhat recalibrates what is "true" or "accurate" in this study in that participant recollections are true to them and thus meaningful.[12] They talked me back to their homeplaces, across oceans, and around their literate lives in the United States. What they believe they did and do with their literacy, and what those experiences mean to them, are the data of this study.

Analyzing Movement

The story of this study's analysis is a constant turning over of what movement and literacy mean. Once I had gathered my data, I faced many puzzles about what exactly was moving in that data and how I could best understand how it affected literacy. I especially wondered what I should trace in the assemblage of things on the move. Should I trace the writers with their practices? Their practices alone? Should I follow their texts across locations—in or out of the United States? Could I look at how their practices move among their languages in their texts or just in their descriptions of their practices? What would best show why writers sometimes succeed and sometimes struggle—not in their writing per se but in what they wanted to *do* with their writing?[13]

A central tension in researching migrant literacies is the need to fix, or pin down, a mobile phenomenon in order to study it. Researchers continue to grapple with this tension, redefining analytic tools and frames such as context, scale, practice, and event.[14] This tension is particularly marked in new literacy studies, which has relied on the notion of socially situated practices to move analytic focus from autonomous to ideological literacies. A seeming imperative to investigate the local community or situation from which literacy practices spring can confound observations of literacies that move in, out, and among situations.[15]

In my data analysis I hoped to avoid these impasses by focusing on movement itself. Following the lead of literacy scholars who propose studying literacy's durable, material, and mobile qualities, I endeavored to investigate not a single site, community, or language but instead literacy's uneven movement across sites, languages, and communities.[16] In other words, I attempted to treat movement itself as a literacy situation and site of study. I analyzed not just how literacy moves across locations but how literacy is bound up in paradoxical relations of movement as it is put into practice by migrant writers. This analysis especially sought to maintain the tension between emic descriptions and etic ideological inference: practice as a description of what participants are doing with literacy (emic) analyzed together with participants' perspectives and my own small theories about those activities (etic).[17]

Therefore I chose analytic procedures that could honor my initial questions—I did not know exactly what to look for until I dug into the data. Contemporary grounded theory's constant comparative analysis honored this process. Rather than adopt Glaser and Strauss's early procedures, I used the "flexible heuristic strategies" that Charmaz has elaborated from the original methodology.[18] Her flexible qualitative approach to analysis aims not for representative categories or generalizable results but for saturated patterns in the data, implicit lines of theory coming to the fore through comparison, and surprising turns in original assumptions based on focused coding. My analysis was exploratory to the extent that constant comparisons evolved as I revisited and reframed categories over and over again (see Appendix D for detailed coding procedures).

Rounds of focused coding followed the paths described in Appendix D. I spun out potential theoretical threads by pursuing focused codes on correspondence practices and contexts (Lorimer Leonard, "Writing"), codes on connections between present practices and past political contexts (Lorimer Leonard, "Rhetorical Attunement"), and codes on values, all of which inform the theoretical structure of this book. This accumulation of codes always revealed fluctuating tensions—between social structure and individual writer, between fluid and fixed practices, between social and economic values—that had originally remained hidden under codes that only named the agentive action of individual writers. Furthermore, these tensions pointed across the data, showing what almost all of the codes shared—a constant friction between the fluidity and fixity of practices, mediated by the social and economic values that manage multilingual practices. In practice, coding rounds were highly iterative, with several rounds occurring during each stage, particularly in tandem with memo writing, and with much of it occurring on the margins of printed-out paper copies strewn in piles around my desk, on my office couch and floor, and under the warm seat of my ever watchful cat. My sixteen research memos, written in connection to hundreds of codes and participant quotations, became visual records of the point at which coding patterns were reaching saturation—when there was enough data for an idea or theme to evolve into an argument—and almost all of them became major sections in each chapter of this book.

A Transnational and Feminist Analysis

In *The Mind at Work*, Rose says his research approach is "eclectic and synthetic," using theory and methodology from a variety of fields to "[shine] a particular kind of light on a remarkably complex cognitive and social reality" and "make partial sense of the swirling whole." While I only aspire to Rose's important work, I built my theoretical orientation to this project through similar mindful synthesis. My analysis is informed by a variety of fields that shed essential light on the "remarkably complex" phenomenon of multilingual migrant literacy. Analysis draws on echoes of terminology across fields, keeping their tensions vibrant rather than reconciled.

I briefly elaborate here two more theoretical orientations (in addition to those mapped in the introduction) in order to clarify how I approached data analysis and arrived at the interpretations that structure this book. My analysis is informed by a transnationalism that finds its starting point outside of methodological nationalism. Methodological nationalism, as an approach, focuses research questions and conclusions on a singular entity like the nation-state. It assumes that the unit of analysis—whether nation, language, culture, religion, or community—is bounded and analyzes or compares within or across these borders. Methodological nationalism tends to reify the singularity of national or cultural experiences, sometimes connecting these to singular languages under study.[19] To see things differently, I located transnational activity not among one country or another but across micro, meso, and macro social scales in multiple locations.[20] Importantly, such analysis does not ignore the borders around cultures, nations, and languages. Instead, borders and boundaries are treated as socially significant but historically odd, not a given, and only meaningful in relation to phenomena diffusing across them.

In other words, moving beyond methodological nationalism involves both the disruption of nation-based analyses and an acknowledgment of the idiosyncrasy of such a world system in the first place.[21]

In this analysis I also aimed to understand how transnational relations of power affect the gendered experiences of the study's participants. My analysis is thus both transnational and feminist.[22] Instead, my feminist analysis aimed to (1) foreground women's lived experiences as a source of knowledge; (2) incorporate researcher reflection and participant interpretation as data; and (3) require an examination of the power relations that create inequality in migrant women's experiences.[23] As noted, women may face an intense set of responsibilities and barriers after immigration. They are often pulled between work and home, face patriarchal limits to education, and are expected to transmit cultural knowledge through home education. Although all women may experience these struggles whether immigrant or not, "institutionalized racism" and "language problems" add elements of exclusion that affect the socioeconomic downward mobility of immigrant women in particular (Sadeghi 218). By centering women's lived experiences, my analysis is mindful of downward mobility but also resists celebrating immigration as the moment of women's complete educational and cultural freedom. Instead, I looked for the give and take of agency in their lived experiences of migration, as they migrated out of economic necessity, family maintenance, or for personal betterment.

Furthermore, the grounded theory procedures I used for analysis, particularly those that incorporate researcher reflection and participant knowledge, have an "epistemological affinity" with feminist methodologies.[24] For example, the use of "in vivo" codes during the axial coding process uses participants' own words as codes themselves (Charmaz, *Constructing*). In one instance I used the in vivo code "mess" from participant Sofia's interview to code every instance of language "mess," "messy," and "messiness" described by participants. Because I had to return to all the data to look for every instance of "mess" rather than just the ones I had originally chosen, this in vivo code helped me analyze the common articulation of "mess," not from my original understanding of chaos or confusion but from the participants' understanding of the word as creative productivity. This code became an entire section in chapter 2. Coding strategies like these foreground participants' own understandings of their experience, supporting feminist concerns that research subjects speak from their own lived experience and play a role in shaping the research process.

Memo writing during data analysis also guided a writing-intensive practice of researcher reflection. For example, I wrote a memo when a particular interview question was eliciting only confusion from participants, causing me to reflect on the way I was asking the question and how a participant might have felt hearing a certain question from a white, middle-class researcher. While some participants self-identified as ethnically white, others commented on feeling no longer white in the United States because of reactions to their hijab or their accents. I wrote a memo on the word "Caucasian" after one participant explained that she stopped identifying as Caucasian, even though she came from the Caucasus, when told by a fellow student that she was clearly "not white." Other memos led me to reflect on why participants would often follow up their responses by asking if that was a "right" or "useful" answer or apologize for their English language skills when they were perfectly fluent. Participants and I were often in a dance of authority, as I was relying on them for their expertise in multilingualism and they were often deferent to me as an English language expert. All of these reflections led me to continually revise my interview protocol, more consciously share with participants my own experiences with language learning, and acknowledge the limits of what I could understand about multilingual migrant women's life experiences.

Finally, my feminist approach to analysis foregrounded inequality and exclusion. As I made sense of the limits and constraints my participants described, I kept in mind the contemporary context of migration, one often driven by fear, hatred, and the pursuit of profit regardless of human consequence. My transnational analysis is feminist in its desire to understand how migrants live under these conditions, particularly its aim to "constantly connect intellectual activity—the study of literature, language, and ideas—to the history and experience of people's lives" (Ritchie 85, 101). My feminist analysis connects theoretical conversations about multilingualism to the actual lived successes and struggles of women writing after migration. As Davis has reminded us, there is no "category of women with which feminists identify and for which they seek liberation," calling this an assumption "built on another one: that a feminist (or anyone else) can *know the truth* about 'women' and then re-present that truth adequately and honestly" (143, emphasis in the original). There also is no singular group called "migrant women" with identical interests and experiences. This study was not designed to discover "the truth" about migrant multilingual women, nor do its conclusions aim to represent a true or comprehensive characterization of all migrant women's multilingual writing practices. I hope to offer one lens through which to view contemporary pressures that shape the movement and stasis of multilingual migrant writing in and out of the United States.

My data analysis process as a whole, and the focused coding on values in particular, produced the findings that organize the book's major chapters into fluidity, fixity, and friction. Findings are supported throughout the book with narration of participants' described experiences, analysis of these narrations, and connections of both of these to theoretical conversations in research on migration and multilingualism. Because researchers can "almost never know" what a piece of data "'really means' to someone," I carefully weighed the potential meaning in participant accounts, narrowing down the range of possible interpretations based on what participants might understand and what they clarified during follow-up interviews (Ahearn 43). In every transcription, code, memo, direct quotation, and subsequent analysis, I endeavored to best represent participant experiences and insights, preserve their personalities, strong wills, and vast life experiences, and respect their willingness to share their thoughts about writing and language with all of us.

CHAPTER 2

FLUIDITY

WHEN WRITING MOVES

Yolanda, a veterinarian from Colombia, describes one of her family's literacy traditions:

YOLANDA (Y): My mother, so, when somebody dies and then the viewing thing? Like when you go see the dead person at the? Yeah she writes on paper, like has message to god. . . . She writes a paper saying, like, "Oh, help me with this. Da da." She folds it very small; she puts it there.
REBECCA (R): In the coffin?
Y: Yes! Where the body is and she says oh the message gets wherever she wants it to go.

With this literate act, Yolanda's mother makes prayer mobile. Yolanda's mother likely does not expect a written reply but instead expects that the message will reach a divine, hopefully interested, reader. Although Yolanda thinks her mother's funeral writing is "cuckoo," a closer look at this literacy practice reveals the social and cultural values bound up in a seemingly small note. Yolanda's mother believes as much in prayer as in the mobility of messages, with paper and coffin as the vehicles that matter. She has faith that writing and text are powerful enough to endure in the afterlife. With scraps of paper flung into coffins, Yolanda's mother thinks "the message gets wherever she wants it to go." She believes that writing itself can move.

Fluid literate acts echo across the literacy experiences of participants in this study. Khadroma believes her role as a health-care interpreter is to "deliver the message" across languages, while Faridah claims that when she can't write, she has "a lot of feelings that [she] can't send to other people." Haneen worries that she lacks the "talent of moving [her] information from [one] head to another" when writing, and Yolanda believes that writing is "part of how the world moves around." For the everyday writers in this study, writing is a courier, moving feelings, messages, and information among readers, listeners, spaces, and heads. This chapter explores how literate fluidity is experienced in the everyday lives of multilingual migrant women. In an era of increasingly mobile people, goods, and information, literacy too is on the move. Migrants bring their multilingual repertoires, including their communication routines, habits, or traditions, with them as they move around the world. These migrant women move for work, for more education, or to make their families whole again. Some move by chance. But these migrants also "move" among their languages when they write.[1] In fact, movement among location and movement among languages are often mentioned by participants in the same breath; one movement sometimes affords or supports another.

This chapter reveals the fluid nature of these movements. Participants repeatedly discussed two kinds of fluidity in their literacy experiences, which I call messy literacy and literacy relays. I analyze the "mess" writers create as they attempt to move their literacy practices among their languages, then I analyze the "relay" created by writers who pass around their literacy, cultural practices, and know-how. Finally, I consider how literate values and fluidity are related, foregrounding how participants themselves explain the potentially productive consequences of fluid literate movement. Each of these sections incorporates voices from a broad representation of participants, then highlights focal writers who experience their literate repertoires in especially fluid ways. Throughout, I explore what fluidity can reveal about the values that support writers' forward movement. The social and economic values held by various agents—teachers, classmates, coworkers, family members, the writers themselves—mediate what multilingual writers are able to accomplish at any given time. Fluid movement especially shows what can happen when writers' values match institutional ones. Writers are at their most productive and innovative as they compose with their full literate repertoires.

MESSY REPERTOIRES

As noted in the introduction, literate repertoires are the complex cluster of reading, writing, listening, and speaking strategies and experiences that multilingual migrants call on to write. Similarly, I use "repertoire" to describe dynamic sets of literate practices learned in specific, lived social contexts.[2] In this understanding, repertoires are not static containers of competence or skills but instead are "biographically organized complexes of resources" that reflect the both formal and ephemeral literate experiences gathered across the "rhythms of actual human lives" (Blommaert and Backus 8). Over time, repertoires include metalinguistic understandings and language ideologies. Thus what may appear to be an incomplete, or "truncated" repertoire, is actually a lived repertoire in process. Here I consider the particularly fluid components of multilingual migrants' literate repertoires, exploring how their messy and connected qualities can have consequences for writers' identities, opportunities, and worldviews. I explore accounts from a broad representation of study participants and then look at two focal writers who describe their fluid literate repertoires in vivid detail.

Alicia immigrated to the United States from Argentina to attend a small liberal arts college in the Midwest. She created a vibrant literacy learning experience for herself while there, majoring in anthropology, studying abroad in Tanzania, and writing a senior thesis in Mexico. As her account shows, Alicia is sharply aware of how and why she writes the way she does, and she maintains an active set of beliefs about the way writing and language should be taught, learned, and practiced. Despite her expansive literate repertoire and the clarity with which she describes it, Alicia explains the development of her literate repertoire as "a total mess." She describes the language varieties among which she communicates as fluid and somewhat random: "I learned Hebrew through Spanish. So Spanish and English are connected, Spanish and Hebrew are connected, but there's no connection between Hebrew and English. [She draws a triangle on the table.] What I'm trying to say is that when I'm talking to somebody that speaks Hebrew and English my mind is a total mess because I feel like I have to listen in English or Hebrew then translate into Spanish, then switch to English or Hebrew, then back. . . . Well I can, but *eeoooo*, it takes double the time."

One dimension of literate fluidity expressed by almost every participant in this study was the "mess" of multilingual experience. Participants describe the movement among their language varieties as anything but tidy. For many, this meant mixed or meshed language use beyond their control, while for others this meant the productive chaos of multilingualism. The broad sampling of participant narratives here shows the frequency of invocations of literate mess as well as the range of its characterizations, as political choice, easier (than monolingual communication), uncontrolled and automatic, or controlled and intentional. Although the multilingual writing of migrants is often treated as error-ridden, unformed, or lazy—too messy to merit response—these writers treat mess as the natural state of language, a set of sometimes chaotic practices that reflect how they believe literacy is experienced in most of the world.

For example, when Nimet, a nurse from Azerbaijan, accidentally speaks Turkish to her American friends, she calls it "bizarre thinking, you know it just comes from your brain . . . automatically." Nimet says this happens for her because she "cannot filter language" so language comes through her no matter the amount of control she attempts to exert. Alicia agrees, saying, "When I'm home I use Spanish and but then sometimes a word in English comes out and it's like, how much language control do you have?" Similarly, Jin, a teacher from Japan, says she and her friends like to "mix it up" by "sort of mixing the Japanese; English plus Japanese verbs kind of together." She says this mixing "feels normal because it's just coming out, naturally coming out."

Fluidity

Paj, a Hmong nurse, and Defne, a Turkish special education aide, echo Jin verbatim, saying that their language varieties "kind of come out" when they communicate, describing uncontrolled literate movement that often escapes their understanding. Defne says when she writes and speaks between English and Turkish that she's "not translating or anything; it just comes out of my brain like that." As Sofia, a store clerk from Ukraine, admits, this uncontrolled mess is common: "I think that it's probably not just me. Many people doing the same thing. You write in a sentence in Russian and bum, one word in English. . . . In Russian we talk talk talk and then bum, English word pops out. Don't know how explain. Mess, just a little bit mess. Which is easy in your mind. You just write it down; when you write it down that list, you don't think, you just write. It's easier."

These writers understand literate messiness to be "automatic," "normal," "natural," and notably "easier." While some might assume that messy writing is the result of struggle, several participants describe messy output as the result of multilingual ease. For example, Paj treats literate mess as ease of articulation, believing like Sofia that it's easier to communicate in both Hmong and English, rather than exclusively in one language or the other. She says, "There are points in Hmong that cannot be expressed in English and there are points in English that cannot be expressed in Hmong, so if I'm speaking with someone who understands both languages then I can use both." If Paj is allowed to draw on the "points" expressed best by either language, the combined result will be eased communication with "someone who understands." For Paj, Defne, Jin, and Sofia, the messy movement among their literate repertoire is not the result of spotty proficiency or yet-to-be-acquired sophistication. Quite the opposite: their messy communication signals clarity in their own thinking and close communicative bonds with others.

Likewise, Haneen, an architect from Palestine, describes a multilingual exchange on Facebook that might appear uncontrolled on the screen—as if the writer is hastily moving among languages—but in fact it is monitored through a sophisticated rhetorical awareness. When discussing Arab Spring demonstrations with a friend, Haneen says she would call a politician a "stubborn donkey." She explains: "But when wrote it down *hamar* in Arabic, I didn't write it as 'stubborn donkey' [in English] because it's stronger when I say it in Arabic, so I did it in Arabic. Then we moved back and we talked about yes, bla bla in English. It comes spontaneously I think. Depend on the one you are talking to. Because you know this word if you say it in different language, it's gonna effect on him, he's gonna laugh about it more, or it's just gonna ring something in his mind . . . the different language will have different effect." Although Haneen says she and her writing friend spontaneously "moved back" to English, this spontaneity occurs together with a refined sense of rhetorical effect. As Haneen wrote between English and Arabic in her Facebook chat, she chose the language that would be "stronger," that would make an audience laugh or produce a more resonant "ring." Thus, for Haneen, the mess of multilingualism operates under a productive order with a rhetorical goal in mind.

In most participants' accounts, messy literacy appears to show writers acting on the productive potential of multiplicity rather than choosing to compose monolingually. Two short accounts about dictionary practices especially characterize the controlled side of literate mess. Sabohi, a teacher from Pakistan, is a habitual dictionary user, a practice cultivated through learning to write simultaneously in Urdu and English. As an avid reader, she notices patterns of word borrowing from Hindi to English and concludes on her own that languages are historical constructs and inherently messy: "Sometimes I went to the dictionary and I saw the first time 'bund' in the dictionary . . . and I was like, yeah, there are so many things that are borrowed from other languages, and English too, so, what's the big deal! I mean, you want to communicate something and you want to write something for pleasure, even if it's literary, as long as somebody understands it and enjoys it so what's the fuss about?" Because Sabohi has always depended on dictionaries to write, it is clear to her that languages that seem standard are really an assemblage of constantly evolving loan words. She understands that borrowing across varieties is not a radical violation but instead a historical inevitability. She also understands composition to be guided by choices made for the ultimate enjoyment of a reader or listener. As a teacher and former journalist, Sabohi is familiar with preferences for standardized language forms. But as a multilingual reader and writer, she doesn't understand what "the fuss" is about when messy forms seem more natural and true to history.

Nimet describes coming to similar conclusions from her dictionary practices. She explains that she cannot translate her first language (Azerbaijani) to her third learned language (English) without the mediation of Russian because of the dictionaries available to her when she learned English: "We used Russian because we had no direct English/Azerbaijani dictionary at that time. Well there was professor who wrote one, but it was not high quality. We have English/Russian or Azerbaijani/Russian. We had a hard time, spent a lot of time to go Azerbaijani/Russian, Russian/English. . . . At the same time you have to learn two words. You have to understand Russian because this way you only can find the other." When she writes now, Nimet still moves among multiple dictionaries, either as habit or as method for making choices: "So I go synonym, go antonym, go homonym, and then come back. My god what kind of word can you substitute this one?!" Nimet moves among word forms and then "comes back" to the meaning she attempts among her choices, a process she describes as intentional mixing to find the meaning she wishes to convey: "Yeah because I mix . . . I mix English, Turkish, Azerbaijani language."

Nimet's dictionary practices reveal how messy literacy can be a product of the mess of politics. The very availability of a dictionary, which was related to Soviet education policy of the time, changed the way Nimet writes today among her languages. She knows that a given language was available to her based on whichever political power felt inclined to grant that access. This in turn led her to believe that official or standard languages were related more to the whims of political change than to hard-and-fast grammatical rules. Sofia, whose literate repertoire was shaped by similar Soviet political forces, explains that in the south of Ukraine "in history, something happened." If they speak Ukrainian, she says, it's a "mess": "it's Russian and Ukraine just together; like not Ukraine, but just like together, mess." In other words, messy politics do not produce messy literacies. Literacies weren't pristine before politics got to them. Rather, messy literacies are an accurate representation of lived language in use before politics tries to tidy them up. Multilingual migrant writers, by virtue of a lifetime of moving among languages and locations in the world, know this well and find literate mess to be a natural state. Thus, messy literacies are not characterized simply by chaos, or control, or creativity. Instead, the mess of multilingual literacy for these writers just is. It is a normal phenomenon grounded in history and manipulated for rhetorical effect. They understand mess in turns as funny, frustrating, unavoidable, and productive. Literate mess does not describe the flagging proficiency of a single language variety, but rather it characterizes an entire repertoire shaped through the life experiences of writers.

Certainly, the mess participants describe has been captured for quite some time in such theories of language alternation as code-switching, code-mixing, code-meshing, and translanguaging. Code-switching has been taken up so widely that it defies neat definition and is often used interchangeably with other terms.[3] Critics point to its treatment of languages as "discrete, identifiable and internally consistent wholes" (Gardner-Chloros 9) and to its limited ability to describe uses of dialects, fragments of languages, or contested identifications across codes.[4] No matter the term, language alternation has always been understood as highly social, with communicative contexts both causing and being created by alternation. Beyond participant descriptions of language alternation as example or challenge to existing terminology, perhaps more interesting is the contribution of this practice to the whole of participants' messy repertoires.

For example, Defne prefers "meshed" rather than "switching" terminology to describe her multilingual repertoire. In response to a question that asked her to describe how multilingualism feels to her, she says, "I would say the first thing that came to my mind is switching back and forth. But it's not. Because sometimes, recently, I don't even know whether I'm talking Turkish or English.... That switching back and forth is not anymore the case for me. It used to be like that. It meshed maybe, being confused, and meshed will be kind of the verb for it, like what those two languages really are." It is not productive to cast Defne's preference for "meshed" as naïve to terminological precision. As a near-PhD in sociology, her own characterizations of her language can be assigned worth, even in a scholarly sense (and they should be even without this education). Defne does seem to associate "switching" with a higher level of control or raised level of awareness than the less discrete, more "confused" notion of "meshed" language—a distinction somewhat aligned with corresponding theories. But here, what matters is how Defne's repertoire feels to her, as the experience of what her languages "really are." She characterizes this feeling as part of a literate repertoire in which languages "just come out," a lack of control that stems not from a lack of proficiency but from the social conditions that have of late shaped her repertoire. As is detailed in chapter 3 Defne lives in a liminal state after immigration. Her meshed Turkish and English are therefore a reproduction of her evolving immigrant identity, a daily performance of how she "really" is evolving as a mother, teacher, and writer in the United States.

Characterizing Defne's and other participants' language alternation practices as "messy" thus shows what their repertoires have in common: fluid literate practices that represent the natural state of their lived multilingual experiences. To ground this claim in more detail, I elaborate messy literacies through two focal accounts below. Alicia's and Tashi's extended accounts show how messy literacy practices develop over time, across language varieties, and around the world to create especially fluid literate repertoires.

ALICIA

Alicia, the high school ESL and social studies teacher introduced earlier, spoke, read, and wrote among Hebrew, Spanish, English, and Arabic as she grew up in Argentina. Her grandparents were Arabic-speaking immigrants to Argentina, so Alicia's use of their Arabic phrases is a family tradition. She attended a private Jewish bilingual Spanish/English primary school and a Jewish technical high school, which exposed Alicia to nine years of written and spoken Hebrew. In the context of these multilingual schools, Alicia wrote often to understand religion, history, and culture, using the Western academic methods she was taught early on. She took French in high school because she was "curious" and learned basic Portuguese from the "bunches of books" her family would buy when they traveled to Brazil. Alicia moved to the United States to attend a small liberal arts college and graduated four years later, marrying a fellow student and finding a job as an ESL teacher in the Midwest. But this brief biography belies the intricacy of a literate life in practice. As Alicia says, the literate repertoire she has developed over time is "just complex."

The earliest writing assignment Alicia remembers is an elementary school project in which she wrote about the resources and history of a region in Argentina: "The idea was that we had to explain the resources of the area, and then I remember using tracing paper for different layers [to show] the resources, the geographic features." The project's tracing image is an apt description of Alicia's early understanding of her literate repertoire: she believes languages have layers to be traced through time. She furthered this understanding in high school by joining an extracurricular oral history group with whom she wrote and conducted interviews with local Jewish communities. Alicia describes interviewing Holocaust survivors and others caught up in Argentina's military dictatorships. She traveled around the country to "Jewish colonies" interviewing the elderly. She was a young student then, so her teachers did most of the analysis of interview results. But Alicia's written experiences with these groups exposed her to evolving multilingual immigrant histories. Her transcription of narrated histories of conflict, displacement, and cultural belonging initiated a practice of ethnographic writing and opened a self-reflective window into her own family's Jewish and literate history in Argentina. Because the oral history group had developed a relationship with a small liberal arts college in the United States, Alicia applied to this college and was accepted, deciding to major in anthropology. As she immigrated to the United States, aided by an international relationship between an Argentine high school and a U.S. university, Alicia traveled with a highly developed repertoire of multilingual literacy practices.

After migration, Alicia was largely successful in calling on her Argentinian and Spanish-language practices to write in the United States and in English: "[My professors] were pretty proud of my writing skills considering the fact that I had only been in the states for like six months." But she did have help. She describes meeting with her English professor, "one of the toughest professors with his corrections," at least once a week to talk through her essay writing, and regularly visiting the writing center on campus. These one-on-one meetings, she says, taught her to read closely for the structure of writing in English. Eventually, she "understood, okay this is the way they write. . . . This is how their reading looks like, so this is what I should be doing." She developed a metalinguistic awareness of her writing in Spanish and English through talk-about-writing that facilitated ongoing comparison. Like almost every Spanish speaker in this study, Alicia's comparisons led her to conclude that in Spanish, "our sentences are so long and kind of messy in comparison to English that it makes your writing obviously that way too." She very much believes that "messy" writing is not "bad" writing. Rather, Alicia understands mess in Spanish to be *culta*—that is, "sophisticated . . . like you know what you're talking about"—in opposition to the "chop chop chop" of English's preference for short, efficient sentences.[5]

Alicia explains that the analysis strategies she began to be able to name after her college general education courses—analyzing "what does this mean in the time period," "who are the people that wrote that," "making general assumptions like what does this mean and taking it further from there"—were skills that she was able to apply in the United States "regardless of whether [she] learned them in English or Spanish." Furthermore, her self-identified ability to "think a lot about the context" initiated in her oral history group was carried over and applied to her assignments in the United States. These literate practices moved with Alicia from Argentina but became named entities in the United States, facilitating a critical understanding of language and audience. This helped her reflect on the way she understood and reacted to multilingualism in her own family history. Alicia says she became "very conscious about the way that [she was] pronouncing things and the word choice" during college and became "very picky and conscious about who [her] audience is."

The repetition of "very" throughout Alicia's narratives is revelatory of the confident and self-aware persona that regulates her strong convictions about language. Alicia has had a very interesting literate life. Because she has moved her literate repertoire among her languages and the places she has lived, Alicia revels in literate fluidity even as she regulates her multilingualism according to audience expectations. In fact, a heightened audience awareness is one of the most salient elements of Alicia's literate repertoire. For example, describing an experience seeing friends in Argentina after studying in the United States for several years, she describes navigating the potentials and the constraints of her evolving multilingual repertoire. "How do I translate like the phonological system of the Neanderthal? I just learned this in biological anthro, but I don't know how to explain this in Spanish. So there were certain circumstances when I was like, oh I wish I could just open my mouth and use English on this occasion or I wish I could open my mouth and speak Spanish in this occasion, but sometimes the audience prevents you from doing that so you have to be selective." Alicia did not interpret this moment, in which she experienced the limits of language, as a communication breakdown. Instead, she found herself preferring to communicate with an audience who was multilingual like her. The anecdote is somewhat sad in that Alicia wishes to share her newfound knowledge with friends from home but cannot do so in the language they share. True to her personality, however, Alicia brushes off the loss and treats the experience as a lesson in how to be rhetorically "selective."

In another example, Alicia's convictions about audience are framed not as the choice of one language over the other but as the skilled use of a multilingual repertoire. Informed by her courses in teaching ESL, Alicia believes that code-switching is motivated by "showing off your resources and your abilities to communicate in multiple languages." She admits that for her it is occasionally a matter of ease: if she can't remember a word in Spanish or English, Alicia will use the language she can remember even if her interlocutor doesn't share it. But beyond the potential of "showing off [her] resources," she finds her switching and mixing important practices to "use in different circumstances." For example, "blending" with her aunt is more effective than doing so with her father: "I know my audience. With her it's nice to just be able to switch. And if I wanna say something that mixes the two languages, who cares! . . . I know she's gonna understand it and it makes sense. But in other cases, um, like if I'm talking to my dad who doesn't speak a word of English, if I were to say like *troca* . . . I know it's blending of two languages, but he wouldn't realize that. He would just look at me and go, what is that?" Alicia lays out this comparison to show the communicative choices she makes based on audience and anticipated effect. She finds "a lot more freedom" from the ability to draw on her full repertoire in this way; she finds "a lot more ability to play with ideas . . . to use both languages as a resource" when she is the one deciding how she will work with her literate mess. Alicia's use of the singular "resource" here to describe her use of "both languages" might even suggest that she perceives her repertoire not as several distinctly developed languages but as the entirety of her messy multilingualism.

TASHI

Like Alicia, Tashi's literacy experiences show her writing with a messy and especially fluid literate repertoire. Tashi is a former teacher who, after immigrating to the United States, returned to school to become a nurse. She has a master's degree in biology and communicates in Hindi, Tibetan, English, and Kannada, the language of the Indian state where she attended school and then taught high school science. Tashi's soft-spoken demeanor—her voice on our interview recordings was often a whisper—conceals the forceful determination and good humor that has directed her life. Although quiet, Tashi is not withdrawn. Her sharp perceptions about writing show how hyperaware she is of nearly everything: language patterns in texts and conversations, Indian and American classmates' assumptions about her own language use, the potential and eventual effect of the messiness of her own literate repertoire.

As Tibetan refugees in India, Tashi's parents had few resources to support Tashi, so they sent her to an English-medium boarding school for Tibetan refugees and orphans. The school was shaped, as Tashi explains, by India's two-hundred-year experience of British colonialism. English language education began in first grade, starting from "words in the English class in first, second, third standard and lots of vocabularies" and reached full essay writing in fifth grade. However, Tashi's classmates did not use English with each other: "Teacher teaches in English, but students answer in Tibetan or sometimes in English." She grew up speaking, reading, and writing in a highly multilingual environment, even in a school influenced by British traditions and routines. As a daughter of sustenance farmers who did not read or write, Tashi guided her own learning, at times "teaching them back what [she] had learned" as she taught her father to sign his name or helped her mother interpret mail. Eventually, as Tashi's parents let her control her own educational trajectory, her literacy learning became almost entirely self-sponsored.

The literacy practices Tashi developed during this time show where her fluid literate repertoire comes from. During the time allotted for homework at her boarding school, Tashi studied English language newspapers and books on her own, teaching herself the similarities and differences of composing in Hindi and English. She was motivated to begin such study when she realized that "whatever you have in your brain can't be seen by other people. You just have to write it down and show them that what you know." In India, she says, "it's not like here [in the United States], not like multiple choice. Over there everything in [English] essay. So you really need to express OUT all your brain." Early on in school, Tashi felt that her grades suffered because she could not express her Hindi- and Kannada-related knowledge in English language writing. So she set out to learn how this was done, collecting books and newspapers to analyze "how they write . . . how they go about it": "I just marked all the vocabularies and I point out the phrase, how they use it. And then I note how they play with the words. And in contrast, and in literal meaning and in applied meaning. . . . This makes me [understand] how to play around with the words and get the things done. And play around with the sentences. So yeah, then I really learned the skill of how to play around with the words, and I really don't have to have a strict rule doing English."

Tashi's intentional play in writing moves her beyond the "strict rule" of doing language. If Tashi had simply copied grammatical patterns, or noted the organization of newspaper stories to follow their structure, the mess of her self-taught writing practices might not be apparent. But she looked specifically for how these writers "used" the vocabulary and phrases she marked, how these were used to make "literal" or "applied meanings," and how one might "play around" with English to "get the things done." The repetition of "play around" shows her open stance to understanding how a piece of writing is put together—one imagines her turning a text this way and that to understand its inner workings. Her solitary study initiates her ability to recognize rules and then move beyond them.

After immigrating to the United States to join her graduate student husband, Tashi was able to move these literacy practices with her. Her multiple degrees did not transfer, but she felt she "should not be just ending up like any other thing who have not studied," so she entered a community college nursing program. Although she found much of the coursework to be repetitive with the science courses she had already completed in India, her dual degrees in education and biology gave her fluency in what she identified as nursing's "main language": to be "compassionate, ready to help." Tashi already knew how to read and write for science courses. As she explains, her existing literacy practices "made it really easy to study psychology, sociology, and all because I can express especially easy when it's writing." Her existing facility in essay testing, which she prefers "more than doing multiple choice," helped her "get across some concept" in writing, "elaborating" on points, "analyzing it and coming to the conclusion." These were all practices she created for herself among multiple languages in India and was able to maintain in her English-dominant U.S. courses.

Tashi also shared the practices she developed in India with other multilingual students she encountered in community college writing courses in the United States. For example, she advised a fellow immigrant student from India who "hated whichever class had writing" on how to enjoy learning to write:

> I was telling her, "No it's not like this, you just have to take an essay and analyze how it is done. Once you get to know, like if you really develop that from your heart, you will really love it. And whenever you see a piece you wouldn't read for the content, you will read for how the structure goes. How it's played around." And once you get grip hold of it, you can manipulate whatever you want it to with the language . . . and you know how things going around [swirling hands on the table] and then you understand for yourself how it works . . . how it plays, how the words go around.

Tashi's repeated use of "play," in this excerpt and the one above, shows her acknowledgment that writing is slippery, not always precise or under control. This is why she doesn't "have a strict rule doing English." Now that she feels she has a "grip" on English, she delights in manipulating it to accomplish "whatever [she] wants to with the language." In her analysis of how language "plays, how the words go around," Tashi exhibits the "curiosity toward the language, [and] the ability to intuit linguistic rules from observation of actual usage" of a highly practiced multilingual writer (Canagarajah, *Critical* 134). This willingness to work with language, to read for semantic and syntactic play, shows how Tashi's writing activities are both messy and fluid. She "understands how writing goes . . . how the words go around." And she aims to pass on these practices to others in the United States because she knows how negotiating the mess of literacy can help.

Tashi, Alicia, and the other writers with fluid literate repertoires are highly aware of and, for the most part, fond of multilingual mess. When asked what they think colleagues, neighbors, or classmates should know about multilingualism, their responses range. Yolanda says that her colleagues should know "that language is a huge barrier, but you have to learn how to break it." Defne wants her neighbors to know that "there're always mistakes, so . . . it's never going to be perfect." Yolanda and Defne project more or less control over their literate repertoire, but both want others to know that broken and imperfect language is a normal literate state. The mess of mistakes, mixed, and meshed language creates a chaos for these writers that is at once uncontrollable, productive, accomplishable, and important.

LITERACY RELAYS

Literacy has a relay nature. As another dimension of literate fluidity, literacy relays show how literacy practices and ideologies are handed off and passed around. More than simply the untethered circulation of texts or arguments, literacy relays bind writers to other writers, as one writer passes a practice to another. Relays are the handoff, bestowal, or delivery of literate strategies, skills, and habits developed over the course of a lifetime on the move. In this way, literacy relays are not races or games but are "serious" literate work, as one participant says.

Building on theories of literacy sponsorship, in which powerful interests grant or deny literacies to writers (Brandt, *Literacy*), literacy relays show how practices flow among powerful institutions and writers. Literacy relays plot the movement of literacy. Examining the relay nature of literate fluidity reveals the chain that links parents to children, teachers to students, coworkers to colleagues, as writers actively and consciously hand off their hard-won literacies. These literacy relays are particularly visible in the lives of multilingual migrants for a variety of reasons: the stakes of maintaining literate heritage are raised in a context that asserts assimilation pressure; migrants wrestle with and gain a heightened awareness of their multilingual identities in a monolingual-dominant culture; multilingual teachers feel obliged to pass on literate survival strategies to migrant or newly arrived students with whom they identify. Literacy relays are thus deeply imbued with pressures of difference, discrimination, and desire that motivate a writer to hand off literate help to another.

Below, participants describe literacy relays in two main ways: as mothers who pass down literate heritage, and as teachers who pass around their own language and literacy strategies. Literacy relays are examined through a wide range of participant voices and elaborated through focal narratives from Alicia, Yolanda, and Nimet. In all participants' accounts, literacy relays show the progression of accumulated knowledge that, if allowed to fluidly move, can lift up writers who pass and receive literacy.

Literacy Relays in Families

As one dimension of literate fluidity, literacy relays show how literate heritage is passed from parent to child. All of the mothers in this study (eighteen of twenty-five participants) include language in the family and cultural heritage they hope their children will inherit. These mothers are happy when their children use what they call their "first" or "native" languages and worry when children understand these languages but respond to them in English. Some mothers describe struggling to pass on literate practices to their children, as one mother says, "pulling them" through "learning both languages." But when viewed through the lens of a literacy relay, it becomes clear that more than syntax and vocabulary are actually being passed on in families. The literacy relays mothers create in their families pass on identities and ideologies together with the traditions and habits they hope will shape their children's literate repertoires. These ideologies are not anti-assimilation—that their children should maintain home languages to the sacrifice of learning school English—but are pro-assimilation and pro-dissimilation. These multilingual mothers believe their children can grow up multilingual *and* American, proud of their family's heritage *and* proud of who they are in the United States.

For example, the literacy relay described by Alandra, a social worker from Brazil, is multivalent, containing English/Spanish/Portuguese multilingualism, Brazilian American identity, as well as an awareness of linguistic and cultural difference. She says she is "very proud" that she could "instill that value" about "different languages and different cultures and different ways to ask for those things." "Whether they're English-only speaking and I have to say, 'Hey, people come from different places,' or my Spanish-speaking people and say, 'It's okay, I can help you translate,' and sort of translate the system or translate the understanding, not only what's being said, but understanding." Alandra describes modeling for her daughter how cultural and linguistic difference can be understood. When Alandra models conversations about difference with "English-only speaking" monolinguals in front of her daughter or translates for Spanish-speaking clients at her social services job as her daughter sits nearby, she is passing on a patient, empathetic, and "understanding" approach to language diversity. Alandra enrolled her daughter in a dual-immersion school not only so she will learn how to write among her languages but also so that she will learn in an environment where it makes "more sense that other people spoke different languages." So although Alandra worries when her daughter calls her "Mommy" rather than Mamãe and frets when her daughter tells her, "I don't want you to speak Portuguese," she feels "very proud" that she is passing on the language ideologies she has learned from being multilingual in the United States and in Brazil.

While the literate heritage traced here may recall terms like "heritage language," my use of "literacy relay" aims to avoid the pitfalls scholars have identified in some heritage language movements.[6] Immigrant communities have a long tradition of creating programs like Saturday schools to help their children maintain or learn heritage languages alongside the English they learn in school. But critics of institutionalized heritage curriculum say it misses the fact that some users don't identify with their heritage languages because of, for example, social class or racial identifications. In fact, language users may purposefully reject their linguistic inheritance (e.g., working-class white adolescents with standard English or ethnic urban youth with Vietnamese), or may affiliate with several simultaneous varieties at once. Other scholars say heritage movements distill complicated affiliations into single othered languages, pointing out that communities don't automatically "inherit" language expertise and traditions and in fact may not affiliate with their family languages at all.[7] For example, García notes that Spanish is not a heritage language of a foreign land but a language long present in the United States, one that is part of active bilingual identities of millions of U.S. citizens ("Positioning" 603). Use of "literacy relay" here therefore aims to acknowledge the heritage desires of many participants but also avoid romanticizing or homogenizing language affiliations.

In the case of Alandra, a literacy relay acknowledges why she might want to pass on Portuguese to her daughter. She is motivated less by cultural continuity than by cultivating tolerance or "understanding." But she also intuitively knows what studies show: language loss does occur, especially in schooling contexts that devalue or place low status on home languages.[8] A literacy relay shows how these high and low values are passed in the context of specific life experiences. Somewhat like Kesler Rumsey's theory of heritage literacy, which traces how "certain practices, tools, and concepts" are transferred across generations and how communities adopt or reject generational change (575), literacy relays show how heritage happens, in family and extra-family contexts, showing what *is* passed on and why.

Every participant treated literacy relays in families as an additive experience—no parent expressed wanting their children to forego English language learning to maintain a heritage language or to practice United States–based writing to suppress literacy informed by their religious or family backgrounds. Importantly, participant accounts also show that literacy relays don't originate with these writers. Relays often start elsewhere, moving through participants' lives, linking family, cultural, or geographic histories to children's literate practices in the United States. For example, Defne helps run a Turkish Saturday school with community parents to teach their children about Turkish language, history, and culture. She says that even if they have a "vague idea of Ataturk and independence, it's good enough, because it's part of their heritage . . . and I'm really happy about that." Khadroma, a Tibetan nurse from China, brings her daughter to Tibetan cultural events to "pass that on," hoping her daughter will use Tibetan when she grows up. Khadroma and Defne are aware that their daughters will become fluent in English by virtue of attending U.S. schools, so they direct extra energy toward literacies in other languages. They model and practice with their daughters songs, prayers, stories, and sayings learned through writing and often eventually performed. Khadroma explains: "It's what my parents did to me. I went to Chinese school but I spoke Tibetan at home. So I'm still very fluent in Tibetan." Thus Khadroma contributes another move in an existing literacy relay: her heritage practices did not start with her, but came from her parents and now move through her to her daughter.

Similarly, Alicia feels her family's complex cultural history move through her when phrases in Arabic appear suddenly in her speech: "When somebody in my family gets something in their throat we go *Allah, allah*! And I was like holy shit, we're saying *Allah Allah*! We're Jewish, what the hell? Doesn't make any sense! But that's the way my great grandparents did it, the way my grandparents did it and then the way they did with my parents. And that's the way I learned to react to that." Alicia explains that her great-grandparents immigrated to Argentina in the 1920s and brought Arabic with them. Alicia's grandparents spoke a little, and select phrases and words remain in Alicia's and her parents' interactions, teaching Alicia to "react" in Arabic in specific situations. She explains that moments like these solidify for her "an amount of pride" in her family's background, something she sees as "very special about [her]." For Alicia, the story of Arabic in her family begins on another continent and several generations back, but remains an integral part of the literate heritage that was passed down to her from her family. She includes these pieces of language when describing her literate repertoire, calling Arabic a "half or maybe one quarter" language that she uses in speaking and in writing.

Both Sabohi and Tashi narrate literacy relays through evolving historical links. Their long excerpts track the events they link to make sense of their family's literate repertoires. Sabohi locates the English language origins of her repertoire prior to her own life. When asked her opinion of the dominance of English in Pakistan, she says:

> Well it goes back to India being English colony. And it is like that slave mentality, I mean this is my understanding of the things. It's just Indians were enslaved and they were treated really badly. And even though they resented the English, but they were made to call them masters, masters, masters, and actually masters are like superior and you tend to imitate that thing and you tend to be more like them or something. And that translates, that travels down because if I had been living in that era and then I was independent, I would like to be like the English master. Then if I had a son, I would definitely want him to be like that. And then I am inculcating in him that mentality and he in turn grows up with that mentality that passes on to next generation. And next generation. And until now it is about convenience because English is, everybody understands in India, outside India, most of the world, half of the world probably speaks English. So it's again, convenience.

In Sabohi's narrative, literacy "travels down," from colonialism to contemporary globalization, creating a literacy relay in which language ideologies are handed off—and also imposed—from one generation to the next. Although her explanation of a son's colonial English knowledge is hypothetical, her shift from the conditional to the present tense shows that she is also describing her own son's current English language practices in the United States. Sabohi treats her family's English history with pragmatism and ambivalence, acknowledging its colonial past but understanding its power in the present as convenience. So as she speaks now to her son in English and Urdu and enrolls him in an Arabic/English Islamic school, she also passes down colonial-inflected language histories. Again, Sabohi's language practices and values did not start with her but come from regional, global, and family experiences that "travel down" through her to her son.

In other words, literacy relays clearly pass on more than heritage languages. In another example, Tashi explains that she "feels good" that her daughter can speak Tibetan as well as English. "That's good for her," Tashi says, because "if she goes and meet her grandmother in India, she won't have a communication problem." Because Tashi's daughter speaks with her grandmother in Tibetan every day on the phone and is surrounded mostly by Tibetan-speaking adults, a unique literacy relay has formed in Tashi's family: "I think it changes with the generation, you know, like my parents and their cohort they speak Tibetan so pure. In India we were born and our generation we speak like 90 percent Tibetan but like 10 percent mixed. And then goes to, let's see, now the kids were born in America are most kind of losing Tibetan language. Like my daughter she can speak whatever language we use frequently, rich in our vocabularies, but the language that we don't use tend to shrink on those vocabularies."

Like Sabohi, Tashi locates literate knowledge before her time, and in another place, as Tibetan practices move through her to her daughter. But even more, for Tashi, a generational literacy relay begins in "pure" Tibetan in India with her parents, which becomes mixed after immigration to the United States. Although this trajectory indexes language loss, Tashi also accounts for the percentage of mixing that occurs along the way, especially because she says her daughter moves fluidly among all of these registers every day. In fact, Tashi's daughter's Tibetan accent performs the trajectory of her family's migration. "So she can speak Tibetan like our accent, our originality, the words that we use at home, and the communication that takes place among the family. But if I make her sing a Tibetan song, like if I teach something new now, she sings like you know, she sings it like an American singing Tibetan song." Tashi's daughter's Tibetan literacy learning happens through family communication as well as reading and performing songs. What Tashi hears in her daughter's singing is the trace of her family's history: the Tibetan she uses with her grandmother on the phone is the "pure" variety located in India; her Tibetan used among adults at home is the Tibetan used among recently arrived Indian immigrants; and the Tibetan used while singing songs at Saturday school carries an American accent. Tashi embeds an immigration narrative within her description of language change that has an origin in pure language, and an endpoint—the current moment—in language that is "mixed." In this way, Tashi is passing to her daughter mixed, accented, and always changing language practices, rooted in history but fluid in its U.S. context.

As should be clear in these accounts, literacy relays in families are as much about identity as they are about language. They are not just about identity and language maintenance, but about fluid identity and language change. For example, in tandem with passing down Arabic literacy practices like the reading of the Quran, Haneen hopes to pass down complex identities to her children. "I am American cause I have the American passport . . . ," she says, "but I'm American-Arab, I call myself." She hopes for the same identification for her children: "I'm raising my kids like, 'You are American and you are Muslim, you're American, you're all of that.' And they're really adjusting with that, 'cause they're not foreigner. They were born here; they live here." Haneen and her family travel frequently between the United States and Jordan, where much of her extended family lives. These trips are intended to give her children Arabic practice but even more, they are meant to model their complex Muslim-Jordanian-American identities. Haneen seems most concerned with passing on to her children access to "all of that," wherever they are living and whichever language they are using.

Literacy relays thus pass down language and literacy practices—songs, sayings, and prayers practiced and repeated in Saturday school activities and around kitchen tables. But literacy relays also pass on the historical knowledge, colonial legacies, mixed identities, and heightened awareness of difference these writers develop in the United States. Importantly, literacy relays in families are not a defense against assimilation. Rather, parents continue relays to connect their children both to their literate past and to their complicated literate present.

Literacy Relays in Schools

Another way to understand fluid literate repertoires is to look at the handoff of multilingual literacy from teacher to student—that is, literacy relays created in schools. Thirteen of twenty-five participants in this study are or were teachers: one group switching *to* teaching; another group switching *away* from teaching after migration precluded their previous teaching qualifications. By virtue of their multilingualism, many participants found employment in the United States as bilingual teachers or as bilingual resource staff at schools or nonprofits. Of the literate experiences described by participants in this study, teaching is a particularly fraught and fertile relay opportunity. Many of these teachers describe passing down literate lessons to their students through the lens of their own struggles and mistakes. Even when these literacy handoffs are not made explicit to students, they often are implicit in the teachers' approach to classroom discourse and feedback.

For example, Aldene, a bilingual resource specialist from Brazil, compares her own struggles as a graduate student in the United States to the literacy challenges of the high schoolers she supports. She shares her "personal experience to help them understand how to write" because, as she says, she "also had the hard time [with] the way they do it here in the U.S." In one case, although Aldene originally "really hated the format you have to follow" for United States–based citation practices, she now "ends up transferring that to [her] students that are not used to using traditional APAs or MLAs." She admits that in a U.S. school context, she has "just learned how to do that and learned how easy it makes their writing too." But Aldene doesn't force students into English monolingualism in pursuit of "the way they do it here in the U.S." Instead, she tells her students to "just write." She says, "Even if you have to put like some Portuguese or whatever language mixed up, just try. It's just a start." Aldene shares with her students the writing strategy she developed in the United States—using "language mixed up" to start. Aldene's relay shows what else she passed to students together with literacy: strategies for writing among languages, information about literacy norms in the United States, and support for rather than judgment of writing with "mixed up" language.

Other teachers describe similar relays. Tashi describes showing the science students she taught in India how to use their native Tibetan to learn to write in English: "Since I was teaching science, I was telling them, 'If you know the concept and if you come short of English, you can just express in few Tibetan words.' . . . So I give them some flexibility for them, keeping in mind their language strength." And Faridah, who teaches beginning Arabic in an Islamic elementary school, uses a similarly flexible approach, hoping to pass on the habit "to work two languages." She says: "You know sometimes you do some mistakes, which is not really mistakes. Because even now I'm teaching Arabic and the kids they are really sometimes confusing between, because Arabic from the right to the left and English is from the left to the right. . . . But with practice, you're gonna have the habit you know, to work two languages."

The commonality of multilingual flexibility among teachers is striking. TESOL and foreign language teaching have long dealt with the tension between teaching only in the target language.[9] Despite that, it is clear from the teachers' multilingual practices in this study—and more important, the way they intentionally pass these strategies on to their students—that multilingual fluidity can help students, as Aldene says, to "just write." Two focal accounts show how literacy relays in schools are motivated by teachers' beliefs in the benefits of a fluid literate repertoire. These accounts from Alicia and Yolanda show how they pass on to students distinct kinds of information: experiences with U.S.- and English-based writing customs, strategies for writing among languages, and ways of being multilingual writers in the United States.

Alicia

Alicia currently works at a Midwestern high school in multiple capacities: she is one of the school's Spanish teachers; she serves as a bilingual resource specialist at the school, observing and consulting with other teachers who have students designated ELL; and she supports ELL students in classes or in small pullout groups. When Alicia works with students in all of these capacities, she relays to them the practices she has developed for writing in English and writing essays in the United States. She also shares knowledge she has gained over a lifetime of writing with her multilingual repertoire.

Like all of the six Spanish-speaking participants in this study, Alicia's understanding of writing in English begins with sentence length. Alicia tells her students, "You're used to reading very long sentences, but here is not the way to do it. In Spanish it's fine; it's acceptable. But in English most people won't be okay with it. They will find it too confusing or overwhelming or would actually categorize it as bad writing skills." Alicia's comparison of expectations "here" in English and those her students are "used to" in Spanish endorses her belief that her students should learn English in the United States and justifies her position in the school. But the comparison of English to Spanish also reflects the processes Alicia used to come to her own conclusions about what she understands to be "acceptable" writing in the United States. She says that "just from comparing and from remembering how hard it was to understand the English way of writing," she realized that Spanish users, in her opinion, "don't have it set up so rigorously as it is in English." Like her use earlier in the chapter of "mess" as productive chaos, Alicia understands "rigorously" in English to essentially mean structured, short, and choppy.

As she describes, Alicia developed these beliefs about English through the English language testing and teacher feedback she experienced in college in the United States. She gathered around her a community of feedback-givers at her university. She met with a literature professor every week to have him explain his written feedback on her papers, she visited the writing center at her university at least once a week, and she had her English-speaking United States–born husband read almost all of her writing. Alicia says when she showed him such texts as job application cover letters, he would tell her, "Ah, well, this sentence is too long; this one is too long, gigantic! The whole paragraph is one sentence." His regular feedback helped her understand that "for somebody that I guess knows already how I write, then it will make sense, but for somebody who's not used to it, then I will maybe have to take a step back and say, 'Okay, let me reword this because I have to think of who's going to be reading this.'" Alicia learned that as she composed in the United States, she needed to "step back" and "try to make it fit for what the purpose of it is."

This is exactly the literacy strategy Alicia passes on to her students. "I tell them, 'You know if this was in Spanish it would make more sense. But because we're writing in English and because you have to remember who's gonna be reading it, then you should phrase this in a way that's more understandable to your audience." She uses the same relay method to help her students understand literacy expectations for U.S. essay writing norms. Speaking specifically of organization, Alicia tells them, "Okay, you need to have your introduction and you need to have your connecting sentence and you need to have you know all these things and your argument, 1, 2, 3." From practicing for and taking the TOEFL, corresponding with U.S. professors who visited her high school in Argentina, completing a master's degree in bilingual education, and now supporting ELL students as a teacher in the United States, Alicia came to believe that U.S. essays are highly structured with concrete steps to be taken throughout, "1, 2, 3." Because she often learns alongside her students, Alicia is immersed in contemporary high school essay-writing practices. She describes helping one ELL student with a language arts essay in a "very English style." She says, "We had to come with the topic sentence and we had to include that in the thesis, like very 1, 2, 3, very rigid. . . . Nobody in college explained to me that I have to have a hook, background, and thesis. I knew you had to have something before the thesis and then the thesis. . . . Now I can structure it for my students so that they can learn it in a standard way that all students do it."

Alicia tellingly associates United States–based literacy practices to "English" practices, often conflating the two. A rigidity of structure and style in both is made explicit by Alicia as she passes to her students what she believes is criteria for success: "the standard way that all students do it." Whether these are the literacy conclusions English teachers and researchers would want endorsed, these are the strategies Alicia developed from her lived experience, and those that she passes to her students. Importantly, Alicia couches all of this knowledge in the context of what it means to be a multilingual writer in the United States. She says, "I don't tell them, 'That's wrong!' I don't talk to them like that. . . . I want them to understand that—and this is what I tell them—it's not that the way you write is wrong, it just doesn't follow the rules of English writing. So that's kinda what I had to learn. I understood, you know, it's not that I'm doing it wrong. It just doesn't fit this language." Alicia passes on a literate lesson beyond simple sentence length or essay organization: right and wrong are based on cultural or, especially, audience-based expectations. United States–based English language essay writing is one practice among many. Alicia shows her students that they are not "wrong" for writing under Spanish stylistic norms, but that they need to better negotiate the multiple valid norms that exist. In this way, her ultimate literacy knowledge is not that all writing should be rule-driven and rigid, but that writers must make choices among their language-based practices according to audience.

For Alicia, this belief is based very much in her multilingual identity, one that she is not willing to give up in the United States. "I do apply some of the things that come just naturally to me if I feel that it's the right thing to do or if it just fits with what I want to say," she says. "I'm not going to completely forget where I come from and what I know to do best. And who knows, sometimes that could be an advantage as well, you know, it makes you stick out or it makes you a little different, which is fine too 'cause we don't want to be all cookie cutters." Perhaps Alicia has a more developed sense of a writerly self than a high school student. She insists she will "still do one or two long run-on sentences here and there because it makes [her] happy." But because she weaves this understanding into her one-on-one and classroom teaching, she is also passing on to her students the connection between run-on sentences, happiness, and cultural origins. For Alicia, these are not separate issues; they exist together in a fluid repertoire that informs how multilingual writers make decisions among their languages.

Yolanda

Yolanda, a bilingual high school science teacher, describes school literacy relays that parallel Alicia's. Yolanda grew up in Bogota, Colombia, in a household dense with literacy, dominated by a mother who highly valued reading and writing. Yolanda remembers as a child reading encyclopedias and Bibles to herself and to her younger brother. She remembers writing "letters to baby Jesus for Christmas to ask for things" and New Year's Eve resolutions with her family, which each family member signed, stored in their wallet, and revisited at the end of the year. (A tradition they continue to this day.) When the family vacationed, Yolanda's mother would pack books with Yolanda's toys, believing that "you always need a book because your books are gonna be your best friends." Her mother believed just as deeply in the power of writing, advising Yolanda that "if you cannot say something just explain it in writing and write what you feel because whatever you say is valuable and you need to be heard." Yolanda's mother looms large in Yolanda's literacy memories, although her family thought of her as radical and a little "crazy": she was the only one in her family to attend college and was the secretly liberal principal of the "very strict" Opus Dei school Yolanda attended. Along with endless energy, Yolanda seems to have inherited many of her mother's literacy practices. She is animated and optimistic as she describes her literate life to me as we sit together at a lab table in her empty classroom.

After secondary school, Yolanda pursued a science education that immersed her in Spanish and English literacy. She attended a veterinary university in Colombia where she read lab reports and scientific articles in English. She composed mostly science writing: abstracts, lab reports, article summaries—all of which she remembers as "super hard." She says she "struggled a lot" and willed herself to "try again, okay try again," working with study groups to get through the majority English-language reading. After graduating, Yolanda worked as a large-animal vet at her father's ranch, where she wrote and read lab reports, analyzed lab samples, and wrote up reports for other vets. When Yolanda moved to the United States to work for a bovine genetics company in the Midwest, she did not intend to stay. She hoped to gain veterinary experience with dairy cows and return to Colombia to start her own farm. Although Yolanda enjoyed working with the cows, she did not enjoy working outside in the Midwestern weather: "I had to go and inseminate cows, and it was so cold. So cold." Instead, Yolanda found a job as a high school bilingual aide, where her colleagues encouraged her to get a teaching license. She returned to school to get her science and ESL teaching licenses and in the meantime met and married an American and decided to stay in the United States.

Because she had attended a bilingual primary and secondary school and was exposed to much scientific English in college, Yolanda assumed that speaking and writing English in the United States would be "easy." But, as she says, "Okay watch TV? Nope. Maybe watch with captions, listen to the radio? No idea." She felt this was due to her being "always kind of bad at English," but nevertheless she practiced with colleagues and classmates and was gratified to receive understanding feedback from her teaching license instructors: "They were so nice. I think they never said that it doesn't sound right. They never said like, 'What do you mean?' They just did an effort to try and understand what I was saying." The generous feedback motivated Yolanda's language learning, and she quickly finished her coursework and found a job as a bilingual science teacher at a local high school.

As a teacher, Yolanda passed to her students literacy and language strategies shaped by all of these literacy experiences. Like Aldene, Faridah, and Tashi, Yolanda encourages her students to use their full literate repertoires to write in English. She lets them "use Spanish . . . they can use both." But because she "needs to know that they know biology," she asks for English in the topics she has taught: "If I'm asking what is 'diffusion,' I want them to use the words 'molecule,' 'concentration,' 'diffusion.' The other words can be in Spanish, you know what I mean?" Like Tashi, Yolanda separates teaching science from teaching English, taking responsibility only for the science. Tashi and Yolanda know that students are learning not content *through* language but content *and* language. As multilingual writers themselves, they know this dual load is hard, and they do what they can to facilitate their students' learning.

For example, Yolanda models her own language learning to help her students understand that struggle is normal. She describes reading along with students trying to pronounce difficult science terminology, showing them that she struggles too. She says, "Hello, I'm teaching biology and I don't know how to say the words we're writing." Yolanda admits what she doesn't know and shows her students how they can set language norms together: "Sometimes I asked the kids when we're reading something scientific, 'How do you think you say this?' And they say, 'I don't know.' . . . They know I don't know how to say it, so I ask them, 'How do you think? How would you say it?' And they find a way to say it, and I say, 'Let's use it.' . . . For kids that speak other languages you know, I have an accent, but look at me, I can do it, so go ahead. 'But what if it's wrong?' Doesn't matter, look at me!" Yolanda encourages students to use a provisional pronunciation, saying, "Let's use it," improvising until later on and knowing they can continue to negotiate meaning until they get it right. Yolanda's "let's use it" shows students how to write within the reality of literate uncertainty: "But what if it's wrong? Doesn't matter, look at me!"

As in her life, Yolanda is lighthearted in the classroom. She thinks her students' lives are hard enough and would prefer to make the sometimes mind-boggling acquisition of English "a comedy for all of us." She hesitates to demand of newly arrived students who are "going through a lot of changes, not only language, but everything, culture and family," to "use this now, now everything gonna be against you." Although her newcomer ESL courses are enrolled with students speaking a variety of languages—primarily Spanish, Nepali, Chinese, and Hmong—she helps the Spanish speakers as much as she can, acknowledging that helping "everybody or nobody" is not actually as fair as meritocratic approaches make it seem. Instead, she helps as many students as she can under "the condition that you have to grow." She says, "Because you just got here, you can do it this way. But you have to start moving on because you have to grow and your language has to grow. . . . You have to move on from that stage, otherwise you're gonna stay there." It is this growth, an action she explicitly couches in movement, that Yolanda wants to pass on most of all. Together with her students she acknowledges that learning English, and learning scientific English, is tough, but she shrugs and says, "Okay, let's move on."

Beyond demonstrating her own struggle, Yolanda moves fluidly among Spanish and English in class to pass on strategies for composing with one's full repertoire. She facilitates improvisation, negotiation, and cooperation among her students and herself. As she says, "There is many things I can not say what I want to say. So I say it in Spanish!" For example, she uses Spanish to express the precise meaning she is after in class. In one example, she uses *papelitos* to describe the little pieces of paper she hands out to students for them to write roles they want to play in dissecting a pig. The students mirror her code-switching, as she asks, "Do I have everybody's *papelitos*?" and the students answer, "You have my *papelitos*!" In another example, she calls a student *sapo*, or toad, when he answers every question she asked the class: "I'm asking the class and he answers; I'm asking the class and he answers." She says, "In Colombia we call that being *sapo*." Because she couldn't access a direct translation in English, she calls on what she has and shows students that lexical borrowing can still produce meaning in context. In fact, this is a strategy supported by research: "extensive empirical evidence" supports "interdependence across languages . . . in language learning generally" and for "literacy-related aspects of language" in particular (Cummins, "Proposal for Action" 588).[10]

These classroom accounts demonstrate the playful approach to literacy Yolanda strives to pass on to her students. She lets students practice hearing accented English, often emphasizing rather than suppressing her accented pronunciation. She has them laugh with her at the occasional comedy of reading and writing across languages and helps them, as she says, "move on" from certainty in a manner that evokes Alan Firth's "let it pass" principle. She finds meaning together with her students—a practice she carried from Colombia, where she and her fellow students worked together to translate their readings into Spanish. But in the process, Yolanda also teaches her students about audience awareness and disciplinary expectations.

Y: I told them to be careful with what you write! You need to read it and remember that English is not my first language, so you are writing this for me. . . . I told them that it didn't make sense to me, and to read it before you [pass it in].

R: So you also taught them about their audience. So if they're writing for you, then . . .

Y: Oh my god I'm so good at teaching writing! [laughing] So I guess yeah, to be aware. Like, guys, you have to remember you're writing like you want me to understand.

Yolanda passes to her students strategies for writing with an audience in mind: being "careful" with what they write; reading it before they hand it to another reader; writing like they want a multilingual reader to understand. Certainly these and the lessons above are simply good teaching. Here, Yolanda is teaching her students about a rhetorical situation and a stage in the writing process.

But these lessons are one part of a relay that reaches back to Yolanda's own literacy learning as a multilingual student in the United States and Colombia. Especially in her teaching courses in the United States, Yolanda fine-tuned her writing strategies for U.S. essay norms. For example, she noticed in peer and teacher feedback the same conventions that Alicia describes earlier: an "introduction, middle, and conclusion" essay organization as well as the desire for shorter sentences. "Everybody told me, 'that sentence is too long!'" she says. "But it's two different worlds and cultures, right?" More than other participants, Yolanda connects a style element as incidental as sentence length to a level of "worlds and cultures." She continues: "It comes with what I told you before about feeling that you are from there *and* from here, so there is something within yourself, within your heart that needs to change for you to not feel that that is offensive, right? Because other than that if it happens too roughly before it is within yourself, you're being imposed to do something you don't believe in, and then you feel offended and you hate it." It's remarkable how Yolanda treats the seemingly minor issue of sentence length as a heightened form of literate expression, one attached to "something within yourself, within your heart." She narrates the process of coming to accept sentence length as a cultural shift that, once mastered, can help a writer feel a part of "there *and* . . . here."

In this rare serious moment, Yolanda offers insight into multilingual writers' resistance to adopted U.S. writing norms. She was not lighthearted in saying the writers might feel "offended" and "hate" writing short sentences if they have not come to "believe in" their purpose. Yolanda came to accept this style as a trade-off: "I understand it's just different culture so you express yourself in a different way. When I live here I'm gonna learn it and I'm gonna do it. But if I was writing in Spanish, I'm gonna do it my way. And if *you* write in Spanish, you do it *my* way [laughing]." By designating short sentences as simply one cultural stylistic choice among others, Yolanda remains confident in the Spanish-language elements of her repertoire, maintaining a repertoire that is "from there *and* from here." She does not exaggerate when she says that writers who are "coming and leaving quick" don't need to use this style, saying that "it's different" for immigrants who come to the United States to stay: "It's like what you are doing with your life, I think."

For Yolanda, style is a choice bound to a writer's transnational identity. In stark contrast to what an instructor might think is a minor slash of a feedback pen, Yolanda believes the choice of a short or long sentence "is just amazing 'cause it's all who you are." And if in that feedback, multilingual writers are made to feel that their long sentences are not "proper English," then "you are not a proper person, right? Even though you can be a very good, giving, generous, good citizen, you are still one level below because you are not proper." Yolanda has learned in the United States that the length of a sentence is absolutely connected to the value of one's identity. She understands the moral heft and class-based prestige that is dependent on one's use of "proper" language, and she believes deeply in passing on that lesson to her students. In other words, the strategies Yolanda passes on to her students prove to be particularly complex. These strategies show that U.S. literacies are options, not universal truths; they imply a quiet resistance to classroom practices that treat multiple languages as separate and standard. Yolanda has cultivated this literacy knowledge over a lifetime—from her mother's respect for literacy to Yolanda's own struggles reading in English in college, to the empathetic instructor feedback she received in her teaching program. This is why she knows her students "need time" to move among multiple literacy norms so that they don't "hate" or "feel offended" using United States–based practices. Like the family relays explored earlier in this chapter, Yolanda's literacy relay starts before her. She simply acts as one important link in a literacy chain that spans continents and languages.

Every teacher in this study who engages in literacy relays is hyperaware of literate expectations in the United States. They know many listeners and readers expect standard language and monolingual communication. They empathize with students as they acquire English, and they push students to develop their proficiency in it. These teachers are not naïve in the face of language expectations in the United States. In fact, by virtue of their multilingualism, they are likely harder on their own multilingual students even as they pass on their own hard-won strategies and habits. Faridah explains this best: "In my class I told them this is my strategy, okay. Like you are going to the war. Okay when it's time to joke, we are gonna have fun time to make joke and laugh like crazy, 'Oh teacher you are funny and you are that!' Okay [clap clap] back to work. It is serious." These migrant women, some of whom were teachers before immigration, and some of whom are brand-new to the classroom, use literacy relays as a central component in their teaching practice. From struggling to understand, acquiring academic language in pieces, collaborating with other language learners, and drawing on the full extent of their literate repertoire, these teachers know that literate practice can be fun and playful but is most of all "serious" business in the United States.

Global Relays

Literacy relays do not only take place in families and schools, of course; they are happening everywhere all the time. Literacy relays also occur on a global scale, enabled by missionary and teacher travel, transnational trade, intensifying communication technologies, and increasingly dense NGO networks. Many of the migrants in this study come from places in the world long treated as in need of services, conversion, or education. Thus these migrants also have participated in global literacy relays, in which powerful individuals or organizations pass around literate practices and ideologies that participants pick up and pass to others. For example, Nimet was a language teacher before migrating to the United States. In Azerbaijan she taught English to high school students and English teachers. She also taught Azeri to Western teachers and volunteers working in Azerbaijan. Her work in teacher training especially reveals the global literacy relays in which she participated.

Early on in Nimet's career as a teacher in Azerbaijan, she understood pedagogy to be directly related to the political system that regulated schools, with writing instruction designed to respond to the correspondence of "Karl Marx, Friedrich Engels, Lenin" as well as to "communism, socialism . . . the history of the Soviet Union [which] they emphasize everywhere, it doesn't matter your major." Curriculum was designed around the materials and practices available under that political system. "During my time," Nimet says, "the Soviet Union education system focus on reading and writing, never listening, speaking, never ever. We have only one DVD or something. We used to go the lab and they put you on wait list because limit equipment and more students." Nimet connected scarce materials to the Soviet system's endorsement of reading and writing over speaking and listening. By extension, she interpreted the Soviet system as wanting to keep these skills separate—Nimet thought the Soviet education system didn't want people to learn how to listen and speak in English. Her teaching experience showed her that this separation inhibited her students' English language learning. She explained: "When I was a teacher, I saw that if you teach the language you have to take this four skills together, otherwise you cannot learn language."

Nimet resisted the pedagogies handed down through political regimes and collaborated with other teachers to change the course of this particular pedagogical literacy relay. With a friend who worked at the American embassy and had "perfect British English," she founded the Azerbaijani English Teachers Association (AzETA).[11] They contacted NGOs for support, but "not our government; government doesn't care." They sought funding from the British Council, the American ambassador's office, the American Council on Education, and the Soros Foundation—all of which had branches in Azerbaijan. They specifically asked for support to write language-teaching textbooks, which they received and used to write a book whose materials were passed around the country. Eventually high school and university teachers joined, and they "saw the result. . . . We begin just twelve people. Now we have eight hundred members." Nimet describes the AzETA hosting conferences of two hundred people from ten regions around the country, "preparing teachers to give workshop," which enabled them to "give workshop to other people." Members of the organization would travel to schools around the country, sometimes supported by British or American embassy funds for bus, food, or materials printing, to "kind of spread the new teaching techniques." Nimet explains that "we need to help—we wanted not just needed—we wanted to help the secondary school and the university to teach effectively because they don't know what to do."

In the background of many participants' experiences in this study, NGOs quietly influence literate practice in many parts of the world. But in this example, Nimet and her colleagues also are agents in this literacy relay—they are the ones organizing, teaching, appealing for funding, creating their own materials, and passing on practices, not the organizations themselves. They work around the government-endorsed pedagogies that emphasize only reading and writing and instead integrate all language learning skills into a book that they write themselves, which they watch produce results in teaching and learning in Azerbaijan. Nimet extends this literacy relay even further when she uses these pedagogies to teach Azeri to English-speaking Peace Corps volunteers working in Azerbaijan. She uses dominoes to teach vocabulary, "just word by word we make that," and creates visual aids to integrate literacy skills. Other teachers from AzETA "put in" and "share" lessons and encourage the volunteers to bring their own to share in turn, "step by step."

Nimet creates "word by word" and "step by step" a literacy relay around the country. She models the collaboration of the Azerbaijan English Teachers Association, encouraging volunteers to bring visual aids to the classes, sharing them and passing them around, which in turn informs the workshops Nimet gives back to the AzETA. While starting and growing such a teaching network is indicative of Nimet's bustling personal and educational activism, it is also an example of the connective quality of literacy. In successive steps Nimet saw a pedagogical lack created by certain political conditions, acted with others to respond to it, appealed to global organizations for funding, and changed the nature of a literacy relay that was spreading language pedagogy around the country. Teachers connected to teachers, to students and back to other teachers. Relays are not purely chronological or generational; they are also lateral and global, as practices move not just from agencies or governments downward but across teachers, writers, and readers.

HOW LITERATE VALUES MOVE WRITING

The potential of fluidity is great. This chapter shows literate fluidity to be the messy, connected, agentive movement of literate practices among languages, writers, and locations around the world. As the accounts show, when writers' literacy practices remain fluid among languages, and when writers can move their practices fluidly to other writers, they gain sharp insight into culture and language, become hyperaware of audience, articulate similarities and differences among writing styles in multiple languages, and occasionally write themselves into altered identities. Many of the lived experiences narrated support scholarly claims that multilingual writers can draw on multilingual resources to successful ends.[12] Their literate repertoires appear to be not only fluid but also mostly reliable—they call on their repertoire when needed and put their practices to the rhetorical use they intend.

The writers in this study understand the consequences of fluidity in specific ways: as potential for language innovation, access to life opportunities, expanded global understandings, and an enriched sense of self. Several participants describe how they believe language to be enlivened by messy literacies. Many writers point to the language innovations created by loan words from other languages or technological neologisms. For example, Alicia enjoys using *googliar* in Spanish (from the verb "to google" in English) as an innovation coming from English and technology simultaneously. Yolanda describes her use of *sadito*, created by adding a Spanish diminutive to English words, in person and in texts with her husband and step-daughters. Nimet claims, opening her hands wide, that writing among languages can give a composed text "broad meaning; broad, broad." She understands broadened meaning to occur as one searches for rhetorical options among dictionaries, writing samples online, textbooks, and multilingual friends. She describes compiling these proliferating semantic options in lists and referring to them as she reads and writes.

Other participants understand the consequences of fluid literate practices more generally, especially as an expansion of ways of thinking or writing. For example, Alicia understands writing among languages to "enhance the experience in both languages . . . [giving] you more creativity and ways to explore language." Defne describes borrowing analogies from Turkish to compose in English, using "that kind of resemblances to other things" to heighten the emotion of her writing in English. Faridah describes this expansion through directionality, saying that when a writer uses "a lot of languages, you are getting the experience of thinking up and down, straight, right, left." She provides a perspectival view of a repertoire, suggesting those who write from multiple languages experience multiple points of view that can enrich writing. Much scholarship theorizes what multilinguals know as successful "multicompetent" communicators (Cook, "Going Beyond" 24).[13] But the consequences of literate fluidity go beyond what multilingual migrant writers' know about literacy to what they can do in and understand about the world. The accounts in this chapter suggest especially a critical sensibility toward linguistic and cultural difference and an awareness of a system of discourse beyond themselves.

Furthermore, many participants understand the consequences of literate fluidity to mean increased access to people, jobs, knowledge, and cultural understandings. Defne's view of access is quite specific. She believes that "using two different languages" is not only "good brain gymnastics" but helps her connect with her monolingual American boyfriend. Without English, she says, she might have lost "the opportunity of [her] life." Sabohi has a more general idea that a multilingual writer has access to "a lot of stuff that is in other languages." For her, this stuff is "resources besides English" that help multilingual individuals "move around" in their writing. Khadroma similarly frames access as movement, saying her work as an interpreter exposed her to "different people from different countries," making her realize, "Well, I should keep moving . . . I don't know where I go or where is my destination, but I'll just keep doing what I've been doing." As is clear by such statements, many of these writers experience multilingualism *as* movement and need fluid literate repertoires to harness their full literate potential.[14]

Finally, participants understand literate fluidity to expand, solidify, or actively remake their identities.[15] Sabohi believes that because she can "read and write in more than one language," she is "more powerful . . . more competent . . . more confident." So does Aldene, who was both daughter and professional translator for her parents while traveling in Argentina. When her parents were "totally lost," she was able to take care of them, which was "just cool; it felt powerful." For Yolanda, living as a Spanish speaker in the United States solidified her identity as a transnational multilingual migrant. In the United States she likes "to be known because [she speaks] Spanish." She likes standing out for her multilingualism and plays up the multiple belongings it signals. She says, "Maybe that's why Spanglish so much; it's a way to show . . . you're not from here *or* from there but you're from here *and* there." She calls the shift from *or* to *and*, from immigrant to transnational migrant, a "transition that happens in your heart." Yolanda feels deeply, in her physical center, that she is a different person now in the United States.

Haneen's life in the United States solidified her identification with where she came from rather than where she is now. When she first moved to the United States, she wasn't a practicing Muslim. She didn't wear a hijab and wasn't praying regularly. But moving to the United States made her "more attached" to Arabic and Islam. A change came as she began to attend Quran study groups, reading and writing alongside "American converts . . . whatever Canadian, Americans, Egyptian, Palestinians, Jordanians . . . who just wanted to learn Arabic for the love of Arabic language." She continues:

> That's not their own language and they say it better than me. I was so ashamed seriously about it. And after that I started to kind of explore my religion and some of the magic of the Arabic language through them. . . . I thank god that I moved to the U.S. to get this opportunity to know what I have. Seriously. When you're there you don't know who are you, but when you move here and you see other people who love you, what you have, they're attached to what you have and you're not, you're getting far but some other people are getting close.

Haneen, the daughter of a liberal Jordanian family, felt "far" from her language and religion until she saw how "close" and "attached" others were to it in the United States. So the solidification of her Muslim identity wasn't oppositional; it didn't develop in reaction to stereotypes or negative interactions in the United States. Rather, her burgeoning pride and affiliation with Islam and Arabic was a result of positive interactions that caused her to reflect on how her language and literacy practices were connected to who she was. Haneen's simultaneous movements—literate English/Arabic and geographic there/here—demonstrates the fluidity that brought her back to herself. Without migrating to the United States, she might have remained further from her culture, religion, and language, not closer. This movement made her want to embrace her Arabic rather than abandon it for English-dominant assimilation.

This chapter suggests that social and economic values have something to do with writers' innovations, access to opportunity and knowledge, and altered identities. Multilingual repertoires become meaningful when social values (family, community, and personal designations of importance or respect) converge with economic assignments of value (the use or profitability of literate commodities). These accounts show how this process of literate valuation leads to fluidity: when writers' social and economic values are similar to institutional social and economic values, then fluid movement occurs. In other words, when the values held by Alicia, Yolanda, Tashi, match those of their teachers, classmates, coworkers, and family members, these writers prove to be productive and innovative with their full literate repertoires. Like-minded individual and institutional values seem to smooth the way for fluidity, enabling movement with and within multilingual repertoires. This is a process of valuation that for the most part leads to writers' success. They are able to accomplish what they set out to do with their repertoires. For example, when readers—institutional or otherwise—value messy repertoires as much as writers, writers' fluidly compose among languages. Haneen and Sabohi write for readers who understand them only *because* they too value multilingualism as a norm. Yolanda's family delights in her texted bilingual neologisms along with her. She receives helpful feedback from an instructor who doesn't mind her written accent. Alicia likes communicating with her bilingual aunt because it is "easier" than the monolingual communication required with others. Tashi, Khadroma, and Haneen find belonging in communities defined by multilingualism; their membership in multilingual groups who value literacy like they do fosters pride in who they are as migrants in the United States. A felt outsider status becomes productive rather than destructive. As Alandra's insights show, valuing one's nonmainstream literacies creates moments of metalinguistic awareness about what they do with their language and why.

Matching values also pave the way for productive literacy relays. Alicia and Yolanda are both hired for their multilingualism; their employers seem to economically value their repertoires as much as they do. NGOs in Nimet's accounts value the kinds of English language literacies Nimet preferred teaching. They figuratively (socially) and literally (economically) sponsored the movement of Nimet's literacies around Azerbaijan. From the United States–based professors who visited her school in Argentina, Alicia intuited U.S. values around individual achievement and hard work. When she deployed these values while writing in college in the United States, determinedly visiting professors' office hours and the writing center weekly, indeed she was rewarded with good grades. In particular, Alicia, Yolanda, and Tashi all perform a conflation of "English" writing and "U.S." writing in a way that matches up with monolingual values in the United States. These details show that multilingual writers' success occurs not simply when writers are proficient in English or when instructors grant them the freedom to move among languages in their writing. It is not just serendipitous social conditions. Rather, multilingual migrant writers experience fluidity when they mirror the social and economic values of the conditions they find themselves in. Looking closely at fluid literacies in writers' lives lets us see how values affect what writers can do and offers insight into their struggles and their successes. The process of valuation shows the rewards that are granted when writers know how to play the literate game.

CHAPTER 3

FIXITY

WHEN WRITING STALLS

As Blommaert has suggested, one problem in studies of multilingualism is that "repertoires are studied" as if they "are 'fixed,' so to speak, in space and time" (*Sociolinguistics* 4). The previous chapter shows that migrants' literate repertoires can be anything but fixed as they move fluidly with writers among their languages, across continents, down through families, and from one writer to another. However, this claim—that repertoires do travel—can belie the complexity of repertoires and the conditions through which they move. A close examination of the lived literacy experiences of multilingual migrant writers shows that fluid and fixed literacies are deeply relational: as a motionless partner to fluidity, fixity is a kind of movement itself. It is literate movement that has stalled. Literate repertoires exhibit fluidity through space and time, but now and then, literate practices, as well as the identities shaped through them, are indeed fixed.

An excerpt from the literacy history of Sofia hints at this complexity. Describing her early language learning experiences, she says, "Parents could get permission that the child release from language where they are because people just, people moving and they didn't want the child stressed. So, for example, two years in Belarus, two years in Ukraine, two years in Georgia. . . . School was in Russian, and every child could learn own language, except with military people because they had this situation with moving." "This situation with moving" is the condition of migration, whether intercountry or intracountry, transnational or regional. For Sofia, the conditions of her family's migration across the Soviet Union meant that she was monolingual in Russian growing up. She was "released" from learning one language after another as her military family moved around the Soviet states. Her family's migration also meant, however, that she did not learn Ukrainian. To this day, Sofia feels less proficient in Ukrainian—her language of identity—than in Russian or English. Here is one relationship between fluidity and fixity.

Because Sofia was so geographically mobile, she was "stuck" in language. She describes the lesser role of Ukrainian in her literate repertoire as a kind of loss, a blow to her identity. Like many of the writers in this study, Sofia cannot easily move through her life in the United States nor move back to her life before immigration. She doesn't feel fluent in the language of power in the United States or in her home country. This affects not only her willingness to migrate but also her willingness to write. In this way the stakes of lost and stuck literacy are high: migrant writers cannot use the expansive repertoires accumulated over a lifetime of multilingual experiences; their motivation is low as they attempt to compose without their existing resources and against institutions that attempt to stall their progress; they find their literate selfhood devalued in the United States. This chapter shows the clear loss of human and intellectual potential when institutions and writers themselves fail to value, or work to actively shut down, their rich repertoires.

Although chapter 2 emphasized the fluidity of literate practices—the literate "mess" created by multilingualism and the literacy relays enacted by writers passing around their practices—this chapter considers a different kind of movement. While scholars from a variety of fields see contemporary global conditions as a full-scale release into fluid mobility, many transnational migrants experience immobility in their multilingual and geographic movement.[1] Writers' literate repertoires can also become stuck, hidden, or elusive. As Blommaert (*Sociolinguistics*) suggests, scholars have argued that any phenomenon of mobility contains elements of immobility as well—fixity within fluidity, boundaries always blocking the movement of some. This acknowledgment highlights the "differentiated" quality of mobility, in which some people more than others are "in charge" of movement.[2] Heightened periods of global movement counterintuitively can coincide with tightening borders, increased regulation of migration, and intensified xenophobia.[3] Recognizing these contradictions hedges romantic versions of literate mobility. Binding fixity to fluidity emphasizes "differentiated (im)mobilities, opportunities, and levels of (un)safety" that migrants experience in the United States (Carrillo Rowe 118). This relationship of fixity to fluidity, complicated by who is allowed to move with which repertoires where in the world, should complicate our understanding of literacy.

In the accounts detailed in this chapter, I analyze the literacy experiences of several multilingual migrant women to show how their fully developed literate repertoires are mediated by values that slowly shut down their multilingual practices in the United States. Writers describe their literate habits, traditions, conventions, and identifications as "lost," "stuck," "nowhere," "frozen," or "gone" in patterns of fixity that demand as much attention as that given to fluid multilingual writing. By analyzing this literate loss as fixity, I reframe multilingual writers' struggles. Stalled movement assumes that movement existed before and that movement can happen again. Fixity-as-movement suggests that writers have setbacks that are actually moments in a long trajectory of literate speed-ups and slow-downs. These setbacks have political, emotional, and physical histories that inform how writers see a way forward. Furthermore, fixity points beyond literacy lack to the agents and conditions that benefit from controlling literate movement. The values held by teachers, advisors, colleagues, and writers themselves can also mediate how repertoires move. This is not to say that powerful institutional values simply shut down writers' practices. Rather, the values held by both writers and powerful agents together muddy movement. In the case of fixity, this seems to happen because the values held by both seem mismatched. In other words, while the writers highlighted in this chapter genuinely value their reading, writing, and multilingualism, their values are not always shared by powerful others. These are deeply literate writers, but they don't have the knowledge or energy to navigate the literate game in the United States.

I examine why and how certain literacy practices become immobile through several dimensions of fixity: designated spaces for different language practices, seemingly failed linguistic and writing knowledge transfer, and altered identities due to lost literacy practices. The chapter incorporates voices from a broad representation of study participants and highlights several focal writers who experience their languages and literacies in especially fixed ways. The overview of participant insights begins to identify and define the social and economic values that hold writing back, while the extended accounts of Defne and Faridah show how these values play out in individual lives. Each section narrates a progressive loss of writerly agency, with writers choosing to put language "in place," but then becoming "stuck", and finally feeling lost among their writing practices. The chapter ends by considering the consequences of literate fixity and the values that mediate it.

LANGUAGE IN AND OUT OF PLACE

In an interesting response to the fluid messiness described in chapter 2, participants describe at length the neat relegation of different literate practices to designated spaces, times, and interlocutors. When describing practices, many writers treat their languages as carefully placed—controlled, structured, and delineated according to learned rules or received messages. This emplacement shows some writers controlling their practices—aiming where they go and to what effect. These writers are shrewd in their recognition of messages that endorse monolingualism or one dominant language over another. They can play that literacy game.

Other participants are the objects, rather than the subjects, of fixity. For them, languages kept in place make them feel out of place. For example, in Sofia's description, languages are assigned to bounded states, as children are "[released] from language where they are" in Belarus, Ukraine, Georgia. Russian, as the language of power, could transcend boundaries, but children's access to their "own language" was fixed according to national borders. So for Sofia, Ukrainian belongs in Ukraine, but it does not necessarily belong to her. During a visit to Ukraine as an adult, Sofia's "situation with moving" became even "scary": "They are saying everything in Ukraine language. And my god I see everything in English. I notice signs. I thought to myself good in English 'cause it's a little bit easier for me to understand than Ukraine. . . . Everything in Ukraine I don't understand. I said, oh my god I can't learn Ukraine, it's enough to do English for me!" Sofia was overwhelmed by the language dynamics in Ukraine during her visit because the country had changed, moving away from Soviet Russian and toward a recuperation of Ukrainian on public signs and in schools and other institutional settings. At the same time, English had gained a presence as a global lingua franca on some signs and public notices. This was comforting to Sofia, who communicates in Russian and English, but it still left her feeling estranged from her native country that had experienced so much political change in her absence. Responding to people who say "It's your country!" Sofia replies, "Yeah it's my country, but what I can explain? I don't know the answer to give to people because they don't understand this, this situation." Before her visit, Sofia understood Ukraine to be the Russian space it was when she left. But the country's politics were more fluid than her literate repertoire, which proves to be stuck in the past rather than serving Sofia in the present.

These themes especially recall Scribner and Cole's observation of the Vai delineating Arabic, English, or indigenous Vai scripts depending on the function of the literacy practice. Another understanding of language-in-place might be closer to diglossia, the use of separate codes for distinct purposes and people. Linguists describe diglossic situations as those that call for certain codes based on topic and interlocutor—a description that has been extended into domain-specific code-switching models like those developed by Fishman ("Bilingualism").[4] Diglossia does explain some participant literacy activities in which they choose among languages according to their interlocutor or reader for texts, e-mails, notes, Facebook messages, or class essays. Yolanda, for example, texts with her husband in English but her brother in Spanish; her class boardwork when teaching is in English but her communication to parents is in Spanish. Nina, a former chemist from Ukraine, describes in one night e-mailing her daughter in Russian, reading her pharmacy textbook in English, and writing a note to her husband in Spanish. Participants describe communicating in certain languages according to topic: Yolanda requires her students to write in English only on biology topics, as explored in chapter 2; Defne writes academic genres only in English and poetry only in Turkish. However, writers' literate activities are emplaced for reasons beyond reader and topic. Diglossia does not fully explain why writers choose language according to memory or feeling. Multilingual migrant writers also make choices depending on their location inside or outside the home or home country, for particular memories, and for written versus spoken communicative tasks.

Inside and Outside

The notion that writers would choose how to communicate according to home/outside domains is as commonly acknowledged as diglossic choice based on topic or interlocutor. However, participants describe these choices in ways that reveal the social pressures also keeping their languages fixed in place. An inside/outside discourse echoes across participant narratives: Shirin, a stay-at-home mom from Pakistan, describes barring English in her home so her children will continue to learn Urdu, saying to her children when they speak English at home, "No, I cannot understand it. Can you please speak in Urdu?"; Ishtar says she and her family are used to "using English mostly outside"; Nina describes using Russian almost exclusively on the days when she stays at home but, as she says, "when I'm working [at the mall] only English English English English."

In this way, home ("inside") is consistently opposed to "outside" spaces like school and work. Participants describe assigning specific literate practices to each of them. But this easy fixity was complicated over time or within domains themselves. For example, the detail Sabohi offers in describing her language acquisition growing up in Pakistan shows complex fixities: at home before starting school she learned to speak (but not read or write) in Kashmiri but did learn to read and write (but not speak) in English. When she went to school, she learned to read and write in Urdu, the "language which is official in the state," but also spoke more frequently in English. So, as Sabohi says, "I was speaking Kashmiri at home, but some Urdu sometimes with my siblings. And then in the school using English and Urdu." Sabohi's early experience moves beyond domain- and topic-based emplacement. She describes these choices as quite delineated, "not a conscious effort, [but] something that automatically came to us." When she entered the school building, she and her cousins "would start speaking Urdu and English," but when they left the building to go home, they would "automatically" use Kashmiri. She describes her cousin's multiple names as an example of this unconscious switching: "We used to call her a different name at home . . . she had a pet name that we used for her at home only, not outside. So just the family members and I would automatically switch to her other name at school. I called her Gazala at school and Shenoa at home, automatically."

Whether it is remarkable that someone would have home- and school-based nicknames, Sabohi finds it remarkable how the switch happens automatically, without conscious effort, at the entrance to the school. The delineation is firm at this point—Kashmiri and Urdu for home; English and Urdu for school—and is symbolized in her cousin's designated inside/outside names. These are the early literate experiences that condition how Sabohi places language now. But though she tries to mirror this practice in her own household in the United States, she cannot get her own young children to respond in Kashmiri or Urdu at home. As is common in many descriptions of second-generation immigrant language practices, Sabohi's children understand her communication in Kashmiri and Urdu but respond only in English. As the "outside" pressures change for Sabohi, the ability to control the language use "inside" wavers.

Yolanda, describing this phenomenon from the point of view of a teacher watching her students, hints at the social pressures that govern these choices:

YOLANDA (Y): I think there's a lot of pressure on the outside. 'Cause we are talking about kids that are fourteen years old, right? You want to keep your friends happy. But you want to keep your parents happy. So I think there's a lot of pressure. . . . School and friends English, most of the time; at home the Spanish.
REBECCA (R): And yet they are writing in Spanish at school.
Y: Because they know I might be a little bit of home. Yeah.

Yolanda's narrative blurs the line between inside/outside domains because she represents for her students "a little bit of home," an inside space. Yolanda treats her bilingual biology class as an "inside" space within the "outside" domain of the school. She says she does this intentionally to give relief to the "pressure" of social expectations from parents, friends, and school and the everyday pressure of being a bilingual migrant teen in a majority white, monolingual town.

Inside and Outside Borders

In an extension of inside/outside delineation, the writers in this study also place language practices inside and outside political spaces and borders. Discussing the language context of the United States, Khadroma explains that she'd like her Tibetan-fluent but English-dominant daughter to learn Spanish next "because it's more popular here" in the United States. Kunthi explains that she is "trying to do [her] best" to learn English because, as she says, "I'm not living in Indonesia again; I'm living in here." And Aldene says if she returns to Brazil, she could return to her "old ways . . . of writing," but for now in the United States, she says, "you gotta adapt to the environment that you are in." For the majority of the study participants, to live inside the geographic boundaries of the United States means to respond to the powerful pressure to use English first and other languages second. As Alicia says, the message to multilingual migrants is clear. Mimicking the discourse of immigration debates, she says, "We are letting you in, so now assimilate. And that would mean reinforcing the idea of English only, like you are choosing to come here, so you gotta learn it. You gotta live in English and write in English and speak in English."

Alicia echoes the belief that the U.S. borders contain an English-only zone in which people are speaking, writing, and living only in one language. That this zone is thought to be maintained by agents "letting" in migrants who are "choosing" to move shows how simplified this belief is. However, many of the migrants in this study agree; they believe that immigrants should learn English in the United States. But, importantly, they don't agree that English should be learned to the detriment of migrants' other languages, nor required outside U.S. borders. For example, Aldene admits that although she's willing to adapt to English-only assumptions in the United States, this should not be a universal expectation. She admits that English "is everywhere" but not "everybody is speaking it or able to read and write in it." She says, "English is not the universal language! And there is still people that refuse to learn English. They wanna keep their language or they just can't learn. So if you want to be able to communicate with everybody or most people, you gotta learn the languages of the places you are going to." For Aldene, language is very much placed. She believes languages should be learned according to "the places you are going" rather than to English's assumed ability to transcend place.

Similarly, Alicia assigns expectations for mixed or fixed language use to "here" in the United States or to "there" in Argentina. The passages below show the progressive softening of her view about whether language should be "mixed" in any place. She begins by saying she disagrees with language "mixing" because "you stick to the language; you stick to the language": "If you go to a native speaking country, they are going to look at you like you're a dumbass. And so that's very hard for me because when I'm home [in Argentina] I use Spanish and but then sometimes a word in English comes out and I feel like, oh, am I doing what my students are doing in a way? Am I the dumbass?" Her thinking evolves as she decides that in the United States she uses mixing "as a resource": "When I'm here I use it because I'm trying to communicate a message so I think it's okay. But when I'm in the native Spanish-speaking country, yeah, I would look like I don't remember my words, which is probably the case." Alicia's choices about sticking to or mixing languages seems to be based on interlocutors—those who might "look at you like you're a dumbass." But she locates the lookers in one "native speaking country" or another. Her decision is based on interlocutor, but even more on the interlocutor's place. In other words, the distinction she makes is not between communicating only in English in the United States and only in Spanish in Argentina. She distinguishes instead between the mixed practices she can't help but use in the United States "as a resource," and the mixing she will avoid at home in Argentina. Eventually she modifies her belief about "[sticking] to the language" to be less a universal rule than a communicative choice she makes in one place rather than another.

Fluid Speech, Fixed Writing

When it comes to languages chosen for oral or written communication, participants' descriptions were even more complex. Beyond placing languages according to space, context, topic, or subject matter, writers also placed languages in either spoken or written modes. This isn't to say that participants assigned Spanish to speech and English to writing, but rather that they assigned multilingual fluidity to speech and monolingual fixity to writing—languages were blended in speech but kept separate in writing. Many of them had a loose approach to language mixing in oral communication, recalling the "messy literacies" of the previous chapter. But writing, for many of them, is a mode that either *requires* languages to stay in place—not mix, not mesh—or else is a mode that *can be used as a method* of keeping language in place. Defne, Shirin, Paj, Sabohi, Alicia, Alandra, Aldene, and Yolanda all describe writing as calling for monolingual communication while describing speech as fluid. They shared a general resistance to using more than one language in the writing practices they understood to be more serious or more consequential than speech.

For example, when I asked Yolanda what it felt like to move between languages when she spoke she said, "Fun, like youthful and different." When I asked her if she moved like this among languages when writing, she said:

Y: Wow, no. I like writing to be more serious. Okay, it's gonna be on paper forever.
R: Why is that? What is it about writing?
Y: Why is that? I don't know! I've never thought of this before but this is how I feel. What is it about writing?

Among the rich descriptions of fluid multilingual literacies and deeply felt opinions about identities constituted in multiplicity, there is a shared, mostly slight but sometimes quite stark, backing-off of these ideas in the context of writing. For Yolanda, writing is a material reflection of herself "on paper forever," so for her it is not a mode to be taken lightly. She thinks writing is "something more serious, more academic" because "it's gonna be there." In opposition to "fun" and "youthful" talk, writing is a permanent self, represented in words and often circulated beyond the writer's control. She evaluates this stark separation of writing and speech of hers as "weird" but hangs on to her conviction that "what's written down is very important." Somehow, for Yolanda and others, this importance requires monolingualism.

In several accounts, writers describe placing their languages in writing, using journaling and letter writing to either control the placement of language or to resist the multilingual mixing that often comes naturally to them. For example, Aldene describes writing a series of letters to her husband to chronicle their relationship for their anniversary:

ALDENE (A): I decided to write . . . ten different letters of different experiences or promises, or ten good memories. I grabbed the paper and did that. Most of the memories were within English. There were some occasions that I wrote in Portuguese but like 95 percent was in English.
R: So what was in Portuguese?
A: Parts related to Brazil. So, for example, like a specific beach or there was a part I wrote in Spanish because it was related to—we went to this bonfire and there was a specific song that I wanted to write about. But those was really specific situations that I had to change into a language where I felt like okay there is a connection there with that language.

Aldene writes the letters mostly in English because most of the memories—the content of the letters—happened "within English."

The idea of events occurring "in" or "within" a language is not unique to Aldene's account. Rosalia says she met her husband "in Spanish" rather than "in Guatemala" to explain why they communicate mostly in Spanish. In this way the languages themselves dictate the shape of the memories and are deemed appropriate for recalling or retelling later on in writing. In Aldene's case, she chose to use Portuguese or Spanish according to the space of the recalled scene—Portuguese for Brazil memories and Spanish for bonfire songs. These designations become meaningful when Aldene relegates languages according to past spaces in a way that contradicts her previous endorsements of multilingual mixing. Here in this literacy event, Aldene parcels out language for effect, keeping English-experienced memories in English and others in other languages. The languages are placed not randomly but intentionally according to geography, feeling, and chronology. As a whole, the letter set is multilingual, but in its content the letters are neatly delineated and languages are kept distinct.

In another practice of emplacement, Alicia describes an activity that she took up while on a college research trip to maintain what she believed were her flagging Spanish skills. During the summer after her freshman year she studied in Tanzania for six weeks with a group from school. She realized that she had been communicating almost entirely in English her first year in the

United States without much Spanish, and she was worried she would lose even more in Tanzania without being able to communicate with her family by phone. The passage below shows the evolution of her thinking on the matter of monolingualism.

> My solution was . . . to keep a journal and I was only gonna write in Spanish. That was tough. It was tough. Because I was like, "Okay, I'm just gonna stay to Spanish," but then again I wanted to add some English words in there, switch and then back and then switch and then back, I just wanted to do it. But I had made this thing that I wanted to write in Spanish . . . so I made this deal that throughout the day everything English; at night when I wrote my journal it had to be in Spanish. But it was tough because during the day I was exposed to English English English and now actually Swahili at the same time. So Spanish was way off my mind and at night I was like forcing myself to write in Spanish. . . . But by week two or three I was like, "Okay, I'm just gonna mix some English in there 'cause that's just the way it makes sense right now."

Alicia uses the written journal as a disciplining mode. She is "forcing" herself to write in Spanish only and resist the "switch and then back" that she desired. She knew her usual opportunities for Spanish—talking with family on the phone, chatting online and emailing with friends—would be few in Tanzania, so she designated the space of the journal as the place where Spanish would occur and used writing to maintain the language boundaries of that activity. Interestingly, this fixed mode eventually breaks down as Alicia describes, with resignation, that language mixing got the best of her. She admits that mixing in some English just "makes sense" in a context where she was exposed to "English English English." In a way the attempt is as interesting as the outcome: Alicia decided that writing, especially journal writing, was the practice that would get her to "stay to Spanish." Her solution makes sense given the lack of Spanish-speaking interlocutors in Tanzania. But a Spanish-only journal makes even more sense to one who believes that writing is a powerful practice for language separation rather than language combination.

Aldene's and Alicia's examples point back to Yolanda's musing about the significance of writing, showing that it is not just formal, academic writing that takes on this status. Writing is often treated as a serious practice or event, an activity that contains or controls languages through its generated material. In this way, writing joins the previously described home, school, and national spaces as a bounded domain where language is kept. This bounded quality complicates the free-flowing language movement writing researchers suggest for socially just, or at least accurately described, literacy in use.[5] While Alicia's account shows that writers end up with this fluidity in practice, reinforcing Scribner and Cole's caveat that delineated languages "are often blurred" in daily literacy practices, the entirety of this section's accounts show that language boundaries also have a powerful function in the social and political contexts through which writing practices move (129).

Therefore, it is appropriate to ask why writers, in addition to their fluid literate practices, value language in place. Certainly they are responding to dominant pressures to do so and are wise to the political histories that endorse powerful languages over others. Migrant writers also have received the school- and publicly circulated messages of access to jobs, cultural capital, and citizenry granted by the acquisition of standard languages. As professionals employed for their multilingualism, they very much value the tidy literate practices that provide this access. This section has described a group of writers who exhibit varying levels of control or management over their own multilingual literacies. Although language borders blur as writers move among them, the breakdowns described happen under writers' control. But as Alicia asks in chapter 2, "How much language control do you have?" One also wonders who else benefits from controlling language movement. What is the relationship between keeping language practices in place and keeping in place language users? While these writers are the agents, the subjects, of fixity, others are the objects, held in place by powerful pressures.

STUCK AMONG LANGUAGES

When the writers in this study describe being "stuck" among their languages, the word is often aligned with frustrated motivation, stalled learning, or literacy lack. In describing her frustration in her slow English literacy learning, Sofia says, "So you have to move, move; try; push yourself. Now I am stuck a little bit." Sabohi describes her worry about her pediatrician's claim that her son was "confused between languages," saying, "I stuck to English then—I stopped speaking in other languages with him—but now we are again and . . . he doesn't know how to make sentences in Urdu, but he can understand." Shirin says, "If somebody says to me to write a big essay in Urdu . . . I will definitely be stuck in some words . . . and sometimes I might get stuck in English as well." This form of literate fixity is a result of writers' perceived inadequacies and widely held values regarding accent, motherhood, or immigrant identity.

Literate practices stuck among languages—practices not moving from one language to another or one context to another—are sometimes described as failed language or writing knowledge transfer. Studies of writing transfer seek to understand how writers use or adapt prior writing knowledge in new or different writing situations or to fit new contexts, while research on language or linguistic transfer, also approached as "crosslinguistic influence" (Kellerman and Sharwood Smith), studies how knowledge of one language can affect the learning or use of another.[6] Transfer among languages that facilitates acquisition has been understood as "positive transfer," while transfer that inhibits acquisition has been called "negative transfer" or "interference." This would be the basis of Sabohi's doctor's fears that her son was "confused between languages." But in contemporary studies of both writing and language learning transfer, literate practices are viewed not as static possessions that can be carried and applied but as emergent and in-process activities sensitive to an immediate context.

Similarly, the everyday experiences of the participants in this study show more complicated dynamics for fixity than simply failed or negative transfer, or the interference of one language on another. For these writers the roots or dimensions of feeling stuck among languages are more complex—occasionally more agentive or more productive—than failed or negative transfer can explain. For example, Aldene describes "missing" and "slowly losing" her "formal writing in Portuguese" or "losing [Spanish] a lot" when using Spanglish with her students. "Most of the time," she says, "it's just using words or sentences that can only work either in English or in Spanish or in Portuguese. So sometimes I get stuck on something 'cause you are like, okay, I'm trying to say this word. It's not working. I know it in Portuguese, I know it in Spanish. But it doesn't access." Aldene is describing a common understanding of being "stuck" among her languages: She can find the words to write in two of her languages but cannot access the third. As she says, "It's just a word exists in one dictionary and not the other." What she wants to say doesn't exist in the metaphorical or literal dictionary of the language.

But in a subsequent interview, when asked to elaborate on this point, Aldene says that when she doesn't use a language "it doesn't necessarily mean that [she] lost it." She explains: "So when I write to myself whenever I write in a more personal way, like to my husband or my family, I definitely let it go. I don't really care about spelling or I don't care about structure, I usually just write it the way I want it to be." Here, Aldene's "it" that she doesn't use (but does not lose) is Portuguese writing conventions. She describes avoiding the "really long" sentences with "lots of details" common in Portuguese prose and is more accustomed to "always chopping [her] sentences a little more to be more the formal way that it should be here" in English. Aldene believes that although she doesn't use a "really long" sentence style with "lots of details," she has not lost it; instead, she chooses when and to whom she will "let it go." Aldene knows which "words or sentences . . . can only work either in English or in Spanish or in Portuguese" and can transfer this knowledge even if she cannot always "access" the English vocabulary she is reaching for.

Other participants describe being "stuck" as a temporary and productive condition, wherein the mind "confused" among languages might lead to a learning milestone. Ishtar, a Syrian teacher, describes how she understands being stuck between Arabic and English when she writes. She says she is occasionally "kind of confused between Arabic and English."

ISHTAR (I): I'm writing in Arabic, I see myself putting some English words. So it's a little confusing, you know what I mean? We're used to speaking English . . . so you're kind of used to the language to express what you wanna say. So now it interferes.

R: The English does?

I: Yes, the English does. . . . It happened to me maybe two weeks ago, writing and then I stopped, "Okay, I don't want to do this." I can't really focus on one language to do it.

Ishtar's description of her stalled writing process echoes theories of interference but describes English interfering with her Arabic maintenance rather than the other way around. Much research seeks to understand the interference of a first language on a target second language (for example, the interference of English language learners' Spanish on their English acquisition), but Ishtar inverts this process to describe her English as a powerful influence on her desire to continue writing in Arabic.

Ishtar further complicates the situation when she elaborates on the previous writing scene. She says, "Even when I'm stuck sometimes with some tricky words and spelling, at least when I find the right way to write it, 'Okay, I have learned something new now!'" So perhaps for Ishtar, language confusion is less stuck-as-loss and more stuck-as-stalled-for-now. She seems to describe her stalled movement as an opportunity to learn and eventually a triumph when movement begins again. Ishtar turns her confusion into production and passes that strategy on to her students and children as well, telling them, "Don't take it as something difficult and I'm struggling with it. Take it as something like, like gaining something, learning something new." Ishtar is able to put a positive spin on being stuck. Her temporary lack of motion motivates her to learn further.

But for other participants, language fixity is described as a social and emotional state of slowed-down, muddied, stalled progress. In this way, "failed" transfer or learning occurs not just from writers' literacy lack but also from gendered, classed, and cultural values that contribute to fixity. These participants describe their motion among languages as a complicated stop-and-go process, which is very deeply felt in their sense of self and imagined possibilities for their future in the United States. For example, Nimet describes a writing process that, in a conventional classroom situation, might appear stuck or confused. But a longer chronology refigures a stall as simply one snapshot of a painstakingly slow and ongoing writing process. Speaking of composing essays in a college general education course, she says, "That's why it is hard for us. Not hard, I cannot say it's only hard. But also take our time more. If *you* write this one page—one hour. This page I can spend sometime five, six hours. My teacher she asked me how many hours you spend for that? I said twelve hours. She is surprised. I said, I don't think so; this is not surprising." Nimet describes her writing process on an hourly scale, explaining that it takes her time to "think, to concentrate, to bring the sentence together, and reading, get information, take notes, brainstorm." These tasks are more than just "hard," they are time-consuming: "Every single thing require time!"

Nimet spends hours on her writing because she is writing from a repertoire that includes not just languages but also cultures. She says: "It is the other; sometimes we think in our own language and then convert in our brain to the other. Sometimes it's the cultural clash. You can't use it, you won't, you don't, you cannot express the sentence. And you stuck there, how can I express? I want to tell this idea. You want to say that this is this. This is that. But again, takes time." Nimet emphasizes the material practicalities of having to "convert in [one's] brain to the other" language while writing. Moving among multiple languages while reading, taking notes, brainstorming, and so on extends time and increases cognitive load. But when Nimet slides out to a cultural scale, placing composing in a context of cultural values, she reveals that being stuck among languages is not just a matter of staring at a screen. It is also a matter of converting how one values writing. This takes time. It is no wonder, then, that what looks like stuck or stalled writing production on paper may be simply one stage in a life-long process of multilingual composing.

Defne

An extended understanding of Defne's literacy history similarly complicates what it means to be stuck among languages. Defne is a thirty-five-year-old Turkish woman from an upper-middle-class family. Her life in the United States has been more challenging than she anticipated. Her interview transcripts are full of emotion and strongly held beliefs about what should or should not have happened after her arrival in the United States. She moved to the United States for graduate school but left her graduate program to teach part-time as a lecturer at a community college. Defne's literacy practices were developed in Turkish, German, and English throughout her primary and secondary schooling years. She says she was "always reading reading" by herself, especially the translated work of Gabriel García Márquez. "Day and night with no sleep . . . ," she says, "I tried to make sure that I read all of his books." Defne explained that her mother would take her and her brother to book fairs in the small, conservative Turkish city she grew up in. She also wrote poems in a journal her professor mother gave her, writing about things that "bothered" her, "those images that kids see. . . . Yeah, it was just this emotion stuck in there that made me." Defne's early memories are saturated with literacy, and she identifies strongly as a highly educated woman.

Defne learned German simultaneously with Turkish because her family lived in Germany for the first three years of her life. German was her first language, but she experienced loss and gain with the language her whole life: she "forgot it" until she returned for three months in middle school and "it just came back"; she lost it again in her "very poor" high school German class but practiced again in Austria for two months during college; but because of the "overwhelming presence of English in [her] life," she "lost it" and "can't read or write." She describes the presence of English as a parallel learning experience: at seven Defne began learning English, singing songs like "Brother John" and "London Bridge" in school, and in high school she visited Cambridge for a summer English immersion program. She says during this trip "it was the first time [she] was exposed to actually thinking creatively, writing things." Defne says she wrote well in these classes, receiving "very positive feedback" from her teachers who were "kinda impressed by the quality of the writing." Her rich and literate repertoire was supported by her family's privileged movement between countries and languages. Because of the back and forth travel Defne experienced, her repertoire's languages are of varying levels and usefulness. But she is aware and proud of the repertoire her literate life has created.

After immigrating to the United States, Defne continued to move between her literacies and languages in a highly conscious way. When asked how learning to write in Turkish influences how she writes now, she answered, "It's not about how I write, it's about how I think." She said: "I am using a lot of uh, how do you say in English like the using, for example, softness, the way the snowflakes fell on your arm? You use that kind of resemblances to other things, right? Yeah, I might be using a very Turkish way because it's very cultural. . . . And I do carry it to the English language for sure. 'Cause I don't see it as an obstacle. I see it as a resource." Defne knows she "carr[ies] . . . to the English language" the "resource" of her analogic thinking from Turkish. She knows her thinking in Turkish governs not only her Turkish composing but her English composing as well; she is proud that her writing contains "a lot of artistic, a lot of poetic" qualities afforded by this thinking. She offers the example of writing an e-mail to a friend and including "the Turkish way" of an analogy she wrote in English: "I feel like all the cells in my body are crinkled." She delighted in the poetic qualities her Turkish thinking added to her English e-mail writing. Defne is as aware of her multilingual habits as she is of dominant essay-writing conventions in standard American English, saying, for example, that she would always include in her scholarly essay introductions "a brief summary, what's my argument, you know I'm gonna talk about this argument." She has had school success with both, pushing the boundaries of academic writing into creative spaces when writing her master's degree thesis, which she says her advisor "loved" and "thought it was one of the best theses she received."

However, even with a long history of valuing literacy, a heightened rhetorical awareness and fluid movement among her languages including fluent academic English, Defne feels stuck when composing. For example, when writing notes to her family, she writes to her daughter and her Indonesian husband in English rather than Turkish. "Sometimes it comes in Turkish," she says, "but it's not as it was before, so that's something definitely I lost." She feels her note writing in Turkish is "a broken Turkish I feel like. I don't feel like it's flowing." Because her audiences are English-dominant and because Turkish is not "flowing" as it was before, Defne believes that even in the home-based informal practice of note writing, "it's easier to write in English now for me." Similarly, in the highly formal academic sphere of writing in graduate school, Defne struggled to access her full literate repertoire to compose. She explains that because she was "trained with the English language" as an academic she struggles to write Turkish academic pieces in the United States because she feels not "capable in [her] native languages." But she also explains that if she wanted to write "poetic" in English "it would sound, like, stupid because . . . however much you know the language, it is not your native language." She explains these struggles with mastery not as a factor of literacy lack or confusion, but as a result of disconnection: "It's not really connected to my soul anymore, let's say that way."

For Defne, this disconnection comes from multiple social pressures but has roots in the pressure of writing in graduate school as a single mother and an immigrant. She describes interactions with her PhD advisor as very painful, especially regarding her academic production and the expected pace of progress in her program. "Well they trashed me. Their assumption of the grad student and the work that was supposed to is based on a functioning family who had kids or a single who have nothing to do but just TA and study a lot, study work a lot. And in my case I had this small baby girl. I was all alone. I was immigrant. I had no social connections. I felt lost for a long time." Although Defne had received positive feedback on her writing during her MA, she could not keep up with the literate expectations of academic writing in English once she entered the pace of the PhD program, which seems to have valued fast writing, high productivity, full devotion to an academic lifestyle. She felt "lost" in this process not because she did not have the literate resources but because of the social conditions in which she found herself as a graduate student in the United States. She alluded to the "sheer quantity of books" and the "process of put them in the paper," which she called "work that I can't do with my realities, not as a mother."

Defne frequently used the word "gone" to describe what had happened to her literate practices in the United States. After leaving graduate school because of the incompatibility of advanced study and her life, her realities became more rather than less difficult. "Immigration-wise," she says, "I couldn't get divorced immediately because I quit the PhD and my immigration status depended on him. And if I get divorced, I'm gonna be deported. So I had to prove [the dangerous conditions of her marriage in her written visa documents], but there will be no hundred-percent guarantee that I will get the permission of residence just for that. So I was kind of stuck in this marriage." For much research on language, literacy, and education, these details of Defne's life might not be considered relevant. That she was "stuck" in her marriage and immigration status might not be a factor with much explanatory power on her stuck writing. But, as Defne says, "that's where I am as an immigrant. If that's relevant." It is: if transfer is mediated by contextual influences, including "attitudes, motivation, sociocultural context" (James 859), then Defne's everyday life in the United States does affect how she is able to call on the rhetorical and academic resources she described. This in turn affects her ability to produce academic English prose, which leads to her current altered life situation.

Defne's stalled writing in English is not the result of failed transfer, nor is it the product of a "confused" multilingual repertoire. Instead, the audiences to which Defne was attempting to write—graduate school advisors, multilingual family members, immigration bureaucrats, and herself—value certain kinds of literate productivity in certain varieties that her life didn't allow for. These readers are shutting a writer down but also demanding a writer speed up. Writing under social conditions that do not recognize her own literate values, Defne feels immobilized: "So I kind of stopped, something happened to me, who knows why. And I stopped." This stoppage caused Defne's literate practices, honed over a lifetime of languages and travel, to become practices "not recognized as institutionally legitimate"—they lacked worth when presented slowly, or in the accented English or forms influenced by Turkish (Luke, "Genres" 330). For her, "sociology writing" in graduate school was not only "too intense" with "a pressure to express yourself in a certain way" but was also literate activity completely divorced from—and more highly valued than—her own "social connections" to poetry and literate play. This matters in Defne's case because she explicitly attaches the full extent of her identity to her writerly output: while writing a rare personal essay toward the end of graduate school, she found herself saying, "Oh! There you are! I'm writing again." For Defne, to write is to be herself. And to write fluidly among her languages is to experience her full sense of self.

After migration to the United States, Defne has become stuck. Her multilingual literate repertoire, highly valued as she grew up, has become revalued in the United States as a repertoire with what Luke ("Genres" 330) calls "no guarantees . . . of fair rewards." And Defne knows this, as is clear from her mention of no guarantees. Of being multilingual, she says, "there are positives, but it's not an easy thing. In many ways it's a lot of sacrifice and loss that comes with being multilingual."

LOST WRITING

Writers in this study describe experiences in which lost literate practices alter their identities. These participants' literate repertoires become uniquely fixed as they run up against social conditions that change or erase the multilingual writer they feel they used to be. In participant accounts, lost literacies are often described as a kind of disorientation, with participants connecting literacy lack to lack of navigation. For example, Kunthi, a teacher from Indonesia, says that "the pressure" to speak English in the United States makes her feel like "in here it's not Indonesia and I am lost somewhere." Aldene agrees that her frequent transnational movement between the United States and Brazil makes her feel like she's "really lost." When returning to Brazil, she struggles with people thinking she's "not from there" because of what she calls her "thick" English accent. She equates not being able to navigate big Brazilian cities with not being able to read. Khadroma understands this disorientation as a fact of globalization. She says people are "compelled to learn more things" like languages if "you don't wanna get lost" in a fast-moving world. Sofia agrees that "we must learn for orientation and life; not just for education, for orientation." She believes that learning to write is a matter of orientation—knowing where one is and how to move forward—more than simply a matter of education. Indeed, the sense of loss accumulated comes from an expressed inability to navigate literate norms in the United States.

However, participants' most fixed sense of loss comes from who they feel they are after migration. Their previous understanding of themselves as readers, writers, and thinkers is lost in the United States. For example, Khadroma says she's "very funny" in Tibetan, but without fluent English, she says, "I just give up and I'm not funny anymore." Kunthi similarly explains that without knowing how to write in English in the United States, "it's different, it's like blind; . . . you not comfort with yourself, . . . I feel like, is that me or something?" Yolanda witnesses something similar in her students, saying "they feel that if you read, write, or speak another language, you are losing a part of yourself, you're losing part of who you are and that attachment to your roots." She says her students, perhaps with more malleable teenage identities, push back on that loss, often writing in Spanish rather than English to make a statement. "Their English is better than mine," Yolanda says, "but they write it in Spanish." While Kunthi and Khadroma in a way shrug and resign themselves to altered identities in the United States, Yolanda's students actively resist an

English-based identity as they write. This is the complexity of identity in lost literate repertoires after migration.

Ishtar explains that after moving to the United States and starting a family, "I got busy and everything, so basically I stopped writing." She is doubly hard on herself for this loss. "I should have done way better than what I have done so far," she says. "But you know with kids and responsibilities and everything, I mean, you're not free. You can't just go whenever you want and take whatever classes you need to take. Your hands are kind of tied a little bit." With tied hands, Ishtar cannot continue her education. She stopped writing when her family responsibilities made it hard to "go whenever" and "do whatever" she needs to improve her writing in classes. Instead, she stays at home and misses the communication that would get her moving again. Because she "always feels kind of guilty" for this, expecting quick literacy learning from herself, she is doubly weighed down by feelings that she "should have done better than this" after migration.

Nimet, for her part, attributes her lack of writing in her college courses in the United States to the pressure to write quickly and to call on English-based resources that she has not yet developed. "When I take the clinic you have to write something yourself, improve your writing skill," she says. "If you don't do this, it's kind of frozen I would say. . . . If I don't have enough information, I just sit there. I say no I cannot do this now. I cannot write this one because I have no idea." As a nursing student in a clinical setting, the pressure to quickly write care plans and reflective journals is high, and Nimet and other nursing participants in this study expressed shutting down under what they identified as United States–based classroom values around production. But Nimet's feeling of being "frozen" also seems to stem from having "no idea" of what to write about. She does not necessarily have the lived history in the United States that her classmates do to call on for content. She feels she needs to "know more word phrases" to write faster, "more sentence structure" or "groups of words that you have to use right place." Nimet says she lacks the vocabulary and grammatical intuition that would help her quickly express her ideas about content when they do come. In other words, Nimet's stalled production is influenced by cultural context, misunderstanding of or low interest in content, and elusive academic English resources. These pressures are both common—many monolingual, nonmigrant college writers would describe their writer's block similarly—and unique, as the multiplication of these pressures causes Nimet, and other multilingual migrant writers like her, to decide "I cannot do this now" and walk away from their writing.

Sabohi understands her lost writing to have far-reaching motivations and outcomes. She says as a school principal she only writes the school newspaper and parent and teacher e-mails. She says writing so little, compared to her previously intense literate routines as a journalist, has caused her to start "losing that grip" she had on writing. Her lengthy comment below shows her relating her writing struggles to her struggle knowing "what is going on around in the world these days."

> Now if I sit down and think I'll write, it doesn't come that easily now. It doesn't. It never was that easy for me. It will always take me some time and so many drafts and redrafts and stuff like that. But now sometimes I, it's like the point when I give up, I say okay forget about it. . . . Definitely when you are in practice you are a much better writer. And you constantly try to strive to do it better. Try to read more, try to see what are the new words, and what are the new techniques, what is going on around in the world these days. And like okay. Fine. It's not affecting. . . . Earlier I would be, 'cause then I would think I might read about this, I might write about that.

Sabohi narrates the loss of her "grip" on writing, a process that frustrates her enough that she gives up. This loss could be understood as simply logistical. She spends her energy now as a principal on the school texts and communication. But in the context of her further elaboration, it seems that losing a grip on writing also means losing a connection to the larger world. She describes her previous writing practices as "[striving]" to be a better writer, reading more, seeking out "new words" and "techniques." She connects this active, engaged writing with access to "what is going on around in the world." She says this engagement was "affecting" her sense of the world, motivating her to think about what she might read, write, or discuss with others. Sabohi describes engaged writing as something she does "miss sometimes," but since she is usually "too busy with stuff" at home and work, she is resigned to her lack of writing and loss of engagement. Thus Sabohi's lost writing is not the slipping away of a literacy practice, but also distance from a world of discourse in which she was formerly immersed as a journalist. This is certainly an altered identity for Sabohi after migration to the United States.

Yolanda offers an important reminder that "people who can't write find a way . . . to live their lives." So the loss of writing is not the loss of everything for these women. Instead, a lost sense of literate fluency more subtly alters how multilingual migrant women understand themselves and their potential in the United States. Like Defne above, Faridah's extended account elaborates the complex conditions that bring about these shifts in identity. Faridah's fixed literate repertoire is mediated by work, class, and gender values to the extent that she cannot see how her vast literate potential will be realized in the United States.

Faridah

Faridah is an Algerian woman who immigrated to the United States after her husband received a visa in an immigration lottery. In the United States she teaches Arabic part-time at a small, private Muslim school. Her outsized enthusiasm for life fuels her admiration for literacy. She understands and deeply respects the rhetorical power of language: when we met, we spent the first twenty minutes of our interview discussing the Arab Spring, which was gaining momentum then. In reality, I didn't say a word. I had taken out my digital recorder, but Faridah put her hand on it to stop me from turning it on. "Can we just talk for a minute?" she asked. I nodded yes as she burst forth about social protest in the Middle East—its importance, its danger. I seemed to present the opportunity to discuss the power of language with a like-minded thinker. Faridah needed to share her thoughts on the movement, and I was happy to oblige.

Neither of Faridah's parents read or write, but Faridah migrated to the United States with a very developed literate repertoire. She says her parents weren't "after me to read or write, so I was doing the homework by myself." Faridah's early and lasting literacy learning was especially motivated by her mother's desire for her and her four sisters to achieve what she couldn't. Because her mother couldn't "open any book," whether from ability or lack of time, she was "dreaming of having her kids do the things that she can't do." Faridah recalls, "She dreams that she can read or write. You know, like in our country when you are fifteen, sixteen, you start to get the idea of marriage, but my mom, she was really different of these women. . . . Her first thing is to go to college and do a PhD and that and that and that. And reach." Faridah notes that her mother was "really different," and she seems to have passed on to Faridah the value to "reach" for more. Faridah often refers to "reaching" in this way as an action that is the opposite of fixity, an orientation that illuminates a way to move forward in social status, educational accomplishments, or life satisfaction.

Faridah was supported in her English language learning by her older sisters who practiced their English around the house before Faridah began to learn it herself. Faridah developed her reading and writing practices first in Arabic, then in French in third grade, and English in sixth. "It's three languages that you have to do with homework," she says, "with all these things." She explained that it was common and expected to move constantly among these three languages for reading, writing, and homework activities, saying, "You know, you are saying the sentence, it's two words Arabic, two words French and like that [slaps hands together] and it's a word!" Faridah values, almost as a matter of cultural common sense, how languages and literacies are easily malleable and can be manipulated for one's literate aims.

In college, Faridah majored in French translation but disliked what she describes as "the classic one of Shakespeare and Molière and bla bla bla." She instead switched to studying the Arabic language—"how it was, and how it is now. History of language, linguistic, we call it." Such educational choices show her self-identification as a highly literate individual and are further demonstrated in her reported success in essay writing, which was commonly assigned. Faridah describes the writing process she developed in Algerian schools in this way: "So you have to do a map in your brain, the introduction, the subject that you are talking, this is the point that I'm gonna talk, *dut dut dut*. . . . You have to use your brain more than use the information, you know? And because maybe there is some people, they have tons of information, but they don't know how to organize their ideas."

Faridah recalls that when writing one of these essays on the topic of pollution, "we have to do the introduction, what is pollution, then what is the effect of this pollution. Then in the end you give your own opinion." Faridah describes these essays as "really organized" with requirements to leave lines after a "full stop" and two lines after the introduction. These rigid formatting requirements contrast the more fluid approach to the languages used to write the essays. In this essay on pollution she had "a little bit mixed with French, because even sometimes I wanna say something in French and then I'm gonna write it the English way." She explained that her teacher did not critique her mixing because "sometimes you do some mistakes like that, which is not really mistakes. . . . With practice, you're gonna have the habit, you know, to work two languages." At this point in her literate history, Faridah cultivated this work among her languages, treating movement across the full extent of her literate repertoire as productive, habitual, and constitutive of an educated multilingual writer from Algeria.

In fact, Faridah is "more comfortable writing" in multiple languages than speaking them, an important exception to the previous accounts of fixity in writing. Faridah says such a preference for writing gives her time to decide "why I am using this word, this is what I mean from this word." Writing gives her space to decide her intended meaning among her languages. In Arabic "a word has many meanings," she says. "And you can choose this word and maybe it can make this person really mad. You cannot use another word that has the same meaning to make him happy," so for Faridah these decisions require the slow pace and opportunity to revise that writing affords. As a writer, she needs the time to compose carefully because for her this is a part of who she is. She deeply identifies as a reader and writer.

> Me, I was crazy about reading. I found the paper on the floor? I'm gonna get and read it. In primary school there is a paragraph describing spring, I'm gonna read

it. I'm gonna keep the beautiful words here in my brain that I can use them. I find difficult book that big writer? I have to finish it. Like the last time, that I did read, it was Arabic and then translation English. I'm in the bed like almost sleeping, but I have to finish it! And my husband was like, what's the secret about this book? It's that it's, you know, inside you.

Even the rhetorical repetition in Faridah's response reveals her profound valuing of literate culture. Books, reading, writing are "inside" Faridah. But she also believes the importance of literacy exists outside her own experience. She finds meaning for her literacy practices by placing them in a wider network of human literate exchange. "When you are reading the book, you are taking from the book and you are giving. You are taking from the book, you are writing the paragraph, you are giving your experience, your opinion, your feelings too, in the writing." The give-and-take of reading and writing connects Faridah to other readers and writers. She orients to the world partly by "taking" from other writers and "giving" her experience back to them.

But like Defne, Faridah does not feel that her current writing practices have been valued in the United States in ways she hoped. She explains that in Algeria her husband was what she describes as "a genius guy in the university." Faridah taught Arabic at a high school and wrote occasionally for a newspaper. This newspaper in fact offered her a permanent position, but she decided instead to follow her husband to the United States. Now her husband works as a school custodian, and Faridah feels that "joining him here, kind of kill some of your dreams you know. Because here to go back to school it's impossible. It's not even hard, it's no way. I don't know how much you're gonna pay." The social pressures encountered after migration—gendered expectations of supporting one's husband, financial barriers to further education in the United States—have quietly shut down Faridah's literacy practices, with U.S. schools operating as a "meta-field, regulating and constraining the availability, value, and use" of her previously lucrative literate capital (Luke, "Genres" 330). Faridah's husband's immigration lottery—intentional state management of migration that belies the free choice of a "lottery"—set the stage for the institutional management that impeded the further practice of Faridah's literacies in the United States. Because she could not access further education primarily for reasons of time and money, her literate practices do not retain their value in the United States, to others and to herself, and are therefore lost.

A devaluation of these literate practices is a devaluation of Faridah's sense of self: "I feel like if I can't write, it's a lot of things inside me, a lot of feelings that I can't, um, I can't send them to other people you know. 'Cause, uh, I find myself when I'm writing." Without remaining "attached with the books, attached with learning," Faridah says, "you're gonna forget who you are." Such attachments are essential "to show who you are or you gonna be lost." She worries that in the United States she has become reduced to "just clean up do that and that and that . . . as a mom, as a wife." She agrees that "being a mom is good, being a wife is wonderful, but what is you, you know, as a person?" In an echo of Defne's expression of loss, Faridah explains that it is through writing that she is able to find herself and know who she is "as a person." Her sense of literate identity hinges on the opportunity to continue her book-based attachments, which have been foreclosed due to gendered demands—primarily the lack of extended family help in the United States—to "clean up . . . as a mom, as a wife." Both Defne and Faridah share this particular need to write their way back to themselves, explaining why, without that writing, they might not know who or where they are.

HOW LITERATE VALUES STALL WRITING

In these accounts multilingual writers migrate to the United States with deeply developed repertoires shaped by complex literate histories. They manipulate their literacy and language resources to express, communicate, and make gains through writing and accomplish what they need to do in their lives. As chapter 2 makes clear, the potential of recognizing these practices is great: when multilingual writers are allowed to draw on their repertoires when they write, they express sharp insight into culture and language, are hyperaware of audience, articulate similarities and differences among writing styles in multiple languages, and often write themselves into new intellectual and professional status. Conversely, then, the consequences of losing these practices are dire, both for writers and for classrooms, workplaces, families, and communities.

In the accounts of multilingual migrants whose literate repertoires are stuck or lost, there is evidence of much wasted human and intellectual potential. Those who can't move their literacy practices among their languages in the United States are unable to take advantage of multilingual innovations or insights. They also struggle to adapt or reuse the literate resources accumulated over a lifetime of multilingual immersion. Some participants, as chapter 4 shows, are able to maneuver around these literate setbacks to develop entirely new literacy practices in the United States, but others see the effort or material resources required as a futile roadblock. Explained this way, the outcomes of fixed repertoires may change how scholars and teachers understand why multilingual writers feel stuck or lost when writing. As Canagarajah has noted, those of us who teach, research, and treasure language have a tendency to romanticize its potential, making it "appear more diverse, dynamic, and democratic" than it actually is ("Translanguaging" 3). We believe deeply in the power of language and encourage the accumulation of it—more literacies in more languages wielded in more accepting social and classroom situations must certainly mean more power. But participants' accounts show this belief in the fluidity of language does not always play out in the lived experience of literacy. Although these writers have developed their literacy practices among multiple languages and across multiple locations in the world, when they reach for these practices in the United States, their practices sometimes stall or slip away. Why might this happen?

It is important to concede that many of these writers' practices are fixed on purpose. Writers can be savvy in their manipulation of literacy's range of movement. Writers seek to control the movement of literacy, slowing it down, speeding it up, pushing it in different directions. Haneen, Tashi, Yolanda, and others cultivate a very fixed sense of self as they refashion their literate lives after migration. Or writers may simply "[opt] for the most effective strategy of the moment," a mode that at times might be practiced as more fixed or "rooted" than fluid (Lavie and Swedenburg 17). But beyond intentional fixity, the struggle to mobilize literate repertoires is also conditioned by shifting social and economic values.[7] For example, both Faridah and Defne's families passed on deeply developed literate values, but valuing reading and writing was not enough to mitigate loss of their literate identities. Their changing professional and economic status in the United States complicates these conditions further: Faridah's desire to study and translate literature is possible in Algeria because of a family support network, manageable cost of living, and status as a working journalist, while the lack of these in the United States makes further study impossible. Defne was supported in Turkey by a well-educated and economically stable family, but after migrating to the United States for graduate school, starting a family, and getting divorced, she refused her family's further support. She left her PhD program to find part-time teaching at a community college and later on as a special education aide.

While Defne and Faridah's mode of entry to the United States differed greatly, they ended up in similar states of lost identification and fixed future potential. Defne entered the United States in the relatively privileged position of a budding academic, while Faridah entered completely by chance on a lottery visa. Upon losing her student visa, Defne depended on a spousal status to stay in the country; after her divorce she held a temporary worker visa and is working to become a permanent resident. But Faridah's status remained the same while in the United States; she was ever in visa limbo—not a state to be equated with stability. Defne herself agrees that these social values matter: "This [graduate school] is very bourgeois stuff . . . not only bourgeois, but maybe life stage and life development and gender, gender." As a smart sociologist, Defne knows that the flexible schedule of a "bourgeois" student is just as influential on her writing practices as are the gendered expectations of a single mother. She recognizes and lives with the "numerous factors" that impact women's lives after migration, including "capitalism, patriarchy . . . the racial division of labour" and "work/life balance" (Cuban, "Home/work" 82). These "factors" make the value of multilingual repertoires volatile, driving it up or down depending on the position of any given writer.

Because migrant women are exposed to devaluing through multiple forms of labor, the value of their repertoires is volatile. The accounts in this chapter are particularly illuminating of this predicament as literate repertoires are valued as both personal and professional assets before migration to the United States and condemned as racial or cultural deficit afterward. This is why multilingual migrants' reticence to put forth literate effort is not lethargy but self-preservation. While their literacies were previously professionally lucrative and socially respected, in the United States it is their at-home skills that garner social value (although little if any economic value). So the devaluation of their literate potential is strongly related to a felt devaluation of the self. Their selfhood and sense of worth is altered as their social relations with family abroad and new migrant communities in the United States are strained.

The increasing mobility of our times can have a fixing effect. Foregrounding the mobility of literacy shows how literacies on the move have the potential to simultaneously empower and disempower writers. Thus the fluidity and fixity of migrants' multilingual repertoires must be understood as two "profoundly relational" types of movement (Manderscheid 38). The mobility of literate repertoires makes writers both socially mobile and also socially marginal because they are continuously subject to shifting values. In these accounts the outcomes of multilingual writers' literacy and language resources are not secure or guaranteed but are instead mediated by social and economic values of school, work, home, and nation. Chapter 4 sets out to consider how the assemblage of social and economic values held by writers and institutions creates a unique kind of friction that mediates literacy in the United States.

CHAPTER 4

FRICTION

WHEN WRITING STALLS IN MOTION

When a multilingual migrant is fluent in standard English, when she has years of literacy education in multiple languages, when she is deeply attuned to the rhetorical effect of her language choices, why do her literacies still stall? What values might be mediating movement characterized by friction—the simultaneous mobilizing and fixing of literate resources? This chapter explores what a third kind of movement, friction, can reveal about literate values. Here, friction is more than a stage between movement and stasis; friction is both movement and stasis. It is the abrasion, dissonance, or contradiction produced by their simultaneity. Building on Tsing's enactment of friction, which she defines as "the awkward, unequal, unstable, and creative qualities of interconnection across difference" (4), this chapter's use of friction highlights the tension, dissonance, or abrasion in literate movement that, at first glance, appears to be smooth or simply stuck, caught up in the "sticky materiality of practical encounters" (1).[1] For Tsing, friction is "messy" and "unstable," a force that doesn't slow or stop movement but is in fact "required to keep global power in motion" (6). This is the analytic lynchpin of relations of movement: analysis of literate movement can show not simply how values do or don't match but also how their mismatching is a joint venture between writers and powerful institutions.

So far, this book has shown what fluid and fixed literacy practices reveal about literate valuation. We saw how messy repertoires and literacy relays support agency and innovation because writers' values match institutional ones. We saw how stuck and lost literacies inhibit the realization of literate identities and productivity because writers' and institutional values are mismatched. This chapter responds to the question the previous chapters raise: Why do writers both succeed and struggle with their multilingual repertoires? Literacies appear to be both fluid and fixed because they are constantly revalued. Writers' literacies are both present and lost, valued and denied. The social and economic values held by various agents—teachers, classmates, coworkers, family members, the writers themselves—mediate what literacy is able to do or be at any given time. Frictive movement suggests writerly and institutional values that both do and don't match. In these cases, writers know how to play the literate game, but the game keeps changing.

The chapter moves through two analytic sections, one that surveys a broad range of participant insights and another that features in-depth participant accounts. I explore family, school, workplace, and community contexts in which social and economic values meet, showing how participants' literate repertoires across contexts are markers of identity as well as goods for sale. Three extended participant accounts show writers moving across contexts and experiencing the friction of literate valuation. I analyze the assemblage of workplace values that monetize migrants' languages (goods that they often use to get jobs in the United States), family and community values about language heritage, and school values that dictate which literate practices count. Simply put, the first section shows what literate values are and the second section shows how these values work. The chapter explores how literate values and movement are related. Friction proves to be evident everywhere—in assumptions, uncomfortable truths, and contradictions about how literacy is valued. I do not resolve this friction but rather hold it up for scrutiny, aiming to more critically understand how literate values shape multilingual migrants' selfhood, literate practices, and social relations.

VALUES IN WORKPLACES, COMMUNITIES, FAMILIES, AND SCHOOLS

This section identifies the literate values participants described most extensively in the contexts of work, community, school, and family. The broad representation of participant insights shows how context-specific social and economic values determine what writers understand their literate resources to be worth. Literate repertoires are a complex of literate resources, and resources themselves are continuously created over the course of a literate life. Literate repertoires and resources—comprised of volatile literacy, language, and identity components—are open to a process of continuous valuation. Literate valuation is particularly potent for multilingual migrants because they move: as writers encounter shifting social conditions before, after, and along the paths of migration, so too do their resources experience shifting value. This isn't to say that multilingual writers are incapable of calling on their resources as a result of migration. Surely participant accounts show this to not be the case. But treating resources as always undergoing valuation might lift some burden *off* the writer if, in fact, their resources do not bring about the social mobility, political power, or wholesale improvement sometimes promised or expected.

In the Workplace

In many narratives about writing at work, participants describe conflicting social and economic values around multilingualism. They know that their multilingualism can be economically valuable in the United States, but they also know that (often unspoken) social values in workplaces favor standard, unaccented, and nonmixed communication in a dominant language—English in the United States. As demonstrated in Table 2 (see the introduction), workplaces seem to value communicability, efficiency, and security. In fact, in the workplaces described here, social values around multilingualism—support for heritage languages, multicultural respect for diverse ethnicities and religions, teacher-parent bilingual communication—appear to be in tension with the demands for efficient and clear communication or safety concerns that privilege security and surveillance. In other words, participants' multilingual repertoires get them in the front door, but dominant language values condition their actions once in the building. The multilingual migrant writers in this study know what they are being paid to do: work in and toward the dominant English language ideology of the United States.

A contradiction in values is almost assumed in many participant accounts. For example, Defne locates this contradiction in a globalizing workplace. When asked what globalization means to her, Defne set up an open/closed tension: globalization has opened up the world through communication technology but also shut down worldwide diversity through English dominance. When asked how this meaning affects multilingual writing, Defne immediately spoke of the workplace. Setting the open/closed tension in the scene of work, she says plainly that jobs in the United States demand work in the "dominant language." She explains: "In the United States you have to use English at work. So maybe in your little private life you use your own language and you have your daily notes or little writing projects, but you still use dominantly the major language." Defne makes a clear distinction between the literate practices allowed in U.S. work spaces and those allowed in "private life spaces." She separates "English at work" from the "daily notes or little writing projects" carried out in "your own language." She draws a clear line between languages and between the public and the private spaces that dictate their use. Her separations are hierarchical, with a "dominant," "major" workplace English garnering more power than language for one's "little" life and writing. She doesn't address the blurred language boundaries she describes in chapter 3 but keeps the English and her "own" languages distinct. Defne's response may be self-evident to many. English is the dominant language of the United States so U.S. workers use English, goes the logic. But her equation is perplexing given the fact that she has been hired more than once for her multilingualism. Other participants describe a similar puzzle.

For example, when working in Pakistan as a journalist and on-air television reporter, Sabohi was paid for her ability to move quickly among languages with a fine-tuned sense of audience. Describing her work in print journalism, she says it is "even effective to use different languages . . . if you are communicating to the masses . . . and [keeping] their culture, their beliefs, their traditions in mind." Rather than address an audience for whom reading in only one language would be unnatural and, as she says, detrimental to communication, Sabohi knew she would succeed at work by using the full extent of her multilingual repertoire. When reporting on the television news, she would simultaneously read her English script and deliver the news orally in Kashmiri. But in the United States, hired as the principal of an Islamic school where students and their families communicate among at least eight languages, Sabohi says her workplace remains primarily monolingual in English.[2] Sabohi maintains her capacious attitude toward multilingual communication in the school, saying, "if that means there's mixing of a few in school newsletter, for example, I don't mind." But at the same time she creates a curriculum in which all instruction is in English with the exception of Arabic in the Arabic language class. In the United States, Sabohi was hired because she was a multilingual professional who could communicate among a wide variety of language and cultural backgrounds. But as the principal, she is paid to lead a primarily English language school with an English language reading and writing curriculum, in which students are prepared for an Islamic life in the United States.

Schools, especially those that receive public funding and are accountable to public whims, are unique workplaces in that their social and economic values around literacy are tied up in larger political debates, trends, and funding streams. But schools are similar to other participant workplaces like service jobs, health-care work, or nannying in that most maintain implicit English monolingual policies (Tardy). For many participants—Faridah, Jin, Raani, Ishtar, Kunthi, Alicia, Aldene, Yolanda, Defne—school is or has been their workplace, so their understanding of literate values also comes through the curricula they are required to teach. For example, Alicia describes explicit multilingual values and implicit English imperatives in her teaching position at a large public high school. She says that there is "no, no, absolutely no" language restriction in the school, with teachers telling students and families "that whatever language you know they are your resources . . . it's an asset not a deficiency." But, she continues, "the program, the way it's set up right now, yes, the ultimate goal is English acquisition, so it's more of a transitional bilingual program in the sense that we are not really teaching a whole lot in Spanish."

Clearly Alicia is conversant in contemporary approaches to additive bilingualism. Her college coursework in bilingual education shapes what she assumes are desired responses from a progressive bilingual educator. But she also acknowledges the realities of the U.S. public school workplace. She works in a sheltered transitional bilingual program in which the "ultimate goal is English acquisition" and the language of instruction is English for that reason. Interestingly, Alicia signals that the transitional program moves students from Spanish monolingualism toward English monolingualism rather than from Spanish monolingualism toward English/Spanish bilingualism. The program's discourse values the "resources" and "asset" of multilingualism but teaches toward the dominant language. Professed additive bilingualism becomes subtractive bilingualism in practice. This contradiction is shaped by both social and economic values. The school upholds social values around multiculturalism embedded in contemporary teacher training. But the school pays for monolingual English communication (in textbooks, testing programs, teacher salaries), perhaps for what it believes to be the best educational preparation for life in the United States. So Alicia knows that although she was hired for her bilingual background, she stays employed because she can adhere simultaneously to both of these approaches toward literacy education.

Assemblages of social and economic values also appear in employee reading and writing practices at work. For example, in her own bilingual position at a different public high school, Yolanda says, "I'm teaching kids that don't speak Spanish, so it's fair; everything has to be in English. The book is in English, the exams are in English, so I give the information in English." Her understanding that English dominance is "fair" is an effective sleight of hand. As a commonsense claim, Yolanda promotes an English lingua franca but ignores the powerful structure that makes a lingua franca seem "fair": the textbooks that formalize language use, the exams chosen by district administration, the public discourse and elected school boards that funnel commonly held assumptions about language into schools. In other words, Yolanda's adherence to English could be as much meritocratic as acquiescent to U.S. language ideologies. But her understanding of the value of English at work is also shaped by the normalization of workplace surveillance: "I think I always write in English. Even to my Spanish speakers friends in other departments, if it's a work e-mail I always do it in English. . . . I feel like maybe someone might want to read it? It's like, it's a work thing so it should be in English so someone could see it. . . . It is public so it is there. . . . I feel it's more polite to use English so everybody can read it and understand what I'm saying."

At work, Yolanda has in mind readers beyond her Spanish speaking colleagues and friends. When she writes an e-mail that is a "work thing," she chooses to use the language that an unknown "someone" might require. There is an assumption that that someone is a higher-up; there is an assumption that the higher-ups use, and need, English. Yolanda muses that her work e-mails might be read by someone from the "public" and therefore she should politely use the language "everybody" can understand in the United States, English. She suggests she should always compose in English, no matter her own desired language choices, because she never knows who will be scrolling through her text. Implicit language norms that deem English language communication fair, accessible, and open to surveillance in turn define good workplace behavior as English-dominant and accountable to unknown stakeholders. These norms are values regulated through the social: what it means to be a good, useful, valuable American worker.

It is no coincidence that many participants' workplaces value multilingualism; it is those very literate resources that helped participants get the jobs they could discuss. In fact, participants like Khadroma and Nimet are aware of the economic value of multilingualism prior to migration to the United States. They both comment on their own or others' lucrative work as interpreters in China and Azerbaijan, respectively. But as is clear in most participant accounts, languages are the goods that multilingual migrants most successfully leverage for new kinds of professional employment in the United States. This complex assemblage of social and economic values becomes clear when the multilingual resources that make migrants employable are systematically revalued by those same workplaces once the job has begun.

In Community Economies

Multilingual migrants' literate resources are valued beyond what their literate commodities earn in pay. Participants find value in their well-being, self-satisfaction, or furthered literate skills. Their literate resources realize value when participants use them to build relationships or trust in migrant communities. Several participants describe engaging in informal language exchanges with friends or neighbors, acting as literacy brokers for family members or helping as spontaneous interpreters in community settings. Kunthi, for example, describes befriending an English-speaking acquaintance who asked to be taught some Indonesian out of curiosity. As Kunthi says, she "wanted to know if it's hard for [her] or no." Kunthi agreed to teach her "like one word two words . . . like this is the foot" as long as her friend agreed to practice English with her in return. Similarly, Nimet engaged in a kind of language exchange when she volunteered at a nonprofit literacy program to teach basic literacy to community members. She describes tutoring a Spanish speaker who would bring an English grammar textbook that he didn't understand to their sessions. Nimet explains that her tutee wanted her help translating the book into Spanish so he could use it.

NIMET (N): It's hard to translate, and he said just tell me in Spanish, and I said I don't know Spanish. So I bought a Spanish dictionary—not for him, for myself. Just communicating like that he improve!

REBECCA (R): Do you think it improved your English?

N: To explain it helps, it helps! Because when you prepare, you also learn something, you also organize, make a lesson plan and okay it makes sense of course. The best way to learn is teaching. I think so. Because sometime I say [when studying for my own] exam, I need somebody to teach!

Nimet knows her literate resources—in this case, teaching practices, dictionary use, familiarity with language learning processes—are valuable even when she is not paid for them. She set out to volunteer in order to stay involved in the community of language learners that she had benefited from after her arrival in the United States. But in the act of tutoring English, she engages in language practice herself, receiving practice-as-pay. Nimet and her tutee exchange practice and motivation, learning together rather than alone: as Nimet's English and Spanish improves, so does her tutee's. In this way her literate resources become valuable beyond employability or salary. They further Nimet's own literate repertoire and create connections with other multilingual migrants where she lives.

Yolanda gives another example of her literate resources receiving value when she acted as a spontaneous health interpreter during a traffic accident. While driving from one farm to another for work, she encountered an accident with a rolled-over car and an ambulance. The people standing around the car looked to her like they might speak Spanish. Her account shows the value of her multilingualism.

> I stopped. I said, "I speak Spanish, do you need any help?" And you could see the ambulance people were all blonde, blue-eyed, very white. That doesn't mean they don't speak Spanish, but I didn't come to say "Hey, you don't know Spanish." I came to say, "Do you need help." And they were so happy, "oh my god, yes!" They got me in the ambulance; the girl was crying because she was pregnant and she was with the husband and the husband didn't know she was pregnant but she didn't want to tell him. It was a drama. . . . So I ended up at the hospital helping translate until an interpreter came. That was like "move your fingers, move your toes." It was so important for them! And then when she said, "Now I don't know if the baby's gonna be okay, and I don't know if I want him to know now." So I told the ambulance people, "Okay, here's the situation. She's pregnant bla bla." So it was huge! Huge.

Yolanda felt proud that her Spanish resources could support a young couple in a complicated scenario. She was not only a language broker among a wife, husband, and several emergency responders, she was an accidental broker of very sensitive and vital health information. Yolanda was gratified to be able to contribute the goods—language—that could relay this information and keep the wife safe. The extent of her participation with the couple shows how her resources were valuable not only to the people needing her translation but also to herself. She benefited from her repertoire and was reminded of her value as a Spanish speaker in the United States.

Several participants described moments of on-the-spot interpretation, especially in hospitals, stores, with family while traveling, or in airport customs or border control lines. These are moments when migrants' multilingual resources can be especially "huge" in helping themselves, their family, or complete strangers in the most mundane or most high-stakes interactions. Literate resources in these situations maintain high economic value in that they are emphatically useful—their value is some of the most impactful of participants' experiences. When asked to recount a memory when they were proud of their multilingualism, many participants went straight to these scenes. Literate resources in these situations also receive very high social value as actions of relationship-building, neighborliness, or family respect. Even when they are offered for free, these literate resources have high value for multilingual migrants. Offering or exchanging these resources can build community economies among multilingual migrants, which in turn can provide well-being in sometimes hostile community conditions.

With Family

In many participants' experiences, families act as a conduit for social attitudes toward literacy and language. These families are not just passing down practices, as do the mothers detailed in chapter 2, they are also passing down beliefs about the practices, what family literacy activities mean. Family-based educational expectations, class background, and cultural norms especially shape how participants themselves—as children or as parents—value their literate resources as respectable, important, or beneficial. This process of literate valuation is present, for example, in the way Ishtar, Tashi, Defne, and Alandra speak about the resources they hope to pass on to their children. These four, along with the majority of participants with children, value an additive approach to multilingualism wherein their children are learning English while maintaining strong connections to their home culture and languages. These values are present in several participants' memories of their mothers' explicit teaching about how reading and writing activities matter.

Yolanda's mother passed down strong social values around writing, reading, and books. Yolanda remembers her mother designating certain weekends as "reading weekends" rather than "fun weekends." Yolanda describes herself and her brother knowing that reading weekends were the times they played without their mother. Yolanda and her brother knew that they had to "respect that she was reading," which in turn caused them to respect reading and writing in general. Similarly, when Faridah explains that her mother "dreams that she can read or write," Faridah is describing her own literate inheritance. She says these values come "from, I think, my mom." She explains: "In her heart she was dreaming of having her kids do the things that she can't do. She can't open any book. When she's doing cleanup at home, whatever paper, she is saving it because she doesn't know is it important or just a thing, you know? And it hurts her a lot when we go home and say, 'Momma this is just [throws hand aside].'" Faridah's mother places high social value on the reading and writing that she did not have access to. Because her mother feels the pain of not knowing whether a piece of paper is important or trash, she places very high social value on writing, written material, books, and reading habits. She believes deeply in the transformative power of literacy and shows her daughters how to respect and admire a literate lifestyle. These values stuck with Faridah especially because a life saturated with literacy was uncommon where she grew up in Algeria, especially for girls. Faridah continues to foster these values in her own life in the United States, feeling "responsible . . . to have my mom's dream come true . . . to show her that here . . . we can do it." As described in the extended account in chapter 3, Faridah treats reading and writing with great respect and is "crazy about reading" everything from "the paper on the floor" to the "difficult book [by] that big writer." She relies on literacy to "do it" in the United States, to succeed in doing "things that [her mother] can't do."

This is not to say that families' literate valuations always resulted in positive attitudes toward literacy and language. In families like Renan's, in which reading and writing were actively discouraged for girls, literate resources were given low social value. The company she kept with books got Renan, a lawyer from Turkey, in trouble with her family. So she grew up reading under her blankets at night and subsequently valuing literacy as a kind of subterfuge or gendered rebellion. Other families, like Houa's, depended so heavily on their children for literacy brokerage that participants avoided writing as much as possible as adults. Although Houa witnessed how her resources were economically valuable for her family, she placed low social value on writing. She saw writing as simply a labor-intensive burden rather than a form of expression or identity. In families like Tashi's or Paj's, translation was treated not as a prestige- or leisure-based activity, but simply as division of family labor, equal in value to traveling home from college on the weekends to care for siblings' children. This equation of babysitting to family translation is one example of how family gender dynamics complicate the social and economic values placed on literate resources in any given time and place. With the exception of a handful of participants, families deeply valued literacy education for their girls. But for almost all participants, the gendered roles after migration—responsibilities for child-rearing and home-caring—impeded their realization of literate values in refashioned family contexts in the United States.

At School

Participants often use comparison to make sense of literacy in schools. They compare the literacy education they witness in the United States to the literacy education they experienced growing up. When asked about their children's literacy experiences, mothers define what their children do in contrast to what they did as children. When describing their teaching practices, many compare back and forth, describing how literacy in their home countries is valued differently or similarly in the United States. Specifically, many participants intuit that school-endorsed literacies are shaped by unstated economic values. Economic values surface in the form of instrumentalist rationales for teaching literacy and language in ways most guaranteed to lead to employability or further education, what Cuban calls the "elixir for the knowledge-based economy" ("Downward Mobility" 7). From testing, teacher feedback, assignments, and textbooks, participants learn how literate resources are valued. They then use those values to define for themselves what the English language and "English writing" actually are.

Participants assume that schools, both in and outside of the United States, value certain English language varieties and English cultural traditions that linger in postcolonial contexts. For example, Tashi describes in nearly twenty lines of interview transcript a school day scheduled to the half hour, including morning and evening prayer and "4 o'clock tea . . . yeah, we have to have tea." Jin's most vivid memory from her English courses in Japan was "Mr. Brown in the textbook" and his conversational antics she had to memorize. Defne describes learning English in middle school by singing "Brother John" and "London Bridge" from the "Longman Series" and following the lives of characters "Miranda, Terry, and Jim" throughout her English language textbook. Defne says, "It's still funny how the Terry one was really funny—this guy with long hair and from the 1970s style. Now I'm close to someone named Terry and . . . like that's the first name I learned!" Scholars have examined the influence of textbooks in language education, noting their lasting ideological impressions on learners' understanding of what matters in the language.[3] Similarly here, textbooks, and the singing, scheduling, and cultural traditions around them, endorse the English varieties that have long moved around the world through settlers, teachers, missionaries, or more recently such organizations as the British Council and cultural exchange NGOs. That the influence in this group of participants seems to come from England more than the United States may be due to participants' age or region, but it is this form of English—rather than the World Englishes that they use, hear on the streets, or see in their hometown news—that they presume is valued by schools.

However, participants in this study who came to the United States as children—what some call Generation 1.5 or resident ESL students—and occasionally travel back and forth, describe English and writing education through projects, assignments, and grading practices that ring remarkably true to U.S. schooling. For example, Houa says, "In middle school we did bunch of essays on careers [and] in the sixth grade we had a bunch of papers but it was more like, pick a continent and write about it." Houa describes writing book reports, making PowerPoint presentations for research papers, writing a short story for a school contest, and making a book as a class. Harriet describes collaborative writing assignments and school reading and writing taking place on class blogs. As elaborated in the extended account in this chapter, Paj similarly remembers writing "paragraphs about a certain topic [she] would choose randomly from a cookie box," writing about a childhood experience with "at least two or three metaphors," and learning about "how fragments were not complete sentences and . . . if you had a fragment you would get points off." In the company of the majority of study participants who finished their early schooling outside of the United States, the difference is stark. Whereas school-based literacy memories from other parts of the world are about position papers, testing, and, most of all, writing to show content mastery, memories from United States schooling are about rewards, grades, collaborative projects, and a certain kind of structured creativity. No participant offered judgment on whether they thought their writing education was *effective*. Instead, they use these school memories to build a definition for themselves of what English language writing *is*.

Regardless of the location or time of their language and literacy schooling, participants understand English to be "clear" and simple, "easier" and less "complicated" than other languages. For example, Khadroma says, "English is kind of famous for being straightforward." She extends that quality to English speakers, saying, "You know, people are more straightforward; people are more direct." Sofia repeats three times in one utterance that English is "easier" than Russian. She understands this ease through the writing she completes in her ESL courses in the United States. "If we write essay in English, so I did this in Russian; it helps that the idea is the same. But it seems to me in English is more like structure, best is clear. In Russian if you begin writing, you can describe that tree [pointing to a nearby tree], how I say, a lot. You can write A LOT. In English it's more 'bum bum bum' just clear." Sofia acknowledges that her Russian writing instruction helps her in English in general and especially in writing essays. According to Sofia's literacy education, the Russian and

English language essay genre share characteristics, but the language used to write that genre is distinct. Sofia works hard to translate the amplified quality of the Russian language into the "bum bum bum" quality of English, and she extends this quality to her definition of the English language as clear and easy. Several participants define English this way. By "easy" they don't mean easy to learn. Participants like Rukiye and Tashi find English grammar hard and express confusion about the exploratory reading and expressive writing that seems favored over grammar instruction in the United States. Instead, participants seem to understand the clarity and ease of English as an assembly line of quick and simple prose.

Other participants learned in childhood and adult English classes that schools value structured, rigid, and choppy writing in English. Raani, Yolanda, Paj, Nimet, and Rukiye all conclude that quick and concise communication must be mastered in order to write well in English. Paj, for example, defines school-based writing *as* the five-paragraph essay, saying, "I remember how each paragraph should be about five sentence and you should have your main sentence and then supporting points, and an essay was like five paragraphs—your introduction, three body paragraphs and your conclusion—and in the first sentence of your conclusion you should restate your topic." Nimet and Alicia's exposure to English-language writing especially through testing leads them to believe that English-medium schools value speedy and timed writing and the ability to write under pressure. By extension, they assume that the audiences who read English language writing must have short attention spans that writers must please and keep entertained. Alicia explains that her TOEFL "English format-type essays" were "very systematically done." She describes her "contrasting" essay as "just presenting the facts" by saying "on the one hand, on the other hand" and then "some people say that . . . and others think that." Her "opinion" essay was "'in my opinion . . . all teachers should be required to know a second language in order to teach,' you know, things like that." She describes with a wave of the hand these essays as easily memorized format options: "In English I feel like there are some more precise way of doing things with writing, with the organization in general or your thoughts." To define for herself what is valued in English writing, Alicia draws a direct line from her TOEFL test to what it means to think in English.

Several participants taking college courses in the United States interpret similar social values from their writing instruction. They have to come to believe that when writing in English, a writer must express an opinion, but one structured through summary and citation rather than "creativity." For example, Alandra says, "My own critique about writing here [in the United States] is, like, just repeat the same thing, but just like no creativity of what you really understand or what you want to do with that knowledge." Alandra wanted to make creative use of what she read or learned in class but was penalized for writing beyond a prescribed structure for academic essays. She finally realized her professors wanted "not much fluffy fluffy about what you write." As Alicia, Yolanda, and Aldene describe earlier, the emphasis on concise rather than "fluffy" writing is taught at the sentence level, with Alicia asking in the voice of her past English teachers: "Chop chop chop, extra words extra words. No need. Where are your periods and sentences?" Yolanda states simply: "In English you write short sentences; in English long sentences are not very pretty."

Nimet similarly learned that U.S. schools value clear and explicit writing from teacher and advisor feedback on her academic writing. After meeting with a program advisor, she learned that her application essay to her nursing program was "too long" because they wanted "brief information." Nimet was happy to have an advisor tell her that her essay should be short and clear, but she was still puzzled by its purpose: "You have to show something, some question you have to answer. You have to explain why, why you apply for this program. What is your purpose? What kind of benefit you will give to the community? . . . Why, a lot of why." Nimet explains that "a lot of why" felt uncomfortable because the essays she had written in Azerbaijani schools were almost exclusively for end-of-year testing and required her to relay subject matter with no opinion, no "why." One could draw tentative conclusions that a Soviet-organized school did not necessarily value individual exploration in school essays, whereas it is exactly the purpose for a U.S. university application essay. Once she understood the difference, Nimet welcomed the change but remained cautious: "You know, this is different society. I grew up different society. You cannot match them because sometimes you write sentence. This society doesn't understand me and then I need to change to the other. But it takes long sentence. [laughing]." Like Alicia, Yolanda, and Aldene, Nimet knows that writing conventions are found in cultural rather than in universal norms. She understands the "long" amount of language it takes to switch among norms that are driven by social values. Although she is happy to learn new conventions in her U.S. nursing program, she argues for patience in that process, saying that sometimes such communicative predicaments "take a long sentence" to resolve.

Whether all English users agree that writing in English is this tidy, structured, or clear, these multilingual writers have experienced enough literacy education in English to believe this is so. They believe English speakers and writers value structure and clarity above all else. They are pragmatic about the English it takes to get a good grade or gain access to a U.S. university and internalize these values as the defining features of the language itself.

Extended accounts from Khadroma, Tashi, and Paj show how these values and others are instantiated across domains in individual lives. Both Khadroma and Tashi were professionals before migration and migrated to follow their husbands who were attending U.S. universities, while Paj immigrated with her entire family as part of refugee resettlement. All three writers were in nursing school during initial interviews and were employed as registered nurses by the end of the study. All three narrate experiences and events that move across the domains delineated above. Their accounts crystalize a complicated assemblage of personal, workplace, family, and community values that push literate resources through a process of valuation. Analysis of the three accounts together shows how friction, as literate movement, is conditioned by a unique process of literate valuation. Literate resources that appear, at first, to be either fluid or fixed turn out to be both as writers and powerful agents decide what writers' practices are worth.

KHADROMA

Khadroma is a registered nurse from China who has settled happily in the U.S. Midwest with her husband and young children. Both times I interview her, once at her home and once via Skype, she listens and responds with intensity to my questions. Like many study participants, she is passionate about language and very thoughtful about what her multilingualism has done for her as a migrant in the United States. The friction in her repertoire is subtle. Khadroma wields her literate resources well in the United States. But immigration also made some of her experiences and credentials inaccessible. Therefore, the movement of Khadroma's literate resources among languages and locations in the world has both helped and hindered. Because she moves her repertoire, it is subject to revaluation. She just happens to have weathered literate valuation particularly well.

Khadroma grew up speaking Tibetan at home and Mandarin in school. She says she attended kindergarten at age four because she had to go "get [her] Chinese fixed" because she "[spoke] Tibetan at home and at school we were supposed to speak Chinese." After completing her early schooling, Khadroma attended a teaching college where the mediums of instruction were English, Mandarin, and Tibetan. She explains that this multilingual setting was noteworthy for its inclusion of Tibetan language in the curriculum. The multilingual curriculum wasn't "just for the sake of language," or the learning of the languages themselves, she says, but for the sake of understanding sociology, anthropology, and world literature through the lenses of different languages. After college, Khadroma entered an English training program funded by several American NGOs, where she was trained in interpretation and translation. Most of her teachers were from California, which is why, as she says, her "English is probably more like American style." At this time she also was employed as a civil servant for the government, writing eulogies for a newspaper and essays on health information for politically important retirees. Through connections from her Californian teachers, Khadroma wrote translations and interpreted for American NGOs who were doing work in China. Although this was weekend work, she was happy to travel and work in her multiple languages.

Upon immigrating to the United States, none of Khadroma's school credits or credentials transferred, but her interpretation experience became an important resource. She decided to "start all over" and become a nurse, attending a local community college and then transferring to a nursing program at a four-year university. While in the nursing program, she was employed by the county public health department as an on-call interpreter for Mandarin- or Tibetan-speaking patients. The nursing program also asked her to serve in a position called "a Chinese officer," translating policy documents for them and offering interpretation support. Later on she was asked by the university's chancellor's office to assist in document translation in preparation for the chancellor's trip to China. In other words, even though Khadroma lost much in the process of immigration and had to professionally "start all over," her multilingual resources were deemed highly valuable in the United States—not only in her nursing program but by local government and the university's administration.

In fact, Khadroma has been able to carry over her multilingual resources into her new profession as a nurse. In the hospital where she is currently employed as an RN, multilingual patient support is regulated through a handful of policies. She explains that the hospital is "pushing forward" multilingual patient support, printing materials in Spanish and providing on-site interpretation. Hospital policies now require nurses to "ask people if they speak English as a different, second, or third language." These policies are not local; they are regulated by the Joint Commission on Accreditation of Health Care Organizations (JAHCO), "a committee that assesses the quality of care at different hospitals" nationwide.[4] According to Khadroma, JAHCO requires that nurses "ask people if they need language help in terms of their care" and then read a script before starting interpretation services. The script says: "'This is my name, I'm going to be the interpreter; I'm going to interpret from this side and from that side, no matter what you gonna say.'" Khadroma is matter of fact in calling this the "general rule" that is explained to patients who ask for interpretation. She explains: "Whatever you said gonna be delivered to the other person. I kind of like that because, as interpreter myself, people tell me, 'Oh don't interpret what I said,' but it's not fair. Whoever is in the room, I'm here to facilitate the communication. I'm supposed to deliver the message."

Khadroma's literate resources are clearly vast and viable in the United States. Across multiple professional and geographic settings, her facility in Tibetan, English, and Mandarin is economically valuable. Khadroma decides she is "fortunate to know more than one language" as her economic prospects are multiplied in turn. Although she characterizes her resources as uneven, saying her English is not as proficient as her Mandarin and Tibetan, her movement among these language proficiencies is itself a resource that proves valuable. As a multilingual writer, she is noteworthy for her ability to refashion her civil and nonprofit writing work into her new nursing career in the United States by pulling her interpretation skills from one context to the other. But Khadroma's literate resources are made valuable not only through her actions but also by the powerful organizations that stand in the background of many of her memories. Various non- and for-profit organizations value Khadroma's literate work: one company provides bilingual health pamphlets, another provides on-site interpretation, and an accreditation organization regulates both. While Khadroma certainly leverages her resources with skill, institutions also play a role in the process of valuation in both China and the United States. As Luke, Luke, and Graham have suggested, in the globalized new economy, supranational corporations and organizations assign value to language goods and language workers more than do nation-states, which have been left to simply regulate their flows across borders. This is certainly the case throughout Khadroma's literate history as Western language teachers, traveling business people, and government and university organizations deemed her multilingual repertoire economically valuable.

Furthermore, this high value is assigned especially when Khadroma treats her literate resources as standardized skills available for language work. The script she was required to read reveals the influence of what Heller calls "Taylorist" management techniques that synchronize language work like that done in call centers into a "standardized sequence of steps" (Heller and Duchene 12).[5] As Khadroma says, no matter the content of the translation or the desires of patients to control their high-stakes information, she is going to follow the protocol, translating "from this side and from that side." From this point of view the value of her literate resources resides in its status of language-as-skill. Khadroma presents herself as a message vessel through which languages move, there to "facilitate the communication" and "deliver the message."

That Khadroma treats her multilingualism as a tool to be maneuvered, as a skill rather than the identity explored in Tashi's account below, seems to have kept her multilingual repertoire viable. But Khadroma's repertoire is frictive—much is lost in its movement just as much as gained. The friction that shapes her repertoire especially reveals that (1) institutions play an outsized role in shaping what her repertoire is worth, and (2) her resources remain valuable because of the way she uses them. For example, her literate resources are easily carried over from school to work because, for nurses, school is work but also because her resources are compatible with contemporary economic proclivities for flexibility and standardized practices. She maintains this approach even toward literate resources in her family, saying that she would prefer her daughter learn Spanish because "it's more popular here [in the United States]" as a practical, employable skill rather than the Mandarin or Tibetan that grounds their cultural identity.

TASHI

Tashi, the nurse introduced in chapter 2, experiences similar friction when calling on her literate repertoire as a nurse. But she uses her resources precisely *to* ground her identity. Because she uses her literacies in this way, she both can and cannot mobilize her literate repertoire against institutions and powerful agents that work to shut it down. This process of literate valuation is possible because Tashi moves her literacies with her to the United States and continues to move them among a multilingual repertoire. As the extended account of her literacy practices describes, Tashi is fluent in multiple languages including English and has fostered an acute awareness of multilingual writing over a lifetime of self-sponsored literacy practices. In the English-medium boarding school for Tibetan refugees where she grew up, the "only thing [she] was doing was English" from "first standard" on. She explains that she learned math, science, and social studies in English: "The books, writing, everything in English." She repeats over and over: "Physics, biology, whatever I have to convey, I have to convey everything through English." Tashi believes having to "comprehend into English" and then write in English the "main core values or the main theme" of all of this content shaped her proficiency. She considers herself able to "express what [she wants] to write . . . 100 percent in English," while she feels she can write about 70 percent of what she wants to express in Tibetan and about 10 to 20 percent in Hindi. So although in practice Tashi's school was multilingual ("The teacher teaches in English, but students answer in Tibetan"), and she spoke Tibetan and Kannada at home before moving to school, Tashi identifies as an English-dominant communicator.

Tashi's English practices are meaningful to her in the context of her postcolonial upbringing. In college in India she participated in an intercollegiate speech competition with students from colleges across India. For the competition she wrote and revised a speech on the topic of "charismatic leadership": "I went back home that night and I tailored my writing and then I practiced and we tape recorded. My friend pretended she was jury to practice. Next day when I went for the competition, I was the last person to call because my name is T, so they go in alphabets. Every student was taking like ten minutes, so it was long in between. So I was sitting over there and then finally I delivered the speech. And I was the first." Tashi won the competition and felt great pride in her writing: "I won and it was nice. I was like a winner because it's for the different colleges and I am the only Tibetan. All are Indians, so competing against them." For Tashi, winning didn't only mean that her English language writing was valued in the context of a competition. It also meant that her writing skills were deeply meaningful, distinguishing her in a community in which she had previously felt repressed. Growing up in India, she says, "Being a refugee, we have no choice but to follow and be, when you are in Rome, be as Roman, so do as Roman do." She explains: "They just keep reminding us of like being as countryless," saying, "You guys are refugees here, you didn't have your land, you should go back." Her small victory in an English speech competition was an opportunity to prove that she belonged through language, that she in fact used the language better than others. Tashi's literacies are proficient enough to push against literate erasure, fusing her right to write with her right to exist. Her quick and quiet mention of being "the first" shows her humility, but she said it with a smile. Fair as always, she dismisses ill-wishers as "good people" who are just "ignorant" and "showing their humanness."

The experience shows that Tashi was familiar with literate valuation prior to migration. In fact, it is an understatement to say that Tashi has long been familiar with the social and economic values of literacy. At her boarding school the teachers placed especially weighty economic value on students' developing literate resources as these were understood as donor investments. But Tashi explains that her teachers also placed heavy social value on their literate work, reminding students, "You have extra responsibility, you have to struggle to survive." Tashi interprets this reminder as a kind of valuation of the literate history of her refugee community. She says that without the "generations of our grandparents with a good education background with history records," it is up to her and her generation to lay down a literate record. She believes that if she succeeds at this, "younger generation will have a better life," so "that's how we have to think of it."

Furthermore, Tashi's literate resources, self-taught in elementary school and revised during college, traveled well to the United States. She has wielded her literate resources successfully, transferring from a prenursing community college program to a research university (the same path Khadroma took), writing a successful scholarship application along the way that fully funded her nursing degree. Given her English education in India, which Tashi says was very focused on grammatical "rules, policies . . . similar to languages in the books," she was surprised to see that English speakers in the United States "just write . . . put it down as they speak." She says when writing summaries of readings with her nursing study group, "actually it doesn't make sense, doesn't look really good or grammatically right." Tashi is not only aware of the value of her vast multilingual repertoire, she also occasionally identifies as a more proficient writer of academic English than her U.S. counterparts.

But all of this richness, the depths and heights of Tashi's literate repertoire faced revaluation in the United States. Even though she experienced success at school and work, she lost much literate ground because of immigration. Like Khadroma, her master's degree in science education did not transfer to the United States, and she found herself repeating much of her college education. In the teaching hospital where she took clinical courses and now works as an RN, Tashi repeatedly ran up against ignorance about her communicative capacities. She often experienced linguistic discrimination, finding herself in encounters where she felt her accent disadvantaged her. She says if a nurse doesn't use English "as a native, like American people do, then people try to rough you, overlook you, or make you repeat it, like 'What did you say?'" In interactions that "happen quite often in day-to-day life," Tashi felt "not accepted if you don't know that language" by people who "think in the world there's only one language." For Tashi, these experiences are particularly frustrating in light of her English fluency and the fact that she has come to "know that language" through a lifetime of schooling and well-honed academic literacy practices.

In addition, Tashi's Tibetan is not valued in her school and work contexts in the United States. Tibetan is the language with which she identifies culturally, speaks at home with her family, and is proud to be passing on to her two children. But she has found that this part of her repertoire can be a liability rather than an asset. "I had the experience in my class, when I see my partner I speak in Tibetan and the patient felt kind of offended. So my clinical instructor, she called me aside and she was like, '[Tashi,] you are not allowed to speak in your language when patient is there. She was offended.' I was sorry, it was so unconscious, like when I see her face, just comes out." In this moment—in which she was communicating in a high-stakes clinical setting—Tashi's literate resources were treated as dangerous and offensive. Although she saw her partner's face and Tibetan just "came out," the language was treated not as a resource useful for communication or interpretation, but as a threat—the language signaled insider communication that the patient didn't feel privy to. Thus Tashi's full literate repertoire is rendered invisible in a context in which she becomes an othered, transgressive student. The instructor chastises her, saying "your language" violates the hospital space. Tashi's use of Tibetan violates an implicit English-only policy seemingly created to avoid the potential "offense" to a real clinical patient. Tashi says, "I tend to speak to [my partner] in Tibetan as soon as I see her face. And if do this mistake, at the bedside of the patient, that's breaking the policy." But rather than take offense herself, Tashi reflects: "I thought, it can be true because patient like, all patient might not be feeling bad, but still, like some patient do have concern. And in her case like she has a right to feel offended because I didn't ask for permission, so she might have felt hurt and she might have felt isolated or excluded? I told [my partner] sorry, but after that she chose another partner."

The question mark in Tashi's quote (indicating the interrogative rise in her voice) is telling. She is trying to understand: Why must she ask permission for speaking a language besides English? Why is a patient offended by Tibetan? Tashi's instructor seems to assume that other languages don't belong in the hospital or in front of patients, a confusing conclusion given the interpretation services offered in that space. Either way, Tashi became marked as dangerous and her partner chose another. In fact, Tashi's multilingual repertoire both is and is not valuable in the American hospitals that were both classroom and workplace for her. English, the language in which she feels most literate, is valuable in her classroom writing assignments but marks her as an outsider in spoken hospital interactions or on written charts. She succeeds as a multilingual student but struggles as a multilingual worker. The hospital can constantly revalue the English language literacies Tashi has used for a lifetime because of the unique power relations among real-life patients, often-monolingual clinical instructors, and sometimes immigrant, multilingual nurses. Tashi's literate resources, while highly valued in classroom settings, still run up against rules in a clinical setting—school that is also work. Tibetan, the language with which she identifies culturally, is treated not as an asset for interpretation or translation but as a risk. So although Tashi is proficient in standard English, she does not, in the opinion of those she describes, "speak it properly," which, according to Heller and Duchene, requires that "you still need to constantly prove yourself against the measures developed by the dominant group" (5). Her facility in Hindi, Kannada, and "caring" (what she described as "nursing's main language") remains invisible, while neither her English nor Tibetan resources are useful in sanctioned ways.

In the United States, Tashi feels, as a multilingual writer, like a "jack of all trades and master of none"—a feeling that she calls "good" since she can pass as "the average," still expressing herself but not being "pointed out for being too weak." But the average does not serve Tashi in a clinical setting that assumes perfectly clear English language intelligibility to be a matter both of success and safety.[6] She does get pointed out. The friction that shapes Tashi's resources, that both propels her forward and holds her back, highlights how powerfully institutional context dictates values. But Tashi's literate resources are revalued in a different way than Khadroma's. Tashi uses her Tibetan and accented English as varieties of identity rather than utility. Instructors and classmates in her predominantly white and English-dominant university hospital therefore respond by devaluing and effectively erasing the multilingual resources Tashi developed over her lifetime.

PAJ

Paj is a registered nurse in the U.S. Midwest and was in nursing school when she and I met. She is one of the youngest study participants and one of the most mature. Her wisdom about literacy kept our nearly two-hour interview alive with constant jolts of insight. Paj, who describes herself as bilingual in Hmong and English, immigrated to the United States from Laos with her parents and seven siblings when she was five. Her family continued to move around the Midwest as she grew up, and she eventually attended college near where they settled. Like Khadroma, Paj's literate resources have been mostly valued in school and in her community. In fact, she was valedictorian of her high school. Because Paj grew up in U.S. schools, her literate repertoire is an accurate reflection of how literacy is socially and economically valued in the United States. Especially because her repertoire has experienced frictive movement—she often mobilizes her resources as they are simultaneously shut down in certain contexts—her literate life vividly reveals the process of literate valuation.

Paj's early experiences with ESL programs show how these values work in school. Because her parents didn't read in English, Paj taught herself to read and write in English at home starting in kindergarten, by "looking at the words, trying to figure them out, trying to look through my books of how to say the sounds." She also taught herself to read in Hmong from her father's "old little booklets" in Hmong that sat around the house. The literacy practices she developed on her own were revalued as soon as she started school. Paj's earliest school memory was a homework assignment that left her feeling less than literate. She remembers a short homework reading assignment from first grade in which a picture of children seesawing was followed by a paragraph of text. "I ended up coming the next day with it blank. And I didn't get a sticker or a candy. So I remember feeling left out and everyone had their sticker and their candy. And I remember being put in a special education course because they thought I had some sort of learning disability, although the teachers knew I was an immigrant and it wouldn't have been fair to expect me to suddenly know how to read in another language."

Juxtaposed with her intense self-education, it is clear that the school had no way to recognize or value the self-sponsored literacy practices Paj already had. The reading assignment could not evaluate Paj's ability to "[look] at the words . . . figure them out" or reward her desire to search for instruction in her "books of how to say the sounds." Instead, the school used an easily assessable reading comprehension worksheet and missed Paj's nascent bilingual literacies. They then punished her for what they missed—candy and stickers are certainly sought-after objects, but it was the reward routine that Paj caught onto right away. She immediately felt left out, doubly so when she was given "special education" rather than English language support. But she knew rewards meant values—where there were stickers, there were literacies that mattered to the school.

When she did join a mainstream class midway through that same year, Paj was pulled out three times weekly for ESL support. She found this routine embarrassing, feeling "kind of on the spot when they pick you out of class 'cause everyone knows you're leaving for ESL." As a good student from the beginning, she was mostly worried that she was "missing out on something" and she remembered "feeling like now I'm gonna be a little more behind." Perhaps it was just her desire to not stand out, but even this early on Paj started putting together the school's values: She understood the school to value quick and efficient learning and worried if she missed class, even as a first grader, that she might "be a little more behind." But she also understood the school to value the community-building potential of supporting the ESL students together, giving them "little bit of special treatment," which was minor for the school but meant a lot to Paj. This was the "good experience" of the ESL program: the pizza that "you get rewarded if you get good grades" or "you'll get to go out for recess a little earlier or stay for recess a little later." She also appreciated that "you get to be with other students who are also learning English as a second language."

Paj appreciated the social support of the program but not the academic barriers it created. She rephrases her explanation of the potential social support of fellow Hmong-speaking students as also inhibiting her language acquisition: "It was kind of difficult because then you're put in a situation where you're like 'you understand Hmong so I'm just gonna speak Hmong with you.' And the teachers like 'No, we all have to speak English here' even though you guys speak the same language." Pretty quickly in Paj's schooling she was made to believe that English belonged in the classroom and Hmong did not. Just as Hmong was devalued in that setting, so was multilingualism. Paj's attempt to sort out these values is a preview of her later literacy experiences and echoes Tashi's clinical experiences detailed earlier in the chapter. Tashi and Paj's multilingual impulse to speak the language they saw in their fellow students was deemed a barrier to the English acquisition that was assumed to be the point of the classroom gathering. This value rang loud and clear to Paj.

Compared to other participants' early literacy memories from around the world, Paj's literacy memories are markedly of the United States: bringing home reading logs for her parents to sign, which she forged because they were always working; reading "the little red engine or the train, was it? And the caterpillar," and later on Boxcar Children and RL Stine; drawing a "web" with "the circle with your point and other little webs with your minor points to help you brainstorm"; and using an umbrella image to write an outline with "your main point in the umbrella and your supporting points in the handle." Most of all, she remembers writing her ACT essay for which she says, "We were supposed to either go for yes, people should have pink flamingos on their lawns and reasons why, or no they shouldn't have pink flamingos on their lawns and reasons why. And I think for some reason I remember that we were supposed to say yes to the pink flamingos."

In the company of other participants' memories of literacy learning, which almost uniformly are about displaying content mastery, Paj's schooling memories reveal how values manifest in U.S. literacy curriculum. Her schools seem to value creative but routinized activity and structured argumentation around an issue reaching toward the absurd or at least the uncontroversial. These values are built into a reward structure of assignments and testing that requires such tidy literacy. Paj elaborates on the experience in which she was required in middle school to use "at least two or three metaphors" in her in-class essay about a childhood experience. She thought she had done a good job on the assignment—she "even had the five paragraphs and everything." But when she got it back "it had a zero." She says, "I don't quite remember what I did wrong except that my terms or the metaphors that I used were not common metaphors? The teacher said they didn't really make sense; that they didn't fit well together. I don't quite remember what I wrote or how I wrote it, I just remember that. . . . I don't think I was original with my metaphors. I think I probably kind of went off of what I've seen, what I've read through my life. So I felt like maybe I didn't create any out of my own mind." By seventh grade, Paj was completely fluent in English and an A student, so her struggle with the assignment was not due to language deficit or interference. Instead, Paj had failed (getting a zero) to respond to the value of structured creativity and originality built into the assignment: using a metaphor, but at least three of them; using metaphors that were "common" and legible to the teacher, but not too common as to not be "original." Paj can't remember what she wrote about or how she wrote it, but she does remember the failure, and it helped shape her navigation of school values from that point on.

When Paj moved an hour away from home to attend college, she remained very involved with her extended family and Hmong community. Her continued presence at home and in her community recognized the social values with which she was raised. She traveled home every weekend to spend time with her family, often translating her parents' mail, writing family correspondence, and babysitting for her older sister. In continuing to act as a literacy broker for her parents, she built on the basic Hmong reading practices she had taught herself by taking Hmong college courses for her electives, which helped her, as she says, "read and write it really well." These newly acquired literate resources made her "feel good because this is my language" and because it "benefits other people too." Paj says, "There are points in Hmong that cannot be expressed in English and there are points in English that cannot be expressed in Hmong," so she learned to use both in texting and writing as much as possible. Paj associates herself, her family, and her Hmong community with values of modesty, cultural promotion, additive bilingualism, and community support and connection. She follows cultural values of modesty, saying, "I know my stuff, you know" but refuses to "brag that this is easy and this is hard." For her, these social values shape her current literacy and language practices in several ways. She gives speeches in Hmong at her home community center, mainly to encourage a group of newly arrived Hmong refugees settling in the area and to "reach out to the Hmong community in a language they can understand." Her speeches are motivational, both for acculturating to life in the United States and understanding "that it's, you know, possible for English." Paj advises her listeners to find a bilingual English/Hmong mentor rather than an English monolingual teacher, encouraging these new migrants to add English to their repertoire but still maintain their bilingualism.

But the friction in Paj's repertoire—the simultaneous mobilizing and fixing of her resources—reveals how her literacies are revalued. The family and community contexts that gave her literacies meaning were shaped by different values than her college classrooms. Her Hmong community valued modesty, bilingual fluidity, self-sponsored learning, community support, and maintaining and sharing the Hmong language. Her college classrooms seemed to value other things. While Paj felt "it would be okay" if she used Hmong in her sociology courses because the instructors "valu[e] differences and diversity and different viewpoints and different outlooks," she believed most of her other instructors wanted brevity and standard English: "They're always, 'Just say the least you can in the best way you can say it.' So if it's like I say a phrase in Hmong, I'm gonna end up having to write a couple more sentences explaining that phrase. So I might as well just stick to the point." Even though she believes "some things are better said in my culture than anything that I could think of to write" in English, she is highly conscious of time and space. Paj wonders about Hmong, "why would I put it in?" when "the professor wouldn't understand it." She worries that having to write more to explain the intention and meaning of a Hmong phrase "would be taking up space." She is aware of page limits that cause her to "always tend to cut out rather than put in." So to produce the most efficient prose, she decides to "stick to the point." Unfortunately, the assumption is that "the point" has nothing to do with Hmong or what might be better expressed in it.

Instead, Paj is strategic. She decides that if the values of the course—valuing differences, diversity, different viewpoints and outlooks—match her own, she will attempt to incorporate writing that is better said in Hmong. But if peer and teacher feedback expresses different values, she will "cut rather than put in." This reason for revising through cutting rather than development should be an insight into the thinking behind what many writing teachers assume to be unsophisticated revision. Paj is not unsophisticated; she just recognizes the game. She strives to fit her values into those she perceives to be the university's: always trying to, as she says, "act the way they want you to act, talk the way they want you to talk." In essence, Paj is forever navigating the mismatch between her own and the school's values. Speaking of conversations with program advisors and instructors in office hours, she says that institutional readers like instructors and advisors "want us to be really assertive where we would talk about our experiences" and "tell everything about how we feel about the experience." Paj interprets this to mean that the onus of communication is on the students rather than the institution. She explains: "What they say is that you're student. You're paying for your education and you want to get the most out of it. So you do what you need to do and whatever you want to know, tell us." For Paj, these conversations get to the heart of why her community and the school's values don't match. As a writer and communicator, she is not inclined to be "assertive." She prefers to listen to learn rather than "tell everything about how we feel." She prefers to engage with others to identify the goals and aims of an experience rather than deciding only for herself "whatever [she] want[s] to know" and telling the teachers what that is. The school—Paj treats instructors and advisors as speaking for the university—communicates to Paj that you get what you pay for; getting literacy is getting your money's worth. As school literacy becomes defined by price, learned literate resources become socially but also economically valuable. These expressed values are quite individualistic, as the onus of making learning worthwhile is on the individual student rather than the school.

Paj did well in college, but her literate repertoire still experienced friction. She struggled when the professed social values of U.S. classrooms were so clearly contradictory to its practices. She couldn't navigate as well the paradoxical values of institutional multiculturalism and those of her predominantly white, monolingual peers. Purported institutional values around diversity were almost always undermined by stronger, though implicit, values of efficiency and brevity, accent-free clarity, order and organization, and individualism. These values became clear to Paj through a variety of literacy and language experiences in and out of her college classrooms. For example, advisors steered her away from working in a minority-access program for fear that future employers might assume that she was a recipient of rather than a mentor in the program. She completed reading assignments from textbooks that had "two hundred pages and there's one paragraph about diversity." She endured conversations about meritocracy and white monolingual norms: she could never figure out how to respond to white classmates pointedly telling her she was present only because of affirmative action. As an undergraduate representative to a nursing school leadership committee, she sat through meetings with faculty "debating about . . . an English test" or requirements to regulate which students with "pretty thick accents" will "probably be kicked out." She didn't know how to tell faculty that such gate-keeping didn't serve patient safety but acted as discrimination against student accents that, as she says, "we might not be able to fix!" As is clear from Alicia's earlier comments about the TOEFL, tests and programmatic requirements were commonly interpreted by many study participants as true sources of institutional values rather than those given lip service in college marketing or orientation experiences.

Values around accent-free spoken and written communication became clear to Paj most of all through feedback she received on writing. She recalls one experience in "clinical," the hands-on courses required of nurses in training, that made her feel she "wasn't knowledgeable" even though she knew she was "good with reading and writing." A written evaluation from her clinical instructor, which seems to have confused race and accent for competence, told her "that it would've helped [the teacher] to help me better if I had spoken with an accent." Paj interpreted this feedback to mean that if Paj had spoken with a more pronounced accent the instructor "would've understood that English was my second language and helped me more." While Paj remains confused about how she could have met the expectations of this teacher—one wonders if performing an accent to match her phenotype would have merited more assistance—the experience is vivid in her memory for its stark contradiction of supposed program values of difference and diversity.

Paj felt friction in her literate repertoire especially when school literacy values met up with work literacy values in her clinical courses. Like Tashi, in the fused school/work context of the hospital, Paj often mobilized her multilingual literacies against institutional pressures that attempted to hold them back. For example, against monolingual preferences of course instructors, Paj knows her bilingualism has workplace value: "Our instructors look at you like 'Oh, you're not competent' and then you get a Hmong-speaking patient who the instructor cannot speak with at all and then you're like, 'I know this.' You're like, see in this case they can't tell you that you not speaking English is a hazard or you having an accent is a hazard to the patient, when they're gonna face patients whose language they don't speak." In these situations, where economic and social values meet, Paj inverts whose literate beliefs have economic value. The instructor's belief that nonaccented English is necessary for care is rendered moot when Paj places that claim in a real-world hospital context. Paj knows that English-only assumptions are naïve, especially in hospitals that are cross-sections of an already multilingual U.S. diorama. She calls the institution's bluff, saying that no matter their language background, nurses can help patients: "If they come in with a bleeding wound, they go out with it bandaged." In the context of the university hospital, Paj actually thinks nurses can help patients *because*, rather than in spite of, their multilingual backgrounds. She describes "fixing" a Hmong-language public health sign posted in the hospital. The sign described "how to wash your hands and how to cover your mouth when you cough." Every day when Paj passed it she noticed "a lot of spelling errors and they had a lot of words that were not words at all in Hmong. So eventually, she says:

> I just kind of white out their poster that they had. It wasn't like I fixed it on a wide scale or anything. But I just fixed it. . . . So that was a moment when I felt like being able to write in Hmong was gonna benefit me. I felt proud that I was able to do something that showed that this is something that I can use as an asset, as a something extra, a gift that I have or a talent or a skill that I have that other people don't have, whereas I don't have to feel like it's a handicap because English is not my first language.

Picture Paj standing at the wall, white-out in hand, publicly and visibly asserting the presence of Hmong. Although she couldn't undo the unfortunate association of non-English languages with germs (the posters were presented in several languages but not English), she could control how the Hmong appeared in writing. She felt proud to confirm that Hmong belonged, and was already present, in the hospital and shaped its use on her own terms. It is tempting to cast Paj's mention of her Hmong as "something extra," that her "talent," "skill," "gift," of multilingualism is an add-on "asset" to her repertoire. But Paj makes Hmong, and her ability to move between it and English, central to her repertoire and identity. She uses Hmong to trade in language goods but also to push back on the social devaluing of her identity, especially as someone who has "always been into school," who "really [likes] reading and writing," but who struggles as "the only nonwhite person in class . . . [who] feels so much more belittled because you're really a minority now." She places all of this squarely in a purported monolingual context to reveal its hypocrisy. Doing so creates friction. This frictive movement—how Paj mobilizes her literate resources—lays bare the process of literate valuation her literacies undergo.

HOW LITERATE VALUES CREATE FRICTION

These extended accounts show how social values (family, community, and personal designations of importance or respect) meet up with economic assignments of value (the use or profitability of literate commodities) in literate lives. Taken together, Tashi, Khadroma, and Paj's accounts offer insights into how literate values create friction, both pushing forward and holding back multilingual repertoires. Although their literate histories are unique, their lives in the United States at the time of the study shared many commonalities. Tashi, Khadroma, and Paj all experienced success as primary and secondary students; both Tashi and Paj essentially taught themselves to read and write and acted as literacy brokers for their parents; both Tashi and Khadroma are married with young children; they both attended the same community college prior to enrolling in the university nursing program where all three were students; all three are heavily involved in their local cultural community centers; and all three write among multiple languages including (differently expressed but still fluent) academic English. They are all content with and proud of their work and family life in the United States.

Furthermore, because Tashi, Khadroma, and Paj are nurses, together their accounts show how high-stakes writing contexts harbor certain values that promote or stop literate movement. Pre-professional contexts like the nursing clinical, in which school and work come together, are a unique case study of an assemblage of values, in that they fuse, and sometimes confuse, the values of school and work. Value claims like "We believe your accent is a liability" seem to be heightened in such high-stakes settings as health work, excusing discrimination under the guise of safety. Although it is true that teaching hospitals and their adjacent clinical contexts educate amid real patient pain and suffering, and thus justifiably demand the highest of nursing communication skills, actual English proficiency is but one factor conditioning the literate practices of these three nurses (Leki, "Living" 86). Also, contexts like hospitals that serve everyone, and thus mirror social demographics, can reveal how a society manages demographic change. The explicit and implicit school- and work-based language values described—woven into training and procedural routines—assume an English-only hospital public and promote monolingual communication for fairness and safety. But Khadroma, Tashi, and Paj's experiences show that many of the hospitals' doctors, nurses, and patients are multilingual and use often-accented English as one part of their multilingual repertoires.

Even with these commonalities, Tashi, Khadroma, and Paj's repertoires have experienced differing processes of literate valuation, with each woman feeling the friction of mobile literacies to a greater or lesser extent. The reality of their experiences at home, school, and work make it nearly impossible to designate Khadroma, Tashi, and Paj's literate repertoires as either mobile or immobile, completely fluid or fixed. Instead, their repertoires are characterized by the push and pull of stalled mobility. This friction creates an uncomfortable dissonance. Why is Paj's literate repertoire highly valued by grades and testing, yet devalued in daily classroom interactions? How can Tashi have such a unique and deep understanding of writing and yet receive low grades and shallow feedback on her writing? The social and economic values running throughout these writers' accounts suggest several possibilities for these differing processes of valuation. While Tashi's literate repertoire is arguably more abundant than Khadroma or Paj's—Tashi speaks, reads, and writes among more languages than the other women and has studied and taught academic English for more years than Khadroma—it is still a repertoire with more variability than standards. Khadroma learned standard American English from visiting Californian teachers during her college years in China, and Paj writes with the school-driven English grammar conventions learned through fourteen years of schooling in the United States.

But Tashi's accented written and spoken English is not standard in a U.S. context. In a globalizing and increasingly saturated global English language market, linguistic variability like Tashi's encounters the strict standards important for the efficient work contexts mentioned. As languages become useful for global economic goals, they become commodities in markets that demand similarity for even exchange. Even though these writers' accounts occur in local contexts, as migrants they cannot always escape the global associations of their literacy work. Thus they are somehow held accountable to the linguistic instrumentalism of globalization. Language-as-commodity drains language of the variability of actual language users—their histories, accents, speaking tongues, and writing hands—and redefines language as an easily traded fungible construct according to market needs. So no matter the extent of Tashi's literate repertoire or the deft wielding of her language resources, these become less valuable in a standardized language economy. Khadroma's literate repertoire, however, is highly valued at work for its adherence to procedural standards. Khadroma believes the accreditation agency's policies for communication and interpretation to be fair and transparent, and she benefits from these rules. In a "new educational order" in which "individualistic learning for economic purposes" takes precedence, Paj's community-informed literacy practices were undervalued at school, even when they were performed in standard American English.[7] Efficient literacies are quickly completed and easily assessed. They are structured like countable metaphors and literal umbrella brainstorming techniques. In contrast to this speed and structure Paj builds literacies through careful community collaboration and mentoring over time. Even though Paj's literacies satisfy expectations simply because she attended school in the United States, like Tashi, her literate repertoire also has been devalued by discrimination and racism. She felt the effects of unstated literate values becoming de facto institutional policy.

Although all three writers employ a range of linguistic resources, Khadroma is especially savvy in her navigation of them. Her literate repertoire is peculiarly flexible and standard, which may appeal to a global work context that prefers flexible and mobile workers who trade in standard language commodities.[8] While Tashi and Paj both tend to separate and place their languages according to domain, Khadroma blurs the lines between work, home, and community. For example, Paj prefers not to bring Hmong into her school writing where she assumes it is not welcome; instead, she uses it almost exclusively at home and in community settings. Khadroma is flexible about where and when she wields different parts of her repertoire, while Tashi and Paj tend to closely associate specific language resources to specific situations. In Khadroma's case, this navigational skill has a history: she was shown during her years at the American-run language school in China how her languages might be valued by travelers, tourists, and business people in a global economy. Her teachers modeled this navigation by employing her to interpret for their friends early on. The influence of global organizations, valuing the language work of an information-dependent economy, was already present in the late 1990s in China and prepared Khadroma well to leverage her multilingual resources after immigration to the United States.

Finally, although all three writers treat their Tibetan and Hmong as languages of identity—the one with which they identify culturally, celebrate during community gatherings, and hope to pass on to their children—only Khadroma converts her Tibetan into a marketable interpretation skill valued by government and corporate organizations. (She treats her Mandarin simply as a skill, not identifying with the language culturally nor hoping to pass it on to her daughter.) Tashi explains that she speaks Tibetan exclusively at home with her family or among friends at community events. Paj uses her Hmong similarly, even framing her Hmong college courses as knowledge gained for further family and community service. She identifies with Hmong strongly but keeps it out of her school writing. And even though she projects that Hmong will be marketable in future work settings, she has yet to do so and mostly uses this hunch to understand the contradictions inherent in teachers' implicit language policies. As is evident in their accounts, Tashi's and Paj's experiences of literate devaluation reinforce this separation of language contexts. Paj's literate decisions were especially shaped by her clinical instructors' racial remarks that if she had communicated in ways (with an accent) more coherent with her appearance (Asian), her writing would have warranted more support.

Therefore, while Khadroma's Tibetan is valuable both as a language of identity and a language of skill, Tashi's Tibetan and Paj's Hmong are languages of identity, not ones deemed especially valuable by the very same teaching hospital that hired Khadroma to interpret for Tibetan-speaking patients. These differing processes of valuation are no light matter. When participants connect their language to identity in some way, the valuation of language-based identities is particularly fraught. Many experience devaluation of their language as a devaluation of their self-realization in the United States. Because they are writing on the move, multilingual migrants meet one context after another that values multilingual literacy differently. In fact, it is because these writers' practices move with them—a fact usually celebrated—that their literacies are subject to continual revaluation.

CHAPTER 5
DEEP CONTRADICTIONS IN THE VALUE OF LITERACY

In the summer of 2016, the Olympic torch relay included twelve-year-old Syrian refugee Hanan Dacka running the torch through the streets of Brasilia. The *New York Times* compared her run to the troubled previous legs of the relay, reporting that onlookers forgot their distrust of the country's handling of the games as they cheered her on.[1] As I looked at photos that summer of Hanan carrying the torch, I felt relief that her family had a chance to resettle in Brazil, where refugees were, for the most part, welcomed then. But I also thought about her torch. Beyond its reference to Zeus's fire, the Olympic torch is meant to announce the Games in each location it passes through, allowing "the general public to share the Olympic spirit" ("Olympic"). As a symbol, its meaning is open to interpretation, often influenced by who is doing the symbol carrying. When other runners carried the torch through Brazil, some were protested; a few times, demonstrators dumped water on the flame. When Hanan ran it through Brasilia, however, she was lauded. In this way, the torch struck me as a lot like literacy.

Like literacy, Hanan's torch traveled around the world, on the move before reaching her and continuing on after her. Like literacy that travels, the torch picked up meaning as it moved, but those meanings were volatile and shifted with each carrier and context it met. While it has a dominant connotation—the spirit of the Olympic Games—the torch also symbolizes freedom and burden, individual achievement and corporate sponsorship, locality and globalization, the hero and the everyperson, egalitarianism and competition. In its long decades of travel, the torch has been assigned so much meaning that it can't help but be a paradox. Like literacy. Is it possible that I saw literacy everywhere in the summer of 2016 because I was revising this book? Quite. Especially with the phrase "literacy relay" ringing in my ears did I see the affinities in Hanan's torch. But my research-centric interpretation of the torch proves my point: its meaning was what I saw in it.

In this book, literacy is also a paradox. While literacy has a dominant social meaning—the reading and writing of skilled people—it also is so packed with beliefs, values, identities, and histories that it can mean whatever people see in it. In the personal accounts that give this book life, multilingual migrant writers described creating, adapting, and losing writing practices in motion, carrying around highly charged experiences and beliefs that influence the ways in which they are or are not able to write. Throughout the book I have foregrounded the simultaneity of the literacies that are maintained and lost on the move: writers are both impressed and disappointed by their literate activities after migration, proud of and ambivalent about their multilingualism, irritated by and attracted to standard American English. I have shown how multilingual migrant women regularly experience the concrete effects of seemingly fluid constructs—though language and national boundaries may blur, languages and the nation-state still solidly impact migrants' job prospects, program completion, family relationships, and self-realization. The paradox of literacy—its chameleonic tendencies—empties it out and opens it up to such contradictions.

As I have argued, literacy is revalued because it moves, so the multilingual literacy of those who write in motion is especially subject to fraught valuation. Because it contains multiple mobilities—geographic, literate, emotional— multilingual migrant writing heightens the volatility of literacy's value. Each chapter featured a different kind of literate movement—fluid, fixed, frictive— to demonstrate the relationship between literacy and values. Fluidity shows writers' values agreeing with others' (chapter 2); fixity shows how values can be mismatched (chapter 3); and friction shows how writers' values simultaneously do and don't correspond to those of others (chapter 4). In three turns, fluidity, fixity, and friction reframe the consequences of multilingual migrants writing with and against the currents of socioeconomic values. When things work out, as they do in chapter 2, and to a certain extent in chapter 4, multilingual migrants can draw on their multilingual resources and call on their repertoire when needed, using their practices for the rhetorical ends they intend. The stories of Alicia and Yolanda especially show that when writers move fluidly in their literate repertoires, they often innovate with language, access further life opportunities, and accomplish the social and personal desires writers imagined migrating for in the first place.[2] When things don't work out, as is the case in some of chapter 4 and certainly in chapter 3, writers shut down as they attempt to write against the pressure of social and economic values they can't intuit or guess. Chapter 4 demonstrates that multilingual writers experience friction as the bets they make on their literacy resources both do and do not pay out. They maneuver through a complicated literacy game, hoping their literate resources are as valuable as they think they are.

This chapter does not aim to resolve the complicated reality of multilingual literacy. Instead, the book sits with these frictions, pointing toward deep and sometimes debilitating contradictions in the way multilingual migrants' literate repertoires are valued. Often times, social and economic values are directed not toward literacy but toward the literacy user.[3] Like the women in this book, recent migrants and refugees represent a broad range of education, class, and professional backgrounds. They often flee to refugee camps and then, if lucky, on to host countries that issue special or humanitarian visas. Their new home countries are fortunate to welcome insights, traditions, and experiences from all over the world into their borders. But often, little (positive) attention is paid to migrants' journeys or their backgrounds.[4] All migrants, immigrants, or those perceived to be outsiders are lumped into a group assumed to take more than they give, flout a country's laws, or refuse to assimilate (according to much xenophobic discourse permeating Europe and the United States in 2015 and 2016).[5] Even more puzzling is that if migrants appear to need too *little* help, this also is evidence that they do not belong—that migrants' proficient English language skills and cell phone use also make their refugee authenticity suspect. These are the mind-numbing conditions through which multilingual migrants attempt to write, work, learn, and live.

As is clear in the experiences of Tashi, Nimet, Paj, Faridah, and others in this study, these contradictions make writers' lives tough. Recognizing these contradictions may ease some of this struggle. This chapter details four threads of contradiction that run throughout this book: contradictions in the experience of multilingualism, English, agency, and writing. I suggest how teachers, administrators, and other powerful individuals might reflect on the impact of these contradictions and better support writers trying to navigate them.

DEEP CONTRADICTIONS

This book shows how social and economic assignments of value meet up to produce deep contradictions in the way literate repertoires are treated. These contradictions are clusters of literate possibility and constraint: multilingualism is rewarded and punished; accent is both authentic and a liability; global English is imperialist and a migrant opportunity. Sometimes these clusters are intuitive: it is just known that monolingual English communication is expected in Yolanda's and Alicia's school even though policies state the opposite and support for multiculturalism is written into school materials. Other times, writers navigate contradictions between what is said and what is done, or what is implied and what is practiced.

Multilingualism as Contradiction

The role of multilingualism in participant accounts is contradictory, endorsed as both personal and professional asset and condemned as ethnic, racial, or cultural deficit. In Paj's and Tashi's descriptions of linguistic discrimination, in Alandra's comments about her daughter's experiences with language and ethnic stereotypes, or in Yolanda's and Alicia's descriptions of their navigation of bilingual work policies, multilingual literacy often is socially devalued. Meanwhile, Khadroma, Rocio, Alandra, Yolanda, Alicia, Sabohi, and others are hired for education or social service jobs in the United States precisely because of their multilingualism. Furthermore, Paj, Tashi, and Houa's work as multilingual literacy brokers for their parents aids their family's betterment and gives them early professionally valuable interpretation skills.

This "bizarre scenario" in which multilingual writers are pushed into being monolingual English literates while English monolingual writers (especially students) are required to gain credentialing in "foreign" languages creates a contradiction not always easy to navigate as a multilingual migrant in the United States (Cummins, "Proposal for Action" 685). One needs only to think of U.S. graduate education in the humanities, in which monolingual students are required to show "proficiency" in languages besides English while multilingual students are required to take English proficiency tests to determine if their multilingualism or accent will hinder their teaching, to consider how engrained this contradiction is. How is it that some writers are rewarded for this movement between languages (professional literary translators, students in foreign language courses) while others (young bilinguals translating for parents, multilingual graduate students, teachers with accents) are punished?

The sticking point of accent, as aural or written evidence of multilingualism, especially seems to drive a wedge between the high and low valuation of multilingual literacy. Writers who already maintain a level of professional or class prestige are forgiven for their accent, while those striving to earn or gain prestige are granted no favors. For example, as Paj observes, "a lot of the doctors have accents": "They're like Russian or Indian and it's like they have thick accents, but you don't hear nurses telling them or the preceptors telling them like you need to take an English course. So it's like, no. You know they're knowledgeable; the accent doesn't mean anything." Rarely was an assumption of knowledge granted to nursing students Khadroma, Paj, Tashi, or Nimet, the latter three of which were instead cautioned in teacher feedback or referred to pronunciation courses that set them back a semester in degree progress.

School and workplace contexts like these might benefit from reconsidering what the everyday language experience is for most people around the world.[6] Especially in the United States, teachers and administrators are guilty of not treating language as the simultaneously slippery and static phenomenon that this book (and previous research cited throughout) has shown it to be. While dominant discourse in the United States perpetuates the myth of monolingualism, making official institutions and everyday life seem (though it never really has been) monolingual, the daily reality for many people living in the

United States is one of highly diverse communication among accents, codes, and dialects. Beyond recognizing that the constant movement among languages is a norm for literate practice around the world including the United States, policies and pedagogies might strive toward supporting the navigation of a multilingual norm in several ways.

For example, teachers might consider how metalinguistic awareness is cultivated in the movement of a literate repertoire. The goal would be for writers to become aware that they have literate repertoires, that their repertoires have histories, and that their repertoires count. According to the fluid experiences of Alicia and Yolanda, the fixed movement of Defne and Faridah, and the felt frictions of Paj, Khadroma, and Tashi, such awareness can come from a range of experiences, not just from fluid ones. Metalinguistic awareness, therefore, could be supported by facilitating all writers'—whether understood as traditionally monolingual or multilingual—purposeful movement among their literate repertoires. Students might observe the movements of other writers or articulate in writing the movements they call on to compose. Students can observe multilingual or nonstandard language use when such texts are made visible in class. Teachers might use multilingual student papers or published models of nonstandard language use like those in the anthology *Rotten English*.

Students understand the concept of shifting registers for different audiences and are certainly able to apply that understanding to their analysis of movement among dialects or language varieties. Before beginning an assignment, students might be asked to write a reflection about when they have written a similar assignment in other language varieties or educational settings, and how what they wrote then might be different or similar to what they're being asked to write now. Although many of these strategies are implications of research on writing transfer, these practices also might be fruitfully used for writers developing metalinguistic awareness. In this book the writers who most effectively wielded their literate skills were those who could articulate how the effect of a sentence or essay differed across their languages. If writers can think back and forth—move—across the bridges that span their literate resources, perhaps they will develop a more intentional approach toward language diversity that they can pass on to their future students, friends, and families. A research agenda toward these ends might pursue what actually stands in the way of implementing pedagogies or policies that support literate movement. For example, research might examine practice and policy on multilingual literacy outside of the United States, exploring notions of standards, official languages, or disciplinary conventions in locations in which a multilingual norm is not provocative in the least.

Agency as Contradiction

Participants understand themselves to be both in charge and not in charge of their own writing. They are often stumped by a contradiction of writerly agency. They both can and cannot control how their writing moves, among languages, situations, people. Aldene describes relegating specific memories to specific languages in letters she writes her husband. Sofia describes her writing "popping" in and out of English and Russian. They both do and do not benefit from moving their writing in ways they would like. Yolanda feels useful when she uses her entire repertoire to teach her students. Tashi is embarrassed when she cannot control how her Tibetan pops into clinical spaces. In fact, writers and powerful others are often vying for control over multilingual migrant writing.

There has been much made of this theoretically. Under globalization, states are said to be "in the business of regulating the movement of people, internally and internationally" (Suárez-Orozco, "Right Moves" 11), a kind of control that has been understood as "regimes of mobility."[7] As described in the introduction, such regimes not only regulate movement but also benefit from keeping people on the move. For example, regimes of mobility have maintained programs of border control, refugee camps and centers, temporary worker visas, and waves of deportation or immigrant detention. In the context of language and literacy, regimes of mobility might enact language and literacy tests, professional standards of certification and credentialing, or dual-language schooling that keep languages separate and hierarchical. For example, international organizations and corporations attempt to "manage the movement of resources across linguistically diverse spaces" in pursuit of maintaining standards (Heller, "Commodification" 107).

In the context of this book, various agents (including teachers, employers, parents, immigration bureaucrats, and study participants themselves) intervene in the unpredictability and open-endedness of mobility, the perceived free-flowing movement of people, ideas, languages, and practices, in order to exert some control over fluidity or maintain fixed cultural or linguistic identifications for survival. Institutions not only slow down and misdirect writers' literacies, they also benefit from keeping writers on the move, sending them to seek extra support they might not need in a roundabout hunt for native-like English proficiency. They direct writers around bureaucratic labyrinths that often delay their educational or economic progress. Writers and institutions seek to manage the pace and direction of literacy as it moves, expecting writing to be both fast (efficient) and slow (thoughtful). Writers' literate repertoires are not simply shut down by powerful others, they are managed to exert control over language change or maintain perceived cultural or linguistic standards.

The agency of literate valuation—who is in charge of determining what literacy is worth—is located not in individual migrants or in hegemonic institutions but in the social and economic values held by both. Multilingual reading, writing, and communication appear to be sets of managed acts that teachers, employers, colleagues, and the writers themselves direct. The management of movement might also be an attempt to control the contingency of literacy's value under globalization. This means that literacy research should account not just for individual agentive practices or for structural or institutional pressures but, instead, for the interaction of both in the valuation of literacy. In the classroom, teachers might reflect on what their literate values are and how they use these values in their teaching. They could ask themselves how their own values do or do not match the values written into their syllabi and course readings or textbooks. Do these values match or contradict assignments and rubrics? How do they complement or challenge the literate values of the program and school? They might also seek to understand their students' literate values: What are students' literate and geographic histories? In what ways do they value their multilingualism? Their writing in English? Although the literacy autobiography is a fruitful assignment toward these ends, teachers might profitably imagine other ways to include students' literate values in the data, material, or content of a class.

English as Contradiction

Participants experience literacy in English as both a colonial remnant and an opportunity for betterment. The early English language educations of Tashi, Khadroma, Jin, Haneen, Sabohi, Shirin, Raani, Aldene, Alandra, and others are shaped through British or American postcolonial residue.[8] (The histories of colonialism are not just seen in English, of course, since Faridah's experience with French in Algeria point to another language lineage maintained through schooling.) These vestiges of colonization keep alive literacy values through English-medium education, as Sabohi describes. Sabohi states quite plainly: "If you know English, you are literate; if you don't know, you are not." Literacy values in English are maintained through sector and field: Rosalia, Nina, and Yolanda's experiences with English in their environmental, chemistry, and veterinary courses in college in Guatemala, Ukraine, and Colombia, respectively, reveal the demand for English in science-based reading and writing. English reading skills especially allowed access to the scientific knowledge they needed to complete their courses (although Yolanda simply paid someone else to translate it all into Spanish for her).

No participant identified the presence of English in their home countries or the global expectation of an English lingua franca using the word "imperialist," although many did call it "dominant" or "powerful." Overall, these writers experience English as a politically fraught and distinctly powerful language. They witness regional language change and language loss in younger generations. Participants say quite plainly, "I need to learn English because English is a universal language," and "English is the global language." Many participants describe the desire for English in terms of further education, work, or social status as well as an attraction to simple popularity. For example, Haneen says, "All the schools now [in Jordan], they want English . . . People love English. People love American." In a way, for some study participants, the colonial language of the past (or the neocolonial present) seems forgiven for the attraction of the language in the present. Sabohi cites India's move to revert cities back to their precolonial names, a move she says she understands as "people wanting to protect an identity and not keeping up altogether with the times." She recognizes the political power of English but does not seem to blame or want to ban English for this history, although she admits there are many others who importantly do. Sabohi's own understanding of "the times" is one of inevitable language change and a near dismissal of colonial remnants of language practice.

So, as English is experienced as the language of globalization, it seems at times to be the ultimate assemblage of literate possibility and constraint. The contradiction of English, as it is experienced by study participants, is woven as legacy into school and work around the world. The language routinizes legacies of oppression even as it affords English-based work opportunities. In the United States, myths of monolingualism—that is, only English is the key to success—are perpetuated in the teaching, testing, and publishing of one standard language, making it, as Alicia says, "so engrained in some immigrants' head that English is the way to go" that migrants often state they have no other choice but to communicate and write only in English, whether to the detriment of practices in their languages or not. Participants constantly navigate this contradiction. However, their experiences suggest that this isn't illogical but meaningful.

For example, Alicia describes a writing activity from her childhood Argentine writing textbook that was "basically to 'fatten the subject and the predicate.'" She said she adapted this activity for her own students to teach development. But she recognizes the contradictions in her teaching: "I was telling them, I want you to embellish your sentences and then the next class, 'Okay, now we're going to discover runon sentences.' So I was like contradicting myself!" Alicia uses an activity that encourages students to *engordar* their sentences but then the next day teaches students to not let their sentences "run on." She recognizes that it is no wonder her bilingual ESL students are confused. In essence, Alicia locates the contradiction within her own literate repertoire—she understands these languages to be acting at stylistic cross-purposes. When these cross-purposes come out through her own pedagogy, she calls it a contradiction. But in fact, teaching both styles—developed/succinct, long/short, single/multiple clause—has shaped her metalinguistic awareness. In other words, her literate contradictions condition her own understanding of how language works. If other multilingual writers were afforded the same opportunity to name and reflect on similar contradictions, their metalinguistic understandings might be similarly affected.

If English is experienced in the United States through contradictory clusters of possibility and constraint, multilingual migrant writers might be better supported in their navigation of these contradictions through a number of policy and practice considerations.[9] These contradictions point to questions that this book is not the first to puzzle over: in writing courses, how should language be addressed? In ESL or ESP courses, should standard English be the target proficiency? Although this book's contributions will not put these questions to rest, participants' experiences suggest several ways to think about them. For example, administrators should consider the literate values implicitly endorsed by testing, tracking, and institutional credentialing. Many of the study participants describe being placed or tracked into a lower-level ESL class when English was their first or one of the many languages in which they were fluent (Andrea, Alicia, Alandra, Harriet, Houa, Nimet) or describe not being qualified to enter programs because their previous credentials, graduate degrees, or professional experiences did not transfer or count (Alandra, Defne, Jin, Khadroma, Nina, Rosalia, Tashi, Yolanda).

Misplacement or mistracking is a frequent theme in research on L2 writing, especially for Generation 1.5 or resident ESL students such as Houa and Harriet.[10] While many participants did not mind taking extra courses or returning to school to completely begin their careers anew, all of them understood this rerouting to be caused by what universities in the United States value. Participants believed they were placed in ESL courses because of their accents rather than their skills or proficiencies; they described abandoning their master's degrees because a program considered their professional teaching or writing methods to be lesser than those practiced in the United States. In other words, these writers interpreted their experiences at university gates as expressions of academic values and beliefs. Participant interpretations cohere with writing assessment research in which the dictum "assess what you value" (a rule of thumb for test validity) can also be understood as "you value what you assess." In fact, programs, departments, and universities are making implicit arguments with their policies and practices, often with metaphorical megaphones, about what they believe counts as a credential, as English, or as academic literacy.

As shown by scholars in L2 writing assessment, testing is perhaps one of the most effective methods of ignoring or denying a writer's full literate repertoire, especially when assessments are designed to discover skills and knowledge altogether different from those a writer might bring to the United States or to English.[11] Scholars have suggested that methods like Directed Self Placement (DSP) or portfolio systems that articulate with global university partners may mitigate some of this loss. But administrators might also simply ask whether they aim to assess native proficiency in English or aim to assess rhetorical skill and capacity with language. These are different goals, and the latter seems to both more closely adhere to contemporary research and best practices in various fields as well as more adequately draw out the existing literate knowledge multilingual writers bring to universities.

Writing as Contradiction

Finally, contradictions gather around understandings of what writing is for. For multilingual migrant writers the role of writing seems to be simultaneously mundane and deeply meaningful. Rosalia, Houa, and Tashi describe experiencing the paperwork of immigration as banal even as they frame the outcomes of that routine writing as exceedingly important, with Tashi deciding that "this is how writing saves." Both study participants and institutions use writing to control or condition language even as writing is the mode by which constraints are bypassed or broken through. In chapter 3, Alicia and Yolanda describe using writing to tame their multilingual impulses even as Defne, Faridah, and Alandra describe writing to be a powerful form of expression, one of the only practices that helps them remember who they are in the United States.

One understanding of this contradiction could be that these writers are simply inconsistent in their narration. Perhaps they simply change their mind as they engage in conversation with me. Examples like Alicia's journal writing (in which she chooses writing to keep her Spanish in place but succumbs to the "mixing" in of English), or Yolanda's classroom (where speech-based switching is modeled and encouraged but writing is treated as a monolingual activity), or Faridah's essay writing practices (which show her fluid movement among languages but the eventual fixity of her literate identity) all appear to be based in contradiction. But when one looks for meaning in this complexity, one finds that these contradictions are under their control. Both Alicia and Yolanda, although fluid in their multilingual speech and writing practices, believe that writing either disciplines this fluidity or represents its serious permanence. This is not contradiction but an elevated status of writing. Though her literate repertoire appears lost and inaccessible in the United States, Faridah's fluid multilingualism remains a vibrant element of her identity, although one lying dormant during this life stage. The friction here points not to contradiction but to the long-term development of a literate repertoire. Understanding literate friction means tracing geographic and linguistic histories. In research, literacy should be treated as current practice inseparable from its linguistic and geographic arcs. Researchers might study how current practices spring from past practices and how that connection creates a trajectory with consequences. If literate practices have histories, then research should move us beyond observations of the practices with which writers arrive (in classrooms, writing programs, or communities) and toward investigations of the movement that informs those arrivals.

There is no point at which clusters of constraint and possibility somehow resolve for writers. Instead, the moments where literacy is experienced in contradiction appear to be attempts to manage the relations of movement that characterize literacy under globalization. In other moments contradictions open up opportunities for writers and for institutions to gain control in some way. The contradictions that run throughout multilingual migrants' experiences spotlight how values undermine, inhibit, or support migrants' literacy practices. In fact, writers' understandings of what literacy and language *are* come from the contradictions produced by clashing values. As their insights about literacy show throughout this book, migrant writers know very well the contradictions that define literacy. Teachers, researchers, and administrators should take this migrant knowledge seriously. In particular, an awareness of the inequity of literate movement could more clearly shape pedagogy and policy.

Like all research, the study on which this book is based is limited by time and funds. The study certainly would have benefited from more time and travel funds to trace participants' literacy practices across more locations for a longer period of time.[12] The study would have benefited especially from access to more of the texts produced in many of the described practices in order to have more participants show me how the practices they describe play out in their writing. Still, the data that supports this book reveals much about how writers and teachers can cultivate a more nuanced understanding of multilingual literacy. I set out on my own research to explore the mobile activity of literate repertoires—the accumulation of genres, practices, experiences, histories, and texts in a variety of languages—to better understand the inequity built into that movement: whose literate practices were rewarded along the way, whose were not, and why. The denial of multilingual migrant writers' life experience, as competent, professional, creative individuals, undermines their capacity to succeed in the ways they hope. As a group, the twenty-five writers in this study show that many migrants arrive in the United States steeped in literacy practices across a variety of languages, credentialed with educational and professional degrees, ready to contribute to new school, work, and community contexts. The book highlights how much human capital is lost in a society striving for monolingualism and how much could be gained by not only maintaining the existing literate repertoires of many migrants but cultivating multilingual practices for everyone.

APPENDIX A

PARTICIPANTS

Participant	Locations lived (including the United States)	Language repertoire	Work
Alandra	Brazil, Argentina, United States	Portuguese, English, Spanish	Teacher
Aldene	Brazil, United States	Portuguese, English, Spanish	Social worker, graduate student
Alicia	Argentina, United States	Spanish, English, Hebrew	Teacher
Andrea	Venezuela, United States	Spanish, English	Nanny, undergraduate student
Defne	Turkey, England, Germany, United States	Turkish, English, German	Special education aide, former graduate student
Faridah	Algeria, United States	Arabic, French, English	Teacher
Haneen	Palestine, Jordan, United States	Arabic, English	Architect
Harriet	China, United States	English, Mandarin	Undergraduate student
Houa	Laos, United States	English, Hmong	Nurse, undergraduate student
Ishtar	Syria, United States	Arabic, English	Teacher
Jin	Japan, United States	Japanese, English	Teacher
Khadroma	China/Tibet, United States	Mandarin, Tibetan, English	Nurse
Kunthi	Indonesia, United States	Indonesian, English, Arabic	Teacher's aide
Nimet	Azerbaijan, Turkey, United States	Azerbaijani, Turkish, Russian, English	Nurse, former teacher

Participant	Locations lived (including the United States)	Language repertoire	Work
Nina	Ukraine, United States	Ukrainian, Russian, English	Undergraduate student, former chemist
Paj	Thailand, United States	Hmong, Thai, English	Nurse, undergraduate student
Raani	Pakistan, United States	Urdu, English	Teacher
Renan	Turkey, United States	Turkish, English	Lawyer
Riya	India, United States	Gujarati, English	Graduate student
Rosalia	Guatemala, Germany, Spain, United States	Spanish, German, English	Social worker, former environmental planner
Sabohi	Pakistan, United States	Hindi, Urdu, Kashmiri, English	Teacher, former journalist
Shirin	Pakistan, United States	Urdu, English	Stay-at-home mom
Sofia	Ukraine, United States	Russian, English	Retail store clerk
Tashi	India/Tibet, United States	Kannada, Tibetan, Hindi, English	Nurse, former teacher
Yolanda	Colombia, United States	Spanish, English	Teacher, former veterinarian

APPENDIX B
INTERVIEW QUESTIONS

WRITING AND READING MEMORIES

Describe one vivid memory you have of reading or writing when you were young. What kinds of things did you read and write in school? At home?

Did your family read or write at home? What writing do you remember your parents or siblings doing?

Do you remember ever teaching yourself to read or write?

Do you have memories of being tested on your writing or with writing?

Would you say that your experience is typical in _____?

Which languages did you use as you learned how to read and write?

In your opinion, how did learning to write in _____ influence the way you write now?

CURRENT WRITING AND READING

When do you write at work? Who is this writing for?

When are you writing at school? Who is this writing for?

How about at home? Do you ever write or read for self-education? Does your family use writing or reading for any traditions or holidays?

Describe a time when you used your writing practices to get something you needed.

What languages are you usually writing in now? If you met someone new to the United States, what would you say to them about learning to write in English?

How did you feel about writing in English when you arrived in the United States? How do you feel about it now?

How would your life be different if you didn't know how to read? How about if you didn't know how to write?

EXPERIENCES OF MULTILINGUALISM AND MULTILITERACIES

How do you use your writing practices from _____ in your life in the United States? Are there any writing practices you haven't used in a long time?

Describe for me a time when you felt lucky or proud that you used more than one language.

Describe a time when you felt disappointed or hurt by your language practices.

Can you think of one word to describe how it feels to use more than one language when you speak? What do you mean by that word? Does the same word apply when you write in more than one language?

Would you call yourself multilingual? Why or why not?

Is there anything else you'd like to tell me?

DEMOGRAPHICS

Where are you from?

How old are you, or when were you born?

When did you come to the United States and for what reasons?

What languages do you use?

Can you think of other friends or acquaintances who also might be reading and writing among multiple languages?

APPENDIX C
FOLLOW-UP INTERVIEW QUESTIONS

CURRENT WRITING AND READING

Would you say your reading and writing practices have changed since we last spoke? In what way?

What languages are you usually writing in now?

When do you write at work? Who is this writing for?

When are you writing at school? Who is this writing for?

How about at home?

Are you writing many letters or e-mails? To who and for what reason? What languages are you writing them in?

Now after two years, how do you feel about writing in English?

Have you traveled back to _____ since we last spoke? How did you feel your languages shift when you travel? How about your writing?

EXPERIENCES OF MULTILINGUALISM AND MULTILITERACIES

Would you still call yourself multilingual? Why or why not?

Do you think policies (at work, at school) in the United States affect how you use your languages? If yes, how so? Do you think current immigration debates affect how people use their languages?

When I say "globalization," what do you think of? How do you think globalization affects people's reading and writing? How do you think it affects reading and writing in multiple languages?

Since we last spoke, how have you been using your writing practices from _____ in your life in the United States?

How would you describe the writing of multilingual people? Would you say that is different or the same as monolingual people? Do you think multilingual people benefit from their multiple languages or not? If yes, how so?

PARTICIPANT INSIGHTS ON DEVELOPING DATA PATTERNS

My previous interviews showed that migrants to the United States bring many of their reading and writing practices with them, but sometimes work, school, or government policies get in the way of those skills being successful. What do you think about that?

Can you think of a time when you wanted to write in a certain way in a certain language and you couldn't? Why do you think that happened?

Is there anything else you'd like to tell me?

APPENDIX D
DETAILED CODING PROCEDURES

My rounds of coding proceeded in three loose stages: initial or open coding that gave every text segment a code, axial coding that compared codes to look for patterns or themes, and focused or selective coding that refined categories from code patterns and built theoretical arguments from them. To keep track of my evolving coding tree, participant demographic data, and research memos, I initially used the qualitative research software Atlas.ti and then switched to the mixed methods web application Dedoose. Both programs allowed me to link all of my collected data, including participant text samples, to my codes, segmented quotations, demographic data, and memos in ways that helped me make analytic meaning out of the data's connections and disjunctures.

During initial coding, I coded every segment of text that struck me as meaningful according to my research questions, with some segments receiving two to four different codes. I especially sought to name the practices participants described in various writing contexts, in different times of their lives, and among their languages. I coded with gerunds as often as possible in order to focus on the activity of multilingual practices (Charmaz, *Constructing*). Practice codes ranged, alphabetically, from "application writing" to "work reporting" and in the end numbered twenty-six literacy practices. Other initial codes included my attempts to name literacy skills or knowledge as they were practiced in different parts of the world or in different languages.

My initial coding began to turn toward axial coding when it became clear that my codes were only naming the practices that existed and ignoring those that didn't. In other words, my original coding scheme was only able to capture the practices that had moved, that were mobile, and could not capture those that were absent, altered, or immobile. This became physically clear during one night of coding when I was sorting printed-out coded text into category piles on my desk I had labeled "skills," "knowledge," and "awareness." At the end of this sorting activity, I was left holding a thick stack of text that couldn't be sorted—these were examples of practices that did not move, a pile of immobility that led to my early findings in the study and became the basis for chapter 3.

Therefore, during axial coding, I added two higher-order codes to many of the initial codes: possibilities and constraints. This allowed me to describe practice with a full definition beyond just activity, as action mediated by the interconnected values, resources, and materials surrounding and including a text, repeated over time for the sake of routine or tradition. This was an especially productive coding round for memo writing. By comparing across practices defined by possibility and those defined by constraint, I was able to see three characteristics of the data. First, I could see the relationality of mobile to immobile practices because constraints and possibilities often co-occurred or sat together in tension. Second, I could see the symbolic status that many practices carried: practices were the real, lived activities of writing, but these practices were also surrounded by (codes co-occurring with) descriptions of class status, family histories, and imagined futures. Third, I could begin to see how competing values in a wide variety of contexts directed where practices moved and what writers could gain from them as they migrated.

NOTES

PREFACE

1. Favell is referencing John Torpey's research about the passport. Also see Moya and McKeown for arguments that migration is as old as human beings.

2. This is Czaika and de Haas's study critiquing Vertovec's theories of superdiversity in particular.

3. Glick Schiller, Basch, and Szanton Blanc, "Immigrant" 52; Brettell; Foner; Held et al.; Moya and McKeown; and Portes, Guarnizo, and Landolt.

INTRODUCTION: WHY WRITING MATTERS

1. For consistency with other studies of migration, I use the United Nations's definition of "international migrant" as those living for at least a year in a location other than the country where they were born. By this definition, international migrants include individuals with a wide range of life experiences and motivations for migration, including skilled professionals with work visas, refugees, and international students. Clearly these individuals do not experience migration in the same ways, which the study's analysis accounts for. Forty-six million international migrants lived in the United States in 2013, double the twenty-three million who did in 1990. According to data from the United Nations and the World Bank analyzed by the Pew Research Center, the United States remained the main destination country for international migrants from 1990 to 2013, and during this time the country increased its share of the world's migrants who are increasingly from middle-income to higher-income countries (Connor, Cohn, and Gonzalez-Barrera).

2. Throughout the book I use "multilingual" to describe writers and writing primarily because this is how participants described themselves. By "multilingual" I don't mean many complete languages that writers easily switch among but, rather, varied proficiencies in language varieties that writers identify with. I recognize that there is tension in this choice. While "multilingual writer" and "multiliteracies" have been taken up as more accurate or encompassing terms than "bilingual" or "biliterate," such enumerations can create a kind of "multiwashing" that can mask power in its tendency to equate all languages and cultures as many equal entities. Pennycook, for example, sets "multilingualism and multimodality . . . which focus on languages and modes as pluralized entities" in opposition to "translingualism and transmodality . . .

which question the very separability of languages and modes in the first place" (*Global Englishes* 49). See, for example, Pennycook, *Practice*; Brah; Frankenberg and Mani. My hope is that the book's theoretical framework and analysis work against this tendency.

3. The website www.languageonthemove.com is an excellent and active collection of academic responses to contemporary social issues around migration and multilingualism.

4. For example, see Atkinson et al.; Canagarajah, *Translingual Practice*; Matsuda, "Lure"; Matsuda, "Wild West"; Horner and Lu's guest-edited *College English* special issue "Translingual Work in Composition"; Horner et al., "Language Difference"; and Lu and Horner's "Translingual Literacy" to follow the debate on the merits of a translingual approach to teaching writing. García and Wei's book *Translanguaging* is a broader educational take on the matter. For more general thinking about language diversity in college composition, see for example, Canagarajah, "Shuttling" and "World Englishes"; Elbow; Guerra, *Language, Culture, Identity*; Horner and Trimbur; Horner et al.; Lu, "Living" and "Professing"; Jordan; Matsuda, "Myth"; and Perryman-Clark et al. For literacy research that focuses on immigrant or transnational multilinguality, see Alvarez; Baynham and Prinsloo; Creese and Blackledge; Farr; Guerra, *Close to Home*; Lam; Martin-Jones and Jones; Menard-Warwick; Norton; Papen; Warriner, "Multiple Literacies; and Warriner, "The Days."

5. For scholarship that explicitly studies how literacy and language moves, see Blommaert, *Sociolinguistics*; Brandt and Clinton; Kell, "Inequalities"; Lam and Warriner; Lorimer Leonard, "Traveling"; Pandey; Richardson Bruna; Rounsaville, "Genre Repertoires" and "Situating"; Stein and Slominsky; Vieira, "Undocumented" and *American by Paper*; and Pahl and Rowsell's collection *Travel Notes from the New Literacy Studies*. For literacy research that attends to migration or transnationality, see Besnier; Farr; Graff; Kell, "Crossing"; Lagman; Meyers; Mihut; and Stroud and Mpendukana.

6. Analyzing language ideologies together with literacy practices shows how writers position themselves across multiple cultural, linguistic, racial, or ethnic identifications. Because writing instruction in the United States often assumes standard English monolingualism that treats linguistic diversity as a problem rather than a norm, migrant writers in the United States are often attempting to deploy or deny their multilingual resources against the pressures of what Paul Kei Matsuda has called the myth of linguistic homogeneity ("Myth").

7. "Repertoire" is used in this book in ways informed by sociolinguistics, applied linguistics, education, and literacy studies. It is a foundational concept in sociolinguistics that originally indicated the set of language varieties and norms of use among which a speech community chose to convey a desired meaning, a "totality of linguistic resources" including dialects, styles, genres, and acts of speaking (Gumperz, *Directions* 20–21; Gumperz, *Discourse*). Repertoires were understood to be developed within speech communities, rather than within individuals, because the dominant research

method of the time, ethnography of communication, focused on communities and their meaning-making activities. But because ethnography of communication was also able to gather the community's interpretations of its own language use, repertoire has always also included the metalinguistic understandings and language ideologies of language users. See Blommaert and Backus; Busch; Lüdi; and Otsuji and Pennycook.

8. For example, Canagarajah describes a student writer who "considers her background as a resource" and "draws actively" from her "multimodal resources for expression" ("Codemeshing" 407). Bawarshi argues for the need to understand the "resources students bring with them" and how students "negotiate between and make use of their varied linguistic and discursive resources" (197). Horner et al. promote a "resource discourse" over a "rights discourse" when speaking of language diversity, saying that while a rights-based discourse "simply affirms the existence or preservation" of different codes and languages, a resource-based discourse views "language differences and fluidities as resources to be preserved, developed, and utilized" (Canagarajah, "SRTOL" paragraph 8; Horner et al. 300). Scholars studying multilingualism in educational contexts similarly suggest that "there is a need for teachers to draw on the considerable language resources that such students bring with them to class" (Block 80) because multilingual students use "the languages at their disposal as a resource in communication" (Cenoz and Gorter 358).

9. For arguments like this, see Brandt, *Literacy*; Graff; Hernández-Zamora; Kalmar; and Luke and Carrington.

10. Heller shows how this happens in "Alternative Ideologies" and "Globalization." Also see Pennycook, *Practice*.

11. For discussion of multilingual identities, see Belcher and Connor; Cox et al.; Kells, Balester, and Villanueva; Kramsch; Norton; Shuck, "Racializing" and "Language Identity"; Villanueva; and Young, *Minor Re/visions*.

12. I use "move" and "moving" to describe the action of nouns "movement" and "mobility." I treat "mobility" as a higher-order concept than "movement," although both are inflected with power and difference. The relationship of language to movement is long; consider images of the god Kairos with winged feet that "foreground movement, the movement of time, the movement of language . . . mark[ing] the celerity and multi-directionality of discourse" (Hawhee 21).

13. I use "globalization" and "global" to mean worldwide phenomena that have consequences on or instantiate in local contexts (Held et al.; Kearney; Levitt). Under conditions of globalization, changes in economies, communication technologies, and transportation have created a "widening, deepening, and speeding up of worldwide interconnectedness," shaping a world that has become "a shared social space" (Held et al. 2). For example, the temporary quality of work under a global economy has created "the feeling that one might or must always be moving" to keep up or survive (Glick Schiller, Basch, and Szanton-Blanc, "Immigrant" 9). Critics of what sociologist Michael Mann calls "globaloney" say claims for the novelty of globalization are exag-

gerated and historically naïve, the worst kind of "theory for theory's sake" (Favell 393). Particularly suspect are claims that globalized mobility creates new kinds of personal or political freedom.

I use "transnationalism" not as a synonym for international or global but to indicate systems of social relations built across borders. Transnationalism is a set of processes "by which immigrants forge and sustain multistranded social relations that link together their societies of origin and settlements"—a complex of migrant activities that combine national identities or acknowledge a "diminished significance of national boundaries" (Glick Schiller, Basch, and Szanton-Blanc, "Transnationalism" 49). This does not mean that transnationalism does not recognize national borders, but instead acknowledges that they exist at certain historical moments for some but not for others (Levitt and Khagram). A transnational analysis looks not only beyond borders but at cross-border connections—kinwork, affective ties, or long-distance nationalism, asking how these occur among spaces, inclusive of the territory within the United States. Thus transnationalism traces how individuals build social fields across real or perceived borders to accommodate and resist difficult circumstances (Glick Schiller, Basch, and Szanton-Blanc, "Transnationalism") with sustained activities over time and across space (Portes, Guarnizo, and Landolt).

Globalization and transnationalism are sometimes set in opposition to each other, wherein the microapproach of transnationalism is adopted in opposition to the "macroapproach" of globalization (Brettell and Hollifield 104). For many, globalization is a phenomenon of global interconnectivity while transnationalism characterizes activities carried out across contexts and borders, whether "from below" with individuals or "from above" with political, military, and economic organizations (Smith and Guarnizo). Some scholars understand transnational processes to be one aspect of the phenomenon of globalization or an active manifestation of it—a set of practices to be understood as always set in a context *of* globalization (Glick Schiller, Basch, and Szanton-Blanc, "Immigrant"; Levitt). Thus "transnationalism" and "globalization" are not terms in opposition or terms describing wholly separate processes, since one system is bound up in the other. While some scholars would prefer sharp distinctions between the two so that each concept does not become "a muddle" (Portes 876), no matter their terminological nuance, the cross-border practices and activities of migrants are always mediated by a global system of affordances and constraints. Indeed, this book understands globalization and transnationalism to be unavoidably connected. The analysis of everyday immigrant activities shows that cross-border practices and global interconnectedness are naturally intertwined and mutually constitutive. The book follows an analytic line of interrelation, avoiding a neat bifurcation of micro-level transnationalism and macro-level globalization, because both terms are salient on micro and macro levels.

14. Across fields, transnational actors have been characterized as moving "freely back and forth across international borders and between different cultures and social

systems" (Brettell and Hollifield 104). Thus the "new immigration" (Suárez-Orozco, Suárez-Orozco, and Qin-Hilliard), "new migration studies" (Friedman), and "new transnationalism" (Brettell) all are characterized by a fluid ongoingness. For similar theoretical notions, see Appadurai; and Ong. For discussion of a mobilities paradigm, see Adey; Barton; Cresswell and Merriman; Franquesa; Salazar; Sheller and Urry; and Urry.

Scholars in critical theory and cultural studies have long examined how space and territory shape subjectivities and identities—variously deemed nomads (Cronin; Deleuze and Guattari), travelers (Clifford; Cronin), tourists, flaneurs, wanderers, and vagabonds. Each of these subjects has come to represent "a generalized poetics of displacement," dislocation, or dispersion (Jacquemet). Although many of these concepts have become "emblematic of postmodernity" in that they disperse a unified subject as they dislocate the national (Cronin), they remain theoretical or discursive concepts, few of which fully connect the material physicality of movement with mobile language practices.

15. Massey's "differentiated" nature of mobility within transnationalism especially suggests the possibility of multiple kinds of movement. For similar understandings of differentiated mobility in the context of literacy, see Blommaert, *Grassroots*; and Luke, "Genres."

16. See Carillo Rowe; De Genova, "Deportation"; De Genova and Peutz; Freitag and von Oppen; and Manderscheid.

17. Circulation is a kind of literate mobility, although not the one I discuss here. Models of writing and rhetorical circulation are approached as "the circuits of production, distribution, exchange, and consumption through which writing circulates as it takes on cultural value and worldly force" (Trimbur 194) or defined through "trans-situational and transhistorical connectivity" among audiences with "fluid identit[ies]" (Chaput 20).

18. See Cenoz and Gorter; Pennycook, *Practice*. I do think it is important to note that although languages might be social constructs, writers still encounter language borders every day. Whether languages themselves have actual boundaries, the *construct* of a bounded language or nation continues to produce real, material consequences that affect writers' lives.

19. See note 3. Lu, for example, says that transcultural literacy is "the only viable metaphor for inculcating the kind of disposition towards cultural-linguistic differences necessary for building a better world for all" ("Metaphors" 292–93). Translingualism also has been explored productively in literary and cultural studies for quite some time. For example, see use of the term in Lydia Liu; Yildiz; and Kellman, *Switching* and *Translingual*.

20. For more rhetorical theories or literacy studies that emphasize the immobile components of mobility, see Cuban, "Downward Mobility"; Hernandez-Zamora; Hesford, "Global Turns"; Luke, "Genres"; Nunley; Prendergast; and Reynolds, "Who's Go-

ing." Literacy scholars have been particularly helpful in the context of social mobility, showing that gained literacy does not necessarily "promote cognitive advance, social mobility or progress" (Street, *Social Literacies* 24).

21. My formulation of "literate valuation" is shaped first by Bourdieu's situating of the linguistic among sociocultural and economic relationships (*Language*) and second by a Marxist conception of valuation as a material labor process. My use of "value(s)" also is influenced by theories that connect structural values to the human actions that make those values meaningful (Heyman; Munn; Zelizer). Just as anthropologists and sociologists have attempted to infuse theories of value with a more robust understanding of social change (Graeber), so does this book attempt to infuse theories of literacy with a more robust understanding of valuation.

22. See Heller, "Commodification"; Rudby and Tan; Park and Wee; and Wee.

23. Park and Wee argue that in the past language was a marker of identity and not "subject to exchange" while the present language is a commodity that is simply an economic resource divorced from identification (125). But both Heller and Blommaert (*Sociolinguistics*) show how literate resources "follow the predicament of their users: when [they] are socially mobile, their resources will follow this trajectory; when they are socially marginal, their resources will also be disqualified" (Blommaert, *Sociolinguistics* 47).

24. Here I am following Zelizer's theory of a good match, which seeks to understand the "mingling of economic transactions with intimate relations" (153). She theorizes the negotiations that occur in this mingling, arguing that the quality of the match between individuals or groups engaged in these negotiations matters. A good match is not necessarily "equal and just," or approved by all parties, but is "viable: it gets the economic work of the relationship done and sustains the relationship" (153).

25. My notion of games here recalls the "Game of Power" that participants discuss in Cushman.

CHAPTER 1. STUDYING WRITING ON THE MOVE

1. For example, see Clayton and Euscher; Cuban, "Home/work"; Farris; Margolis; and Warriner. Gabaccia tells a nuanced narrative of women's opportunities after migration, noting, for example, that immigrant women's literacy rates are often higher than those of their native-born counterparts.

2. The Organisation for Economic Co-operation and Development (OECD) gives the following overall picture of the United States: from 2007 to 2009, estimates of undocumented immigrants fell from 11.8 million to 10.8 million, numbers of refugees admitted grew but were below quota level, employment-based permanent and temporary visa certifications fell, and nonagriculture temporary workers fell short of the quota cap. Meanwhile, visas granted for employment-based preferences (high-skilled workers) stayed steady, and foreign student and exchange visitor visas increased, exceeding the quota cap, with a 64 percent increase in Chinese nationals.

3. Here I am using 2009 census data to make a comparison with the 2009 data the Brookings report used. The 2010 data shows a growing foreign-born population (7.2 percent from 6.3 percent), growing migrant population without citizenship (67.8 percent from 63.7 percent), and growing population of newly arrived, post-2000 migrants (55.1 percent from 42.9 percent).

4. Work by Castles and Miller; Donato and Gabaccia; and Engle mention this trend.

5. This narrative crosses fields, appearing in work as diverse as Appadurai; Gabaccia; Mahler and Pessar; Mojab; Phillion; Pratt; Ramdas; Robinson-Pant; Sadeghi; Sarroub; Sreeharsha; and Street, *Literacy*.

6. Cuban's work is especially revelatory of these details, particularly her article "Examining."

7. Interviews lasted from forty to ninety minutes and were designed to foreground an emic perspective on migrant writing, drawing out participants' own insights about their writing and migration experiences. The interview protocol was organized into three categories—home, school, and community literacy memories; current literacy practices in English and other languages; and opinions about multilingual communication—with questions aiming to draw out the shape and specificity of everyday writing taking place over the span of a lifetime and across dispersed geographic locations (see Appendix B, "Interview Questions," and Appendix C, "Follow-Up Interview Questions"). All participants expressed a desire to conduct the interviews in English, either because they felt fluent enough or because they agreed to be interviewed precisely to practice their English. Therefore interviews were conducted in English, with occasional switching into Spanish from participants who knew I would understand.

Interviews were digitally recorded and transcribed only by me. In transcription I recorded participants verbatim, maintaining all pauses, laughter, nonstandard phrasing, and backchannel responses. In participant accounts throughout the book, however, I have omitted the repetition of certain backchannel utterances—"mm," "mmhmm," "like," "you know," "okay," and "yeah"—as well as indications of length of pauses, interruptions, or changes in intonation. These choices follow the conventions of several linguistic anthropologists and support the focus of my analysis, aiming to highlight, rather than obscure, participants' contributions (Ahearn; Schiffrin). For example, it was very important to maintain participants' nonstandard constructions in English because these participant utterances—just the way they phrased them—were often rich sites of meaning, both for their own understanding and for mine.

8. I collected varied data to support a rich contextual understanding of the participants' writing lives and to achieve data saturation and theoretical detail. I never explicitly asked for participants' writing. In some situations, asking felt too teacherly; in other situations, undocumented participants were uncomfortable with any request for documents. Therefore I decided to look at texts only when they were offered by participants. I read these for a holistic understanding of the practices that produced them.

9. My treatment of qualitative interviews is especially informed by Bogdan and Biklen; Charmaz, "Qualitative Interviewing"; and Merriam.

10. This focus follows traditions in new literacy studies that focus on what writers are already doing with their literacies rather than how literacy, as a stable entity, has a measurable impact on them. See Barton, Hamilton, and Ivanic; Scollon; Street, *Social Literacies*; and Tusting, Ivanic, and Wilson.

11. For the theories of practice I rely on, see Baynham and Prinsloo; Bourdieu, *Outline*; Pennycook, *Practice*; and Smith and Guarnizo. Kell's work ("Crossing" and "Inequalities") is especially important for understanding practices in transnational, mobile literacy. I did not aim to trace genres, since genres can act as a focus of practice but are not the entire practice itself. A practice includes everything around the genre—traditions, beliefs, purposes—which all together create a practice bound up in the values of a particular family and culture, repeated over time for specific occasions.

12. My use of literacy history interviews is primarily informed by Brandt's work. For further thinking on the promise and challenges of these interviews, see Brandt's discussion in *Rise of Writing* (7–12); Duffy; Prior; Vieira "Doing Transnational Writing Studies" and *American by Paper* (17). My decision to focus primarily on interview data is influenced by Leki's explanation in "Coping Strategies" that are consistent with "qualitative research, narrative elements allow us to see how these strategies play out in real lives" (241).

13. This research was designed to understand how writers themselves defined and measured their own success rather than defining their success through language acquisition, proficiency, or fluency.

14. These definitions and redefinitions are especially interesting in Blommaert, *Sociolinguistics*; Collins, Slembrouck, and Baynham; Kell, "Crossing" and "Inequalities"; and Lillis, "Ethnography."

15. Kell's work is most helpful on this point. Scholars especially claim that overattention to the local can miss global ideological pressures, an impasse variously identified as local/distant (Brandt and Clinton), universalist/particularist (Collins and Blot), or vernacular/hegemonic (Kell, "Inequalities"). Scholars have suggested several approaches to move beyond these impasses, like focusing on the ideological relationship between the local and the global rather than on one site or the other (Street, "What's 'New'").

16. See Brandt and Clinton; Collins and Blot; and Vieira, "Social Consequences."

17. This tension is helpfully elaborated in Lillis, *Sociolinguistics*.

18. In these procedures, rounds of coding support analytic development through inductive and emergent refinement of concepts as laid out in Charmaz, "Grounded Theory" (510), and in Charmaz, "Emergent Method."

19. Methodological nationalism often forwards theoretical conclusions that cannot work themselves out of nationalist conclusions because they depend on and thus respond to nation-based understandings of geopolitical forces (De Genova, "Con-

nections"; Grewal). Some scholars see methodological nationalism implicit in much research across the social sciences and humanities, stemming from academic habits, departmental designations, and government or NGO funding streams concerned with the economy and security of particular nation-states (Glick Schiller and Salazar). Also see Glick Schiller; and Gupta and Ferguson.

20. Analytic approaches from wide varieties of fields do this. Transnational methodology following Spivak moves beyond comparative analysis, stepping beyond Said's "traveling theory" to analyze inequality and power differentials in global and postcolonial contexts (Grewal; Kaplan; Hesford, "Cosmopolitanism"; Dingo; Reidner). Transnational methodology informed by sociology and anthropology pursues affiliations and affinities forged in social fields across national locations, most currently analyzing movement and stasis together "within social and economic relationships rather than in relation to geographic borders" (Basch, Glick Schiller, and Szanton-Blanc; Glick Schiller and Salazar 194; Levitt; and Waldinger). Diasporic methodologies analyze the doubled affective and political ties created by displacement not only among host and home communities but among host communities that share a common home (Brah; Lavie and Swedenburg; see especially the "transnational migrant circuit" in Rouse). In literacy studies Kell has proposed tracing trajectories of meaning-making or undertaking transcontextual analysis of meanings projected across contexts. In applied linguistics, Makoni and Pennycook's "disinventing languages" analyzes the histories and political economies of languages rather than their pragmatic or discursive characteristics, while Otsuji and Pennycook's "metrolingualism" takes the city as a unit of analysis and analyzes the superdiversity of fluid and fixed languages across it.

21. Transnational perspectives on literacy, language, and rhetoric—especially those that study the mobility, networking, or circulation of practices or arguments—can appear to be novel even though they have long historical precedent. If the methodological assumption is static, singular units, then analysis beyond these can feel new. But contemporary transnational perspectives are not always wholly novel and instead are responding to changes in community technology, transportation, and global economies that build on preexisting transnational flows and links. The same can be said of linguistic diversity, which appears to be new to many who live in monolingual cultures or locales when, as Piller has written, referring to superdiversity as perception not reality, "it has been the normal human experience all along" (30).

22. As defined in Dingo; Hesford, "Cosmopolitanism" and *Framing*; Reidner; and Wingard. Feminist methodologies generally share the following epistemological features: treating women's lived experiences as a legitimate source of knowledge, including researcher reflexivity on the researcher/participant role in the research process, and analyzing the workings of power in all forms of inequality while aiming for social action. This synthesis is informed by Campbell and Wasco; Conti and O'Neil; Gordon; Harding; Mohanty, "Feminist Encounters"; Naples; Plummer and Young; and Pratt.

23. I am aware of the potentially trite and "deeply formulaic" nature of self-reflexive moves in critical ethnographic or qualitative research. To say that researcher reflexivity matters to me is to involve my participants in the research process rather than to believe that I have solved any problems by acknowledging my own powerful status (Cintron 939–40).

24. This is an affinity especially noted in sociological studies of nursing, which is not surprising given that grounded theory originated there. For example, see Plummer and Young; Keddy, Sims, and Noerager Stern; and Wuest.

CHAPTER 2. FLUIDITY

1. Here "move" is in quotation marks because writing among languages isn't commonly described in terms of movement. More commonly, it is understood as bilingualism, code-switching, or transfer. I originally used "movement" to reflect the terms that participants used. Their terms stuck.

2. My use of "repertoire" is informed by Busch; Collins, Slembrouck, and Baynham; Lüdi; and Otsuji and Pennycook.

3. Many theories have moved code-switching beyond the notion of rational actors choosing among languages; for example, Rampton's theory of "crossing" traces speakers' switches across ethnic, racial, and language boundaries, often into varieties assumed not to be their own (Rampton, *Crossing*). Code-switching also is understood as a political strategy, in which people can "be two or more things where normally a choice is expected" (Heller, "Codeswitching" 93). Most commonly, code-switching is understood to signal contextual shifts or create meaning in socially or grammatically appropriate ways, while code-mixing is a result of language contact without the pragmatic effects of code-switching. Language borrowing, like that described by Sabohi in this chapter, operates only at a lexical level. See Auer; Gumperz, *Discourse*; Heller, "Codeswitching"; and Myers-Scotton.

4. For example, Canagarajah and V. A. Young each propose that "code-meshing" avoids the stratification of codes they understood code-switching to create between informal/formal genres, home/school contexts, and early/final written essay drafts (Canagarajah, "World Englishes" 594–95; V. A. Young 153–54n9). Also see Makoni and Pennycook for their critique of bounded languages that need to be "disinvented." Other scholars, like Matsuda, critique the loose evolution of terms like these, acknowledging that many scholars use them interchangeably and encouraging the clarification of their use (Matsuda, "Wild West" 133–35).

5. In her study of high school students writing in Mexico, LoCastro similarly finds that length is valued but describes "*la lengua culta*" as that specifically joined through subordination rather than coordination (206).

6. Some literacy research has studied family transmission of literacy practices, such as Taylor's "Family Literacy: Conservation and Change in the Transmission of Literacy Styles and Values." The act of passing down literacy skills, values, and expe-

riences through families and groups has been studied as "language heritage," which has been used to refer to languages of immigrant, refugee, indigenous, or nonmajority groups, with "heritage language learners" referring to students who have developed functional proficiencies in a "non-English" home language or language with which they identify. See Cummins, "Proposal for Action"; Valdés, "Bilingualism" and "Heritage Language Students"; and Fishman, "Heritage Language" and "Mother-tongue." Also see Yildiz's argument about language ideologies encoded in "mother tongues."

7. In "Heritage Language Students," Valdés critiques the term for distilling a complex set of affiliations and proficiencies into learning single non-English languages. García critiques the term for its "rear-viewing" tendencies to romanticize languages supposedly "left behind in remote lands" ("Positioning"). Leung, Harris, and Rampton; Nero; and Rampton, "Displacing," all provide important critiques in similar veins.

8. For example, see conclusions in Cummins, "Bilingual Proficiency"; Valenzuela's important work on subtractive schooling; and Wong Fillmore.

9. As explained in Cummins, "Proposal for Action" 587.

10. Also see Cummins, *Negotiating Identities*; Cook, *Effects*; and Valdés, "Bilingualism."

11. The official website of AzETA expired in early August 2016, but you can read about the organization here: https://www.britishcouncil.az/en/teach/teacher-networks and http://www.visions.az/en/news/127/53d4fa5d/.

12. For just a few examples of research that makes this claim, see Alvarez; Bawarshi; Canagarajah, "World Englishes"; Horner et al.; Lu, "Professing"; Rounsaville; and Stein and Slominsky.

13. For theoretical and empirical work on what multilingual writers know or understand, see Cook, "Multi-competence"; Hall, Cheng, and Carlson; Franceschini; Canagarajah, *Critical* and "World Englishes"; and Hattori and Ching.

14. In an interesting similarity among Spanish speakers in the study, several participants used metaphors about doors to describe this access. Alandra believes that by enrolling her daughter in a dual-immersion school she is "opening the doors for choice." Alicia says that her parents enrolled her in a trilingual school and paid for an English language tutor at home because "you never know what's gonna happen, where you're gonna end up, so I wouldn't close any doors." These writers connect literate fluidity to both opportunity and self-defense—you never know where in the world you might end up, so you should keep all doors, or linguistic possibilities, open just in case. Yolanda similarly parallels the enumeration of languages with doors open to knowledge and cultural understanding: "Every language you know is like a big door in your life. It's like if you have a room, you are born in a room with no doors. Then you learn your first language and a door open, you learn another one another door open, opens, right? So the more languages the more doors." The echo of this metaphor did motivate a follow-up question to participants about a potential *dicho*, a saying or expression, in Spanish about opportunities and doors, but neither Yolanda nor Alicia could think of

one. So rather than a belief based in Spanish, the echo of "doors" seems to be based in the state of literate fluidity itself, supporting a consideration of languages as assets that lead to movement. For them, language itself opens the door that they move through.

15. Much scholarship considers the role of identity in linguistic diversity. For example, see V. A. Young; Cox et al.; Gilyard; Kellman, *Switching*; Kramsch; Matsuda, "Identity"; Norton; Villanueva; and M. Young.

CHAPTER 3. FIXITY

1. See my explanation on this topic in the introduction.

2. This refers to Massey's notion of differentiated mobilities as described in the introduction.

3. My understanding of these oppositional forces is most informed by Glick Schiller and Salazar. Moya and McKeown, and Turner also explore this phenomenon.

4. See Blom and Gumperz; Ferguson; and Fishman, "Bilingualism." One critique of such models for the multilingual writers in this study is the assumed duality of diglossia in which speakers are switching between only high and low varieties based on prestige or formality.

5. See Lu's discussion of translingualism as a socially just metaphor ("Metaphors"). Also see grounding claims in Canagarajah, "Codemeshing"; Guerra, "Putting Literacy"; Horner et al.; and Horner and Lu.

6. For further explanations of writing knowledge transfer, see Nowacek and Yancey, Robertson, and Taczak. For an introduction to language transfer, see Jarvis and Pavlenko. The extensive work of James as well as the exchange between DePalma and Ringer and Grujicic-Alatriste published in the *Journal of Second Language Writing* offers important insight into the coming together of transfer research in these two areas.

7. Socioeconomic backgrounds are often used to explain the struggle of multilingual migrants in the United States. Educational preparation, professional status, social class, and mode of entry all may influence the extent to which these writers can call on their literate practices, but not uniformly so. Several writers whose accounts are explored in this chapter—Yolanda, Alicia, Aldene, Khadroma, Tashi—experience in the United States comparable social and professional status to their home countries and speak just as frequently of their literate fluidity as of their fixity. Nor are any participants' experiences of fixity completely dictated by a lack of literate repertoire or flagging fluency in English. So social factors do not fully explain the variable trajectories of these writers and their similarly fixed practices.

CHAPTER 4. FRICTION

1. See Horner and Lu for an extension of Tsing's theory that accounts for writers' agency as literate labor in the reconstruction of meaning.

2. For example, see Piller's thinking on "the monolingual habitus of multilingual schools" (99–104).

3. See Apple and Christian-Smith; Luke, *Literacy*; Matsuda and Matsuda; Yenika-Agbaw; and You.

4. JAHCO seems to have recently evolved, but Khadroma described the organization in the manner above. Read more at www.jointcommission.org/.

5. Also see Cameron on standardized communication in workplaces.

6. See Leki, "Living through College Literacy," for explanations of how these assumptions play out in the literacy experiences of multilingual nursing students.

7. Cuban also identifies that an attendant focus on accountability and outcomes-based education take precedence over "active citizenship and the common good" ("Downward Mobility" 8). She sees the link between economy, language, and education in governmental demands for evidence-based information and in the seeping into schools of business models emphasizing productivity and competition. Also see Horner and Lu.

8. Heller, "Commodification" 106; and Karakayali and Rigo.

CHAPTER 5. DEEP CONTRADICTIONS IN THE VALUE OF LITERACY

1. Jacobs.

2. The potential or necessity of this kind of imagination is discussed in Appadurai; Hattori and Ching; and Salazar.

3. Many scholars make this point, noting that linguistic discrimination is often more about speakers than the language they are using. See Graff; Kalmar; Piller.

4. One interesting exception is the new *Journal of Interrupted Studies* out of Oxford University, which was founded with the recognition that the "intellectual potential" of "so many very educated" displaced academic refugees is, as editor Paul Ostwald says, "basically just wasted" ("Nascent Journal"). The journal aims to push against the media depiction of refugees as "very pitiful individuals who have a lot of needs but very little to give" by creating a venue for "academic endeavors thwarted by forced migration" ("Nascent Journal"). While the belief that migrants' knowledge is "wasted" is an unfortunate take on the situation, the journal is at least a start (see jis-oxford.co.uk/about.html).

5. Consider legislation like Prop 187 banning bilingual education and services in California or SB 1070 in Arizona or similar immigration laws in Alabama and Georgia.

6. See Barton and Papen; Donahue; Lillis and Curry.

7. See De Genova and Puetz; Glick Schiller and Salazar. De Genova, "Conflicts"; Mezzadra and Neilson; Shamir; and Karakayali and Rigo.

8. In "Linguistic Memory," Trimbur shows especially well the history and impact of this legacy in the United States.

9. By "policy" I mean assessment design, the naming of programs and curricular tracks, the design of curriculum and outcomes, or the creation of teaching materials like textbooks. By "practice" I mean the implementation of all of these—how pedago-

gies, materials, and assessments are put into practice by teachers and administrators and how they are experienced by students.

10. Roberge, Harklau, and Siegel's collection explains this well.

11. For example, see the work of Cushing Wiegle; Hamp-Lyons; Inoue and Poe; Shohamy; and Menken.

12. The project's methodological attention to only women participants also adds an interesting tension to the project's conclusions about multilingual writers. As explained in the introduction, the project focused on women in order to complicate a narrative of women immigrants' downward mobility in the literature in migration studies. However, the same caveat can apply to any concern about representation in empirical work: the project did not set out to represent all experiences but to offer insight into some experiences. This is an essential distinction. The methodological design of this study allowed for a small window into the life experiences of immigrant multilingual writers. It did not seek to represent, through random sampling or distributed demographic representation, all multilingual writers or all of their possible experiences. The sheer number of categories that have been used to describe multilingual writers—ESL, ELLs, resident ESL, ear/eye learners, Generation 1.5, international, immigrant, newcomer, foreign, parachute students, dialect speakers, basic, remedial, developmental—is enough to deter a researcher from attempting to represent them all.

BIBLIOGRAPHY

Adey, Peter. "If Mobility Is Everything Then It Is Nothing: Towards a Relational Politics of (Im)mobilities." *Mobilities* 1.1 (2006): 75–94. Print.

Ahearn, Laura. *Invitations to Love: Literacy, Love Letters, and Social Change in Nepal.* Ann Arbor: University of Michigan Press, 2001. Print.

Alvarez, Steven. "Brokering the Immigrant Bargain: Second-Generation Immigrant Youth Negotiating Transnational Orientations to Literacy." *Literacy in Composition Studies* 3.3 (October 2015): 25–47. http://licsjournal.org/OJS/index.php/LiCS/article/view/96. Accessed December 14, 2015. Web.

Anzaldúa, Gloria. *Borderlands: The New Mestiza.* San Francisco: Aunt Lute Books, 1999. Print.

Appadurai, Arjun. *Modernity at Large: Cultural Dimensions of Globalization.* Minneapolis: University of Minnesota Press, 1996. Print.

Apple, Michael, and Linda Christian-Smith, eds. *The Politics of the Textbook.* New York: Routledge, 1991. Print.

Atkinson, Dwight, Deborah Crusan, Paul Kei Matsuda, Christina Ortmeier-Hooper, Todd Ruecker, Steve Simpson, and Christine Tardy. "Clarifying the Relationship between L2 Writing and Translingual Writing: An Open Letter to Writing Studies Editors and Organization Leaders." *College English* 77.4 (2015): 383–86. Print.

Auer, Peter. *Code-Switching in Conversation.* London: Routledge, 1998. Print.

Barton, David. "People and Technologies as Resources in Times of Uncertainty." *Mobilities* 6.1 (2011): 57–65. Print.

Barton, David, and Mary Hamilton. *Local Literacies: Reading and Writing in One Community.* New York: Routledge, 1998. Print.

Barton, David, and Uta Papen. *The Anthropology of Writing: Understanding Textually-Mediated Worlds.* London: Continuum Publishing, 2010. Print.

Barton, David, Mary Hamilton, and Roz Ivanic, eds. *Situated Literacies: Reading and Writing in Context.* New York: Routledge, 2000. Print.

Basch, Linda, Nina Glick Schiller, and Cristina Szanton-Blanc. *Nations Unbound: Transnational Projects, Postcolonial Predicaments, and Deterritorialized Nation-States.* Langhorne, PA: Gordon and Breach, 1994. Print.

Bawarshi, Anis. "The Challenges and Possibilities of Taking Up Multiple Discursive Resources in U.S. College Composition." In *Cross-Language Relations in Composition*. Edited by Bruce Horner, Min-Zhan Lu, and Paul Kei Matsuda. Carbondale: Southern Illinois University Press, 2010. 196–203. Print.

Baynham, Mike, and Mastin Prinsloo, eds. *The Future of Literacy Studies*. New York: Palgrave Macmillan, 2010. Print.

Besnier, Niko. *Literacy, Emotion, and Authority: Reading and Writing on a Polynesian Atoll*. Cambridge: Cambridge University Press, 1995. Print.

Block, David. "Bilingualism: Four Assumptions and Four Responses: Innovation in Language." *Learning and Teaching* 1.1 (2007): 66–82. Print.

Blom, Jan-Petter, and John Gumperz. "Social Meaning in Linguistic Structures: Code Switching in Northern Norway." In *Directions in Sociolinguistics*. Edited by John J. Gumperz and Dell Hymes. New York: Holt, Rinehart, and Winston, 1972. 407–34. Print.

Blommaert, Jan. *Grassroots Literacy: Writing, Identity, and Voice in Central Africa*. New York: Routledge, 2008. Print.

Blommaert, Jan. *The Sociolinguistics of Globalization*. Cambridge: Cambridge University Press, 2010. Print.

Blommaert, Jan, and Ad Backus. "Superdiverse Repertoires and the Individual." *Tilburg Papers in Culture Studies*. Paper 24. March 2012. www.tilburguniversity.edu/upload/d53816c1-f163-4ae4-b74c-0942b30bdd61_tpcs%20paper24.pdf. Accessed April 10, 2012. Web.

Bogdan, Robert C., and Sari Knopp Biklen. *Qualitative Research in Education: An Introduction to Theory and Methods*. 3rd ed. New York: Allyn and Bacon, 1998. Print.

Bourdieu, Pierre. "The Economics of Linguistic Exchanges." *Social Sciences Information*. 16.6 (1977): 645–68. Print.

Bourdieu, Pierre. *Language and Symbolic Power*. Translated by Gino Raymond and Matthew Adamson. Cambridge: Polity Press, 1991. Print.

Bourdieu, Pierre. *Outline of a Theory of Practice*. Translated by Richard Nice. Cambridge: Cambridge University Press, 1977. Print.

Brah, Avtar. *Cartographies of Diaspora: Contested Identities*. New York: Routledge, 1996. Print.

Brandt, Deborah. "Accumulating Literacy: Writing and Learning To Write in the Twentieth Century." *College English* 57.6 (1995): 649–68. Print.

Brandt, Deborah. *Literacy in American Lives*. New York: Cambridge University Press, 2001. Print.

Brandt, Deborah. *The Rise of Writing: Redefining Mass Literacy*. Cambridge: Cambridge University Press, 2014. Print.

Brandt, Deborah, and Katie Clinton. "Limits of the Local: Expanding Perspectives on Literacy as a Social Practice." *Journal of Literacy Research* 34.3 (2002): 337–56. Print.

Brettell, Caroline. *Anthropology and Migration: Essays on Transnationalism, Ethnicity, and Identity*. Walnut Creek, CA: Altamira Press, 2003. Print.

Brettell, Caroline, and James Hollifield, eds. *Migration Theory: Talking across the Disciplines*. New York: Routledge, 2000. Print.

Busch, Brigitta. "The Linguistic Repertoire Revisited." *Applied Linguistics* 33.5 (2012): 503–23. Print.

Cameron, Deborah. *Good To Talk?: Living and Working in a Communication Culture*. Thousand Oaks, CA: Sage Publications, 2000. Print.

Campbell, Rebecca, and Sharon Wasco. "Feminist Approaches to Social Science: Epistemological and Methodological Tenets." *American Journal of Community Psychology* 28.6 (2000): 773–91. Print.

Canagarajah, A. Suresh. "Codemeshing in Academic Writing: Identifying Teachable Strategies of Translanguaging." *Modern Language Journal* 95.3 (2011): 401–17. Print.

Canagarajah, A. Suresh. *Critical Academic Writing and Multilingual Students*. Ann Arbor: University of Michigan Press, 2002. Print.

Canagarajah, A. Suresh. "The Place of World Englishes in Composition: Pluralization Continued." *College Composition and Communication* 57.4 (2006): 586–619. Print.

Canagarajah, A. Suresh. "Toward a Writing Pedagogy of Shuttling between Languages: Learning from Multilingual Writers." *College English* 68.6 (2006): 589–604. Print.

Canagarajah, A. Suresh. "Translanguaging in the Classroom: Emerging Issues for Research and Pedagogy." *Applied Linguistics Review* 2 (2011): 1–26. Print.

Canagarajah, A. Suresh. *Translingual Practice*. New York: Routledge, 2013. Print.

Canagarajah, A. Suresh. "An Updated SRTOL?" *CCCC Conversations on Diversity* (Conference on College Composition and Communication). N.d. http://cccc-blog.blogspot.com/2010/11/updated-srtol.html. Accessed October 7, 2010. Web.

Carrillo Rowe, Aimee. "Whose 'America'? The Politics of Rhetoric and Space in the Formation of U.S. Nationalism." *Radical History Review* 89 (2004): 115–34. Print.

Castles, Stephen, and Mark J. Miller. *The Age of Migration: International Population Movements in the Modern World*. New York: Guilford Press, 1998. Print.

Cenoz, Jasone, and Durk Gorter. "Focus on Multilingualism: A Study of Trilingual Writing." *Modern Language Journal* 95.3 (2011): 356–69. Print.

Chaput, Catherine. "Rhetorical Circulation in Late Capitalism: Neoliberalism and the Overdetermination of Affective Energy." *Philosophy and Rhetoric* 43.1 (2010): 1–25. Print.

Charmaz, Kathy. *Constructing Grounded Theory: A Practical Guide through Qualitative Analysis*. Thousand Oaks, CA: Sage Publications, 2006. Print.

Charmaz, Kathy. "Grounded Theory: Objectivist and Constructivist Methods." In *Handbook of Qualitative Research*. Edited by Norman Denzin and Yvonna S. Lincoln. Thousand Oaks, CA: Sage Publications, 2000. 509–35. Print.

Charmaz, Kathy. "Grounded Theory as an Emergent Method." In *Handbook of Emergent Methods*. Edited by Sharlene Nagy Hesse-Biber and Patricia Leavy. New York: Guilford Press, 2008. 155–72. Print.

Charmaz, Kathy. "Qualitative Interviewing and Grounded Theory Analysis." In *Inside Interviewing: New Lenses, New Concerns*. Edited by James Holstein and Jaber F. Gubrium. Thousand Oaks, CA: Sage Publications, 2003. 311–30. Print.

Cintron, Ralph. "The Timidities of Ethnography: A Response to Bruce Horner." *Journal of Advanced Composition* 22.4 (2002): 934–43. Print.

Clayton, Pamela, and Gisela Euscher. "Hidden Treasure." *Adult Learning* 13.1 (2001): 244–51. Print.

Clifford, James. *Routes: Travel and Translation in the Late Twentieth Century*. Cambridge: Harvard University Press, 1997. Print.

Collins, James, and Richard Blot. *Literacy and Literacies: Texts, Power, and Identity*. New York: Cambridge University Press, 2003. Print.

Collins, James, Stef Slembrouck, and Mike Baynham, eds. *Globalisation and Language in Contact: Scale, Migration, and Communicative Practices*. London: Continuum, 2009. Print.

Connor, Phillip, D'Vera Cohn, and Ana Gonzalez-Barrera. "Changing Patterns of Global Migration and Remittances: More Migrants in U.S. and Other Wealthy Countries; More Money to Middle-income Countries." *Pew Research Center* (2013): no pagination. www.pewsocialtrends.org/files/2013/12/global-migration-final_12-2013.pdf. Accessed June 12, 2014. Web.

Conti, Joseph, and Moira O'Neil. "Studying Power: Qualitative Methods and the Global Elite." *Qualitative Research* 7.63 (2007): 63–82. Print.

Cook, Vivian. "Going Beyond the Native Speaker in Language Teaching." *TESOL Quarterly* 33.2 (1999): 185–209. Print.

Cook, Vivian. "Multi-competence and the Learning of Many Languages." *Language, Culture, and Curriculum* 8.2 (1995): 93–8. Print.

Cox, Michelle, Jay Jordan, Christina Ortmeier-Hooper, and Gwen Schwartz, eds. *Reinventing Identities in Second Language Writing*. Urbana, IL: National Council of Teachers of English, 2010. Print.

Crawford, Ilene. "Growing Routes: Rhetoric as the Study and Practice of Movement." In *Rhetorica in Motion: Feminist Rhetorical Methods and Methodologies*. Edited by Eileen Schell and KJ Rawson. Pittsburgh: University of Pittsburgh Press, 2010. 71–87. Print.

Creese, Adrian, and Angela Blackledge. "Translanguaging in the Bilingual Classroom: A Pedagogy for Learning and Teaching?" *Modern Language Journal* 94.1 (2010): 103–15. Print.

Cresswell, Tim, and Peter Merriman, eds. *Geographies of Mobilities: Practices, Spaces, Subjects*. Burlington, VT: Ashgate Publishing Company, 2011. Print.

Cronin, Michael. *Across the Lines: Travel, Language, and Translation*. Cork, Ireland: Cork University Press, 2000. Print.

Cuban, Sondra. "The Downward Mobility of Skilled Migrant Care Workers in England." *Migration Letters* 6.2 (2009): 177–84. Print.

Cuban, Sondra. "Examining the Feminization of Migration Concept for Adult Education." *Gender and Education* 22.2 (2010): 177–91. Print.

Cuban, Sondra. "Home/work: The Roles of Education, Literacy, and Learning in the Networks and Mobility of Professional Women Migrant Carers in Cumbria." *Ethnography and Education* 3.1 (2008): 81–96. Print.

Cummins, Jim. "The Development of Bilingual Proficiency from Home to School: A Longitudinal Study of Portuguese-speaking Children." *Journal of Education* 173.2 (1991): 85–98. Print.

Cummins, Jim. *Negotiating Identities: Education for Empowerment in a Diverse Society*. 2nd ed. Los Angeles: California Association for Bilingual Education, 2001. Print.

Cummins, Jim. "A Proposal for Action: Strategies for Recognizing Heritage Language Competence as a Learning Resource within the Mainstream Classroom." *Modern Language Journal* 89.4 (2005): 585–92. Print.

Cushing Weigle, Sara. *Assessing Writing*. Cambridge: Cambridge University Press, 2002. Print.

Cushman, Ellen. *The Struggle and the Tools: Oral and Literate Strategies in an Inner City Community*. Albany: SUNY Press, 1998. Print.

Czaika, Mathias, and Hein de Haas. "The Globalization of Migration: Has the World Become More Migratory?" *International Migration Review* 48.2 (2014): 283–323. Print.

Davis, Diane. *Breaking Up (at) Totality*. Carbondale: Southern Illinois University Press, 2000. Print.

De Genova, Nicholas. "Conflicts of Mobility, and the Mobility of Conflict: Rightlessness, Presence, Subjectivity, Freedom." *Subjectivity* 29 (2009): 445–66. Print.

De Genova, Nicholas. "The Deportation Regime: Sovereignty, Space, and the Freedom of Movement." In *The Deportation Regime: Sovereignty, Space, and the Freedom of Movement*. Edited by Nicholas de Genova and Nathalie Peutz. Durham, NC: Duke University Press, 2010. 33–68. Print.

De Genova, Nicholas. "'We Are of the Connections': Migration, Methodological Nationalism, and 'Militant Research.'" *Postcolonial Studies* 16.3 (2013): 250–58. Print.

De Genova, Nicholas, and Nathalie Peutz, eds. *The Deportation Regime: Sovereignty, Space, and the Freedom of Movement*. Durham, NC: Duke University Press, 2010. Print.

Deleuze, Giles, and Felix Guattari. *A Thousand Plateaus: Capitalism and Schizophrenia*. Minneapolis: University of Minnesota Press, 1987.

DePalma, Michael-John, and Jeff M. Ringer. "Adaptive Transfer, Genre Knowledge, and Implications for Research and Pedagogy: A Response." *Journal of Second Language Writing* 22.4 (2013): 465–70. Print.

DePalma, Michael-John, and Jeff M. Ringer. "Toward a Theory of Adaptive Transfer: Expanding Disciplinary Discussions of 'Transfer' in Second-Language Writing and Composition Studies." *Journal of Second Language Writing* 20.2 (2011): 134–47. Print.

Dingo, Rebecca. *Networking Arguments: Rhetoric, Transnational Feminism, and Public Policy Writing.* Pittsburgh: University of Pittsburgh Press, 2012. Print.

Donahue, Christiane. "'Internationalization' and Composition Studies: Reorienting the Discourse." *College Composition and Communication* 61.2 (2009): 212–43. Print.

Donato, Katharine, and Donna Gabaccia. *Gender and International Migration.* New York: Russell Sage, 2015. Print.

Duffy, John. "Recalling the Letter: The Uses of Oral Testimony in Historical Studies of Literacy." *Written Communication* 24.1 (2007): 84–107. Print.

Elbow, Peter. "Inviting the Mother Tongue: Beyond 'Mistakes,' 'Bad English,' and 'Wrong Language.'" *Journal of Advanced Composition* 19.3 (1999): 359–88. Print.

Engle, Lauren B. *The World in Motion: Short Essays on Migration and Gender.* Geneva: International Organization for Migration, 2004. Print.

Farr, Marcia. *Rancheros in Chicagoacán: Language and Identity in a Transnational Community.* Austin: University of Texas Press, 2006. Print.

Farris, Sara. "Migrants' Regular Army of Labour: Gender Dimensions of the Impact of the Global Economic Crisis on Migrant Labor in Western Europe." *Sociological Review* 63.1 (2015): 121–43. Print.

Favell, Adrian. "Migration, Mobility, and Globaloney: Metaphors and Rhetoric in the Sociology of Globalization." *Global Networks* 1.4 (2001): 389–98. Print.

Ferguson, Charles A. "Diglossia." *Word* 15 (1959): 325–40. Print.

Firth, Alan. "The Discursive Accomplishment of Normality: On 'Linga Franca' English and Conversation Analysis." *Journal of Pragmatics* 26.2 (1996): 237–59. Print.

Fishman, Joshua A. "Bilingualism with and without Diglossia; Diglossia with and without Bilingualism." *Journal of Social Issues* 23.2 (1967): 29–38. Print.

Fishman, Joshua A. "Mother-tongue Claiming in the United States since 1960: Trends and Correlates." In *The Rise and Fall of the Ethnic Revival: Perspectives on Language and Ethnicity.* Edited by Joshua A. Fishman, Michael H. Gertner, Ester G. Lowy, and William G. Milan. Berlin: Mouton, 1985. 107–94. Print.

Fishman, Joshua A. "300-plus Years of Heritage Language Education in the United States." In *Heritage Languages in America: Blueprint for the Future.* Edited by Joy K. Peyton, Donald A. Ranard, and Scott McGinnis. Washington, D.C.: Center for Applied Linguistics/Delta Systems, 2001. 89–97. Print.

Foner, Nancy. *In a New Land: A Comparative View of Immigration.* New York: New York University Press, 2005. Print.

Franceschini, Rita. "Multilingualism and Multicompetence: A Conceptual View." *The Modern Language Journal* 95.3 (2011): 344–55. Print.

Bibliography

Frankenberg, Ruth, and Lata Mani. "Crosscurrents, Crosstalk: Race, 'Postcoloniality,' and the Politics of Location." In *Displacement, Diaspora, and Geographies of Identity*. Edited by Lavie Smadar and Ted Swedenburg. Durham, NC: Duke University Press, 1996. 292–310. Print.

Franquesa, Jaume. "'We've Lost Our Bearings': Place, Tourism, and the Limits of the Mobility Turn." *Antipode* 43.3 (2011): 1012–33. Print.

Friedman, Susan Stanford. "The 'New Migration': Clashes, Connections, and Diasporic Women's Writing." *Contemporary Women's Writing* 3.1 (2009): 6–27. Print.

Freitag, Ulrike, and Achim von Oppen, eds. *Translocality: The Study of Globalising Processes from a Southern Perspective*. Leiden: Brill, 2010. Print.

Gabaccia, Donna. *From the Other Side: Women, Gender, and Immigrant Life in the U.S., 1820–1990*. Bloomington: Indiana University Press, 1995. Print.

García, Ofelia. *Bilingual Education in the Twenty-first Century: A Global Perspective*. New York: Wiley and Blackwell, 2011. Print.

García, Ofelia. "Positioning Heritage Languages in the United States." *Modern Language Journal* 89.4 (2005): 601–605. Print.

García, Ofelia, and Li Wei. *Translanguaging: Language, Bilingualism, and Education*. New York: Palgrave Pivot, 2013. Print.

Gardner-Chloros, Penelope. *Code-switching*. Cambridge: Cambridge University Press, 2009. Print.

Gilyard, Keith. *Voice of the Self: A Study of Language Competence*. Detroit, MI: Wayne State University Press, 1991. Print.

Glaser, Barney, and Anselm Strauss. *The Discovery of Grounded Theory: Strategies for Qualitative Research*. Chicago: Aldine Publishing Company, 1967. Print.

Glick Schiller, Nina. "A Global Perspective on Transnational Migration: Theorizing Migration Without Methodological Nationalism." In *Diaspora and Transnationalism: Concepts, Theories, and Methods*. Edited by Rainer Baubock and Thomas Faist. Amsterdam: Amsterdam University Press, 2010. 109–29. Print.

Glick Schiller, Nina, and Noel Salazar. "Regimes of Mobility across the Globe." *Journal of Ethnic and Migration Studies* 39.2 (2013): 183–200. Print.

Glick Schiller, Nina, Linda Basch, and Cristina Szanton-Blanc. "From Immigrant to Transmigrant: Theorizing Transnational Migration." *Anthropological Quarterly* 68.1 (1995): 48–63. Print.

Glick Schiller, Nina, Linda Basch, and Cristina Szanton-Blanc. "Transnationalism: A New Analytic Framework for Understanding Migration." *Towards a Transnational Perspective on Migration: Race, Class, Ethnicity, and Nationalism*. Annals of the New York Academy of Sciences 645 (1992): 1–24. Print.

González, Norma, Luis C. Moll, and Cathy Amanti, eds. *Funds of Knowledge: Theorizing Practices in Households, Communities, and Classrooms*. Mahwah, NJ: Lawrence Erlbaum Associates, 2005. Print.

Gordon, Deborah. "Border Work: Feminist Ethnography and the Dissemination of Literacy." In *Women Writing Culture*. Edited by Ruth Behar and Deborah Gordon. Berkeley: University of California Press, 1995. 373–89. Print.

Graeber, David. *Toward an Anthropological Theory of Value: The False Coin of Our Own Dreams*. New York: Palgrave Macmillan, 2001. Print.

Graff, Harvey. *The Literacy Myth: Cultural Integration and Social Structure in the Nineteenth Century*. New Brunswick: Transaction Publishers, 1991. Print.

Grewal, Inderpal. *Home and Harem: Nation, Gender, Empire, and the Cultures of Travel*. Durham, NC: Duke University Press, 1996. Print.

Grujicic-Alatriste, L. "A Response to DePalma and Ringer's Article 'Toward a Theory of Adaptive Transfer: Expanding Disciplinary Discussions of "Transfer" in Second-Language Writing and Composition Studies.'" *Journal of Second Language Writing* 22.4 (2013): 460–64. Print.

Guerra, Juan. *Close to Home: Oral and Literate Practices in a Transnational Mexicano Community*. New York: Teachers College Press, 1998. Print.

Guerra, Juan. *Language, Culture, Identity, and Citizenship in College Classrooms and Communities*. New York: National Council of Teachers of English and Routledge, 2016. Print.

Guerra, Juan. "Putting Literacy in Its Place: Nomadic Consciousness and the Practice of Transcultural Repositioning." In *Norton Book of Composition Studies*. Edited by Susan Miller. New York: W. W. Norton and Company, 2009. 1643–53. Print.

Gumperz, John. *Discourse Strategies*. Cambridge: Cambridge University Press, 1982. Print.

Gumperz, John. "Introduction." In *Directions in Sociolinguistics: The Ethnography of Communication*. Edited by John Gumperz and Dell Hymes. New York: Holt, Rinehart, and Winston, 1972. 1–25. Print.

Gupta, Akhil, and James Ferguson. "Beyond 'Culture': Space, Identity, and the Politics of Difference." *Cultural Anthropology* 7.1 (1992): 6–23. Print.

Hall, Joan Kelly, An Cheng, and Matthew T. Carlson. "Reconceptualizing Multicompetence as a Theory of Language Knowledge." *Applied Linguistics* 27.2 (2006): 220–40. Print.

Hall, Matthew, Audrey Singer, Gordon F. De Jong, and Deborah Roempke Graefe. *The Geography of Immigrant Skills: Educational Profiles of Metropolitan Areas*. Washington, D.C.: Metropolitan Policy Program of the Brookings Institution, 2009. Print.

Hamp-Lyons, Liz, ed. *Assessing Second Language Writing in Academic Contexts*. Norwood, NJ: Ablex Publishing, 1991. Print.

Harding, Sandra. "Introduction: Is There a Feminist Method?" In *Feminism and Methodology: Social Science Issues*. Edited by Sandra Harding. Bloomington: Indiana University Press, 1987. 1–14. Print.

Hattori, Tomo, and Stuart Ching. "Reexamining the Between-Worlds Trope in Cross-Cultural Composition Studies." In *Representations: Doing Asian American*

Rhetoric. Edited by LuMing Mao and Morris Young. Logan: Utah State University Press, 2008. 41–61. Print.

Hawhee, Debra. "Kairotic Encounters." In *Perspectives on Rhetorical Invention*. Edited by Janet M. Atwill and Janice M. Lauer. Knoxville: University of Tennessee Press, 2002. 16–35. Print.

Held, David, Anthony McGrew, David Goldblatt, and Jonathan Perraton. *Global Transformations: Politics, Economics, and Culture*. Oxford: Polity Press, 1999. Print.

Heller, Monica. "Alternative Ideologies of 'la francophonie.'" *Journal of Sociolinguistics* 3.3 (1999): 336–59. Print.

Heller, Monica. *Codeswitching: Anthropological and Sociolinguistic Perspectives*. Berlin: Mouton de Gruyter, 1988. Print.

Heller, Monica. "The Commodification of Language." *Annual Review of Anthropology* 39 (2010): 101–14. Print.

Heller, Monica. "Globalization, the New Economy, and the Commodification of Language and Identity." *Journal of Sociolinguistics* 7.4 (2003): 473–92. Print.

Heller, Monica, and Alexandre Duchene. "Pride and Profit: Changing Discourses of Language, Capital, and Nation-State." In *Language in Late Capitalism: Pride and Profit*. Edited by Alexandre Duchene and Monica Heller. New York: Routledge, 2012. 1–21. Print.

Hernández-Zamora, Gregorio. *Decolonizing Literacy: Mexican Lives in the Era of Global Capitalism*. Clevedon, U.K.: Multilingual Matters, 2010. Print.

Hesford, Wendy. "Cosmopolitanism and the Geopolitics of Feminist Rhetoric." In *Rhetorica in Motion: Feminist Rhetorical Methods and Methodologies*. Edited by Eileen Schell and KJ Rawson. Pittsburgh: University of Pittsburgh Press, 2010. 53–70. Print.

Hesford, Wendy. *Framing Identities: Autobiography and the Politics of Pedagogy*. Minneapolis: University of Minnesota Press, 1999. Print.

Hesford, Wendy. "Global Turns and Cautions in Rhetoric and Composition Studies." *PMLA* 121.3 (2006): 787–801. Print.

Heyman, Josiah. "Ports of Entry as Nodes in the World System." *Identities: Global Studies in Culture and Power* 11.3 (2004) 303–27. Print.

Hornberger, Nancy. *Continua of Biliteracy: An Ecological Framework for Educational Policy, Research, and Practice in Multilingual Settings*. Clevedon, U.K.: Multilingual Matters, 2003. Print.

Horner, Bruce, and Min-Zhan Lu. "Toward a Labor Economy of Writing: Academic Frictions." In *Literacy, Economy, and Power: New Directions in Literacy Research*. Edited by Julie Nelson Christoph, John Duffy, Eli Goldblatt, Nelson Graff, Rebecca Nowacek, and Bryan Trabold. Carbondale: Southern Illinois University Press, 2014. 111–26. Print.

Horner, Bruce, Min-Zhan Lu, and Paul Kei Matsuda, eds. *Cross-Language Relations in Composition*. Carbondale: Southern Illinois University Press, 2010. Print.

Horner, Bruce, Min-Zhan Lu, Jacqueline Jones Royster, and John Trimbur. "Language Difference in Writing: Toward a Translingual Approach." *College English* 73.3 (2011): 303–21. Print.

Horner, Bruce, and John Trimbur. "English Only and U.S. College Composition." *College Composition and Communication* 53.4 (2002): 594–630.

Inoue, Asao, and Mya Poe, eds. *Race and Writing Assessment*. New York: Peter Lang, 2012. Print.

Jacquemet, Marco. "Transidiomatic Practices: Language and Power in the Age of Globalization." *Language and Communication* 25.3 (2005): 257–77. Print.

Jacobs, Andrew. "A Young Syrian Torchbearer Highlights Brazil's Embrace of Refugees." *New York Times*. August 5, 2016. www.nytimes.com/2016/08/06/world/americas/brazil-olympics-syria-refugee.html. Accessed August 6 2016. Web.

James, Mark A. "Cross-linguistic Influence and Transfer of Learning." In *Encyclopedia of the Sciences of Learning*. Edited by Norbert M. Seel. New York: Springer. 2012. 858–61. Print.

Jarvis, Scott, and Aneta Pavlenko. *Crosslinguistic Influence in Language and Cognition*. New York: Routledge, 2008. Print.

Jordan, Jay. *Redesigning Composition for Multilingual Realities*. Urbana, IL: National Council of Teachers of English, 2012. Print.

Kalmar, Tomas Mario. *Illegal Alphabets and Adult Biliteracy: Latino Migrants Crossing the Linguistic Border*. New York: Routledge, 2000. Print.

Kaplan, Robert B. "Contrastive Rhetoric and Second Language Learning: Notes towards a Theory of Contrastive Rhetoric." In *Writing across Languages and Cultures*. Edited by Alex C. Purves. Newbury Park, CA: Sage Publications, 1988. 275–304. Print.

Karakayali, Serhat, and Enrica Rigo. "Mapping the European Space of Circulation." In *The Deportation Regime: Sovereignty, Space, and the Freedom of Movement*. Edited by Nicholas de Genova and Nathalie Peutz. Durham, NC: Duke University Press, 2010. 123–44. Print.

Kearney, Michael. "The Local and the Global: The Anthropology of Globalization and Transnationalism." *Annual Review of Anthropology* 24 (1995): 547–65. Print.

Keddy, Barbara, Sharon Sims, and Phyllis Noerager Stern. "Grounded Theory as Feminist Research Methodology." *Journal of Advanced Nursing* 23.3 (1996): 448–53. Print.

Kell, Catherine. "Crossing the Margins: Literacy, Semiotics, and the Recontextualisation of Meanings." In *Travel Notes from the New Literacy Studies: Instances of Practice*. Edited by Kate Pahl and Jennifer Rowsell. Clevedon, U.K.: Multilingual Matters, 2006. 147–64. Print.

Kell, Catherine. "Inequalities and Crossings: Literacy and the Spaces-in-Between." *International Journal of Educational Development* 31.6 (2011): 606–13. Print.

Kellerman, Eric, and Michael Sharwood Smith. *Crosslinguistic Influence in Second Language Acquisition*. New York: Pearson College Division, 1986. Print.

Kellman, Steven. *Switching Languages: Translingual Writers Reflect on Their Craft.* Lincoln: University of Nebraska Press, 2003. Print.

Kellman, Steven. *The Translingual Imagination.* Lincoln: University of Nebraska Press, 2000. Print.

Kells, Michelle H., Valerie Balester, and Victor Villanueva, eds. *Latino/a Discourses: On Language, Identity, and Literacy Education.* New York: Heinemann, 2004. Print.

Kesler Rumsey, Suzanne. "Heritage Literacy: Adoption, Adaptation, and Alienation of Multimodal Literacy Tools." *College Composition and Communication* 60.3 (2009): 573–86. Print.

Kramsch, Claire. *The Multilingual Subject.* Oxford: Oxford University Press, 2009. Print.

Lagman, Eileen. "Moving Labor: Transnational Migrant Workers and Affective Literacies of Care." *Literacy in Composition Studies* 3.3 (2015): no pagination. http://licsjournal.org/OJS/index.php/LiCS/article/view/95. Accessed December 14, 2015. Web.

Lam, Wan Shun Eva. "Multiliteracies on Instant Messaging in Negotiating Local, Translocal, and Transnational Affiliations: A Case of an Adolescent Immigrant." *Reading Research Quarterly* 44.4 (2009): 377–97. Print.

Lam, Wan Shun Eva, and Doris Warriner. "Transnationalism and Literacy: Investigating the Mobility of People, Languages, Texts, and Practices in Contexts of Migration." *Reading Research Quarterly* 47.2 (2012): 191–215. Print.

Lavie, Smadar, and Ted Swedenburg, eds. *Displacement, Diaspora, and Geographies of Identity.* Durham, NC: Duke University Press, 2001. Print.

Leki, Ilona. "Coping Strategies of ESL Students in Writing Tasks across the Curriculum." *TESOL Quarterly* 29.2 (1995): 235–60. Print.

Leki, Ilona. "Living through College Literacy: Nursing in a Second Language." *Written Communication* 20.1 (2003) 81–98. Print.

Leung, Constant, Roxy Harris, and Ben Rampton. "The Idealised Native Speaker, Reified Ethnicities, and Classroom Realities." *TESOL Quarterly* 31.3 (1997) 543–60. Print.

Levitt, Peggy. *The Transnational Villagers.* Berkeley: University of California Press, 2001. Print.

Levitt, Peggy, and Sanjeev Khagram. *The Transnational Studies Reader.* New York: Routledge, 2007. Print.

Lillis, Theresa. "Ethnography as Method, Methodology, and 'Deep Theorizing': Closing the Gap between Text and Context in Academic Writing Research." *Written Communication* 25.3 (2008) 353–88. Print.

Lillis, Theresa. *The Sociolinguistics of Writing.* Edinburgh: Edinburgh University Press, 2013. Print.

Lillis, Theresa, and Mary Jane Curry. *Academic Writing in a Global Context: The Politics and Practices of Publishing in English.* New York: Routledge, 2010. Print.

Liu, Jun. "Writing from Chinese to English: My Cultural Transformation." In *Reflections on Multiliterate Lives*. Edited by Diane Belcher and Ulla Connor. Clevedon, U.K.: Multilingual Matters, 2001. 121–31. Print.

Liu, Lydia. *Translingual Practice: Literature, National Culture, and Translated Modernity—China, 1900–1937*. Stanford, CA: Stanford University Press, 1995. Print.

LoCastro, Virginia. "'Long Sentences and Floating Commas': Mexican Students' Rhetorical Practices and the Sociocultural Context." In *Contrastive Rhetoric: Reaching to Intercultural Rhetoric*. Edited by Ulla Connor, Ed Nagelhout, and William V. Rozycki. Philadelphia: John Benjamins Publishing, 2008. 195–218. Print.

Lorimer Leonard, Rebecca. "Multilingual Writing as Rhetorical Attunement." *College English* 76.1 (2014): 227–47. Print.

Lorimer Leonard, Rebecca. "Traveling Literacies: Multilingual Writing on the Move." *Research in the Teaching of English* 48.1 (2013): 13–39. Print.

Lorimer Leonard, Rebecca. "Writing through Bureaucracy: Migrant Correspondence and Managed Mobility." *Written Communication* 32.1 (2015): 87–113. Print.

Lu, Min-Zhan. "An Essay on the Work of Composition: Composing English against the Order of Fast Capitalism." *College Composition and Communication*. Urbana, IL: National Council of Teachers of English, 2004. 16–50. Print.

Lu, Min-Zhan. "Living-English Work." *College English* 68.6 (2006): 605–18. Print.

Lu, Min-Zhan. "Metaphors Matter: Transcultural Literacy." *Journal of Advanced Composition* 29.1–2 (2009): 285–93. Print.

Lu, Min-Zhan. "Professing Multiculturalism: The Politics of Style in the Contact Zone." *College Composition and Communication* 45.4 (1994): 442–58. Print.

Lu, Min-Zhan, and Bruce Horner. "Translingual Literacy, Language Difference, and Matters of Agency." *College English* 75.6 (2013): 586–611.

Lüdi, Georges. "Multilingual Repertoires and the Consequences for Linguistic Theory." In *Beyond Misunderstanding: Linguistic Analyses of Intercultural Communication*. Edited by Kristin Bührig and Jan D. ten Thije. John Benjamins, 2006. 11–42. Print.

Luke, Allan. "Genres of Power? Literacy Education and the Production of Capital." In *Literacy in Society: Language Description and Language Education*. Edited by Rugalya Hasan and Geoffrey Williams. New York: Longman, 1996. 308–38. Print.

Luke, Allan. *Literacy, Textbooks, and Ideology: Postwar Literacy Instruction and the Mythology of Dick and Jane*. Bristol, PA: Taylor and Francis, 1988. Print.

Luke, Allan. "On the Material Consequences of Literacy." *Language and Education* 18.4 (2004): 331–35. Print.

Luke, Allan, and Victoria Carrington. "Globalisation, Literacy, Curriculum Practice." In *The Routledge Falmer Reader in Language and Literacy*. Edited by Teresa Grainger. New York: Routledge, 2004. 52–66. Print.

Luke, Allen, Carmen Luke, and Philip Graham. "Globalization, Corporatism, and Critical Language Education." *International Multilingual Research Journal* 1.1 (2007): 1–13. Print.

Mahler, Sarah J., and Patricia R. Pessar. "Gender Matters: Ethnographers Bring Gender from the Periphery toward the Core of Migration Studies." *International Migration Review* 40.1 (2006) 27–63. Print.

Makoni, Sinfree, and Alastair Pennycook. *Disinventing and Reconstituting Languages.* Clevedon, U.K.: Multilingual Matters, 2007. Print.

Manderscheid, Katharina. "Unequal Mobilities." In *Mobilities and Inequality.* Edited by Timo Ohnmacht, Hanja Maksim, and Manfred Max Bergman. Burlington, VT: Ashgate Publishing Company, 2009. 27–50. Print.

Margolis, Maxine. "From Mistress to Servant: Downward Mobility among Brazilian Immigrants in New York City." *Urban Anthropology* 19.3 (1990): 215–31. Print.

Martin-Jones, Marilyn, and Kathryn Jones, eds. *Multilingual Literacies: Reading and Writing Different Worlds.* Philadelphia: John Benjamins Publishing, 2000. Print.

Marx, Karl. *Capital: A Critique of Political Economy,* vol. 2, London: Penguin Classics, 1993. Print.

Massey, Doreen. *Space, Place, and Gender.* Minneapolis: University of Minnesota Press, 1994. Print.

Matsuda, Aya, and Paul Kei Matsuda. "Globalizing Writing Studies: The Case of U.S. Technical Communication Textbooks." *Written Communication* 28.2 (2011): 172–92. Print.

Matsuda, Paul Kei. "Identity in Written Discourse." *Annual Review of Applied Linguistics* 35 (2015): 140–59. Print.

Matsuda, Paul Kei. "It's the Wild West out There: A New Linguistic Frontier in U.S. College Composition." In *Literacy as Translingual Practice: Between Communities and Classrooms.* Edited by Suresh Canagarajah. New York: Routledge, 2013. 133–35. Print.

Matsuda, Paul Kei. "The Lure of Translingual Writing." *PMLA* 129.3 (2014): 478–83. Print.

Matsuda, Paul Kei. "The Myth of Linguistic Homogeneity in U.S. College Composition." *College English* 68.6 (2006): 637–51. Print.

Menard-Warwick, Julia. "'The Thing about Work': Gendered Narratives of a Transnational, Trilingual Mexicano." *International Journal of Bilingual Education and Bilingualism* 9.3 (2006): 359–73. Print.

Menken, Kate. *English Learners Left Behind: Standardized Testing as Language Policy.* Clevedon, U.K.: Multilingual Matters, 2008. Print.

Merriam, Sharan. *Qualitative Research in Practice: Examples for Discussion and Analysis.* San Francisco: Jossey-Bass, 2002. Print.

Meyers, Susan. *Del Otro Lado: Literacy and Migration across the U.S.-Mexico Border.* Carbondale: Southern Illinois University Press, 2014.

Mezzadra, Sandro, and Brett Neilson. *Border as Method, or, the Multiplication of Labor.* Durham, NC: Duke University Press, 2013. Print.

Mihut, Ligia. "Literacy Brokers and the Emotional Work of Mediation." *Literacy in Composition Studies* 2.1 (2014): no pagination. http://licsjournal.org/OJS/index.php/LiCS/article/view/42. Accessed December 14, 2015. Web.

Mohanty, Chandra. "Feminist Encounters: Locating the Politics of Experience." In *Social Postmodernism: Beyond Identity Politics*. Edited by Linda Nicholson and Steven Seidman. Cambridge: Cambridge University Press, 1995. 68–86. Print.

Mojab, Shahrzad. "The Power of Economic Globalization: Deskilling Immigrant Women through Training." In *Power in Practice: Adult Education and the Struggle for Knowledge and Power in Society*. Edited by Ronald Cervero and Arthur Wilson. San Francisco: Jossey-Bass, 2001. 23–41. Print.

Moll, Luis C., Cathy Amanti, Deborah Neff, and Norma Gonzalez. "Funds of Knowledge for Teaching: Using a Qualitative Approach to Connect Homes and Classrooms." *Theory Into Practice* 31.2 (1992) 132–41. Print.

Moya, José C., and Adam McKeown. "World Migration in the Long Twentieth Century." In *Essays on Twentieth Century History*. Edited by Michael Adas. Philadelphia: Temple University Press, 2010. 9–52. Print.

Munn, Nancy. *The Fame of Gawa*. Cambridge: Cambridge University Press, 1986. Print.

Myers-Scotton, Carol. *Social Motivations for Codeswitching: Evidence from Africa*. Oxford: Clarendon, 1993. Print.

Naples, Nancy. *Feminism and Method: Ethnography, Discourse Analysis, and Activist Research*. New York: Routledge, 2003. Print.

"Nascent Journal" *National Public Radio*. June 20, 2016. www.npr.org/2016/06/20/482750891/nascent-journal-to-help-refugees-preserve-and-publish-their-research. Accessed August 6, 2016. Web.

Nero, Shondel. "Language, Identities, and ESL Pedagogy." *Language and Education* 19.3 (2005): 194–211. Print.

Norton, Bonny. *Identity and Language Learning: Gender, Ethnicity, and Educational Change*. New York: Longman, 2000. Print.

Nowacek, Rebecca. *Agents of Integration: Understanding Transfer as a Rhetorical Act*. Carbondale: Southern Illinois University Press, 2011. Print.

Nunley, Vorris. "From the Harbor to da Academic Hood: Hush Harbors and an African American Rhetorical Tradition." In *African American Rhetoric(s): Interdisciplinary Perspectives*. Edited by Elaine B. Richardson and Ronald L. Jackson II. Carbondale: Southern Illinois University Press, 2004. 221–41. Print.

"Olympic Torch Relay." www.olympic.org/olympic-torch-relay. Accessed August 6, 2016. Web.

Ong, Aihwa. *Flexible Citizenship: The Cultural Logics of Transnationality*. Durham, NC: Duke University Press, 1999. Print.

Organisation for Economic Co-operation and Development (OECD). "Recent Changes in Migration Movements and Policies (Country Notes): United States." In *Inter-

national Migration Outlook: SOPEMI 2010. Paris: OECD. www.scribd.com/document/217370374/OECD-Migration-Outlook-2010. Accessed April 17, 2012. Web.

Otsuji, Emi, and Alastair Pennycook. "Metrolingualism: Fixity, Fluidity, and Language in Flux." *International Journal of Multilingualism* 7.3 (2010): 240–54. Print.

Pahl, Kate, and Jennifer Rowsell, eds. *Travel Notes from the New Literacy Studies: Instances of Practice.* Clevedon, U.K.: Multilingual Matters, 2006. Print.

Papastergiadis, Nikos. *The Turbulence of Migration: Globalization, Deterritorialization, and Hybridity.* Cambridge: Blackwell Publishers, 2000. Print.

Papen, Uta. *Literacy and Globalization: Reading and Writing in Times of Social and Cultural Change.* New York: Routledge, 2012. Print.

Pandey, Iswari. *South Asian in the Mid-South: Migrations of Literacies.* Pittsburgh: University of Pittsburgh Press, 2015. Print.

Park, Joseph Sung-Yul, and Lionel Wee. *Markets of English: Linguistic Capital and Language Policy in a Globalizing World.* New York: Routledge, 2012. Print.

Pennycook, Alastair. *Global Englishes and Transcultural Flows.* New York: Routledge, 2007. Print.

Pennycook, Alastair. *Language as a Local Practice.* New York: Routledge, 2010. Print.

Perryman-Clark, Staci, David E. Kirkland, and Austin Jackson, eds. *Students' Right to Their Own Language: A Critical Sourcebook.* New York: Bedford/St. Martin's, 2014. Print.

Phillion, Joann. "Obstacles to Accessing the Teaching Profession for Immigrant Women." *Multicultural Education* 11.1 (2003): 41–45. Print.

Piller, Ingrid. *Linguistic Diversity and Social Justice: An Introduction to Applied Sociolinguistics.* New York: Oxford University Press, 2016. Print.

Plummer, Marilyn, and Lynne Young. "Grounded Theory and Feminist Inquiry: Revitalizing Links to the Past." *Western Journal of Nursing Research* 32.2 (2010): 305–21. Print.

Portes, Alejandro. "Theoretical Convergencies and Empirical Evidence in the Study of Immigrant Transnationalism." *International Migration Review* 37.3 (2003): 874–92. Print.

Portes, Alejandro, Luis E. Guarnizo, and Patricia Landolt. "The Study of Transnationalism: Pitfalls and Promise of an Emergent Research Field." *Ethnic and Racial Studies* 22.2 (1999): 217–37. Print.

Pratt, Geraldine. *Working Feminism.* Philadelphia: Temple University, 2004. Print.

Prendergast, Catherine. *Buying into English: Language and Investment in the New Capitalist World.* Pittsburgh: University of Pittsburgh Press, 2008. Print.

Prior, Paul. "Combining Phenomenological and Sociohistoric Frameworks for Studying Literate Practices." In *Literacy, Economy, and Power: Writing and Research after Literacy in American Lives.* Edited by John Duffy, Julie N. Christoph, Eli Goldblatt, Nelson Graff, Rebecca S. Nowacek, and Bryan Trabold. Carbondale: Southern Illinois University Press, 2014. Print.

Ramdas, Lalita. "Women and Literacy: A Quest for Justice." In *Literacy: A Critical Sourcebook*. Edited by Ellen Cushman, Eugene Kintgen, Barry Kroll, and Mike Rose. Boston: Bedford/St. Martin's, 2001. 629–43. Print.

Rampton, Ben. *Crossing: Language and Ethnicity among Adolescents*. Boston: Addison Wesley, 1995. Print.

Rampton, Ben. "Displacing the 'Native Speaker': Expertise, Affiliation, and Inheritance." *ELT Journal* 44.2 (1990): 97–101. Print.

Reidner, Rachel. *Writing Neoliberal Values: Rhetorical Connectivities and Globalized Capitalism*. New York: Palgrave Macmillan, 2015. Print.

Reynolds, Nedra. *Geographies of Writing*. Carbondale: Southern Illinois University Press, 2004. Print.

Reynolds, Nedra. "Who's Going to Cross This Border? Travel Metaphors, Material Conditions, and Contested Places." *Journal of Advanced Composition* 20.3 (2000): 541–64. Print.

Richardson Bruna, Katherine. "Traveling Tags: The Informal Literacies of Mexican Newcomers in and out of the Classroom." *Linguistics and Education* 18 (2007): 232–57. Print.

Ritchie, Joy. "Confronting the 'Essential' Problem: Reconnecting Feminist Theory and Pedagogy." In *Feminism and Composition: A Critical Sourcebook*. Edited by Gesa Kirsch et al. New York: Bedford/St. Martin's, 2003. 79–102. Print.

Roberge, Mark, Linda Harklau, and Meryl Siegal, eds. *Generation 1.5 in College Composition: Teaching ESL to U.S.-Educated Learners of ESL*. New York: Routledge, 2009. Print.

Robinson-Pant, Anna. "Women's Literacy and Health: Can an Ethnographic Researcher Find the Links?" In *Literacy and Development: Ethnographic Perspectives*. Edited by Brian Street. New York: Routledge, 2001. 152–70. Print.

Rose, Mike. *The Mind at Work*. New York: Penguin, 2005. Print.

Rounsaville, Angela. "Genre Repertoires from Below: How One Writer Built and Moved a Writing Life across Generations, Borders, and Communities." *Research in the Teaching of English* 51.3 (2017): 317–40. Print.

Rounsaville, Angela. "Situating Transnational Genre Knowledge: A Genre Trajectory Analysis of One Student's Personal and Academic Writing." *Written Communication* 31.3 (2014): 332–64. Print.

Rouse, Richard. "Mexican Migration and the Social Space of Postmodernism." *Diaspora: A Journal of Transnational Studies* 1.1 (1991): 8–23. Print.

Rudby, Rani, and Peter Tan, eds. *Language as Commodity: Global Structures, Local Marketplaces*. New York: Continuum, 2008. Print.

Sadeghi, Shiva. "Gender, Culture, and Learning: Iranian Immigrant Women in Canadian Higher Education." *International Journal of Lifelong Education* 27.2 (2008): 217–34. Print.

Said, Edward. "Traveling Theory." In *The World, the Text, and the Critic*. Cambridge, MA: Harvard University Press, 1983. 226–47. Print.

Salazar, Noel B. "The Power of the Imagination in Transnational Mobilities." *Identities: Global Studies in Culture and Power* 18.6 (2011): 576–98. Print.

Sarroub, Loukia. *All American Yemeni Girls: Being Muslim in a Public School*. Philadelphia: University of Pennsylvania Press, 2005. Print.

Schiffrin, Deborah. *Approaches to Discourse*. Oxford: Blackwell, 1994. Print.

Scollon, Ron. *Mediated Discourse: The Nexus of Practice*. New York: Routledge, 2001. Print.

Scribner, Sylvia and Michael Cole. "Unpackaging Literacy." In *Literacy: A Critical Sourcebook*. Edited by Ellen Cushman, Eugene R. Kintgen, Barry M. Kroll, and Mike Rose. Boston: Bedford/St. Martin's, 2001. 123–37. Print.

Shamir, Ronen. "Without Borders? Notes on Globalization as a Mobility Regime." *Sociological Theory* 23.2 (2005): 197–217. Print.

Sheller, Mimi, and John Urry. "The New Mobilities Paradigm." *Environment and Planning* 38.2 (2006): 207–26. Print.

Shohamy, Elana. "Assessing Multilingual Competencies: Adopting Construct Valid Assessment Policies." *Modern Language Journal* 95.3 (2011): 418–29. Print.

Shuck, Gail. "Language Identity, Agency, and Context: The Shifting Meanings of *Multilingual*." In *Reinventing Identities in Second Language Writing*. Edited by Michelle Cox, Jay Jordan, Christina Ortmeier-Hooper, and Gwen Schwartz. Urbana, IL: National Council of Teachers of English, 2010. 117–38. Print.

Shuck, Gail. "Racializing the Nonnative English Speaker." *Journal of Language, Identity, and Education* 5.4 (2006): 259–76. Print.

Smith, Michael P., and Luis E. Guarnizo, eds. *Transnationalism from Below*. New Brunswick, NJ: Transaction Publishers, 1998. Print.

Spivak, Gayatri. *A Critique of Postcolonial Reason: Toward a History of the Vanishing Present*. Cambridge, MA: Harvard University Press, 1999. Print.

Sreeharsha, Kavitha. "Reforming America's Immigration Laws: A Woman's Struggle." In *Immigration Policy Center Special Report*. Washington, D.C.: American Immigration Council. June 2010. Print.

Stein, Pippa, and Lynne Slominsky. "An Eye on the Text and an Eye on the Future: Multimodal Literacy in Three Johannesburg Families." In *Travel Notes from the New Literacy Studies: Instances of Practice*. Edited by Kate Pahl and Jennifer Rowsell. Clevedon, U.K.: Multilingual Matters, 2006. 118–46. Print.

Street, Brian. *Literacy and Development: Ethnographic Perspectives*. London: Routledge, 2001. Print.

Street, Brian. *Social Literacies: Critical Approaches to Literacy in Development, Ethnography, and Education*. New York: Longman, 1995. Print.

Street, Brian. "What's 'New' in New Literacy Studies? Critical Approaches to Literacy in Theory and Practice." *Current Issues in Comparative Education* 5.2 (2003): 77–91. Print.

Stroud, Christopher, and Sibonile Mpendukana. "Towards a Material Ethnography of Linguistic Landscape: Multilingualism, Mobility, and Space in a South African Township." *Journal of Sociolinguistics* 13.3 (2009): 363–86. Print.

Suárez-Orozco, Marcelo. "Everything You Ever Wanted To Know about Assimilation but Were Afraid To Ask." In *The New Immigration: An Interdisciplinary Reader*. Edited by Marcelo Suárez-Orozco, Carola Suárez-Orozco, and Desiree Qin-Hilliard. New York: Routledge, 2005. 67–84. Print.

Suárez-Orozco, Marcelo. "Right Moves? Immigration, Globalization, Utopia, Dystopia." In *The New Immigration: An Interdisciplinary Reader*. Edited by Marcelo Suárez-Orozco, Carola Suárez-Orozco, and Desiree Qin-Hilliard. New York: Routledge, 2005. 3–20. Print.

Suárez-Orozco, Marcelo, Carola Suárez-Orozco, and Desiree Qin-Hilliard, eds. *The New Immigration: An Interdisciplinary Reader*. New York: Routledge, 2005. Print.

Tardy, Christine. "Enacting and Transforming Local Language Policies." *College Composition and Communication* 62.4 (2011): 634–61. Print.

Taylor, Denny. "Family Literacy: Conservation and Change in the Transmission of Literacy Styles and Values." In *Language and Literacy in Social Practice*. Edited by Janet Maybin. Clevedon, U.K.: Multilingual Matters, 1994. 58–72. Print.

Torpey, John. *The Invention of the Passport: Surveillance, Citizenship, and the State*. Cambridge: Cambridge University Press, 1999. Print.

"Translingual Work in Composition" (special issue) *College English* 78.3 (2016). Print.

Trimbur, John. "Composition and the Circulation of Writing." *College Composition and Communication* 52.2 (2000): 188–219. Print.

Trimbur, John. "Linguistic Memory and the Politics of U.S. English" *College English* 68.6 (2006): 575-88. Print.

Turner, Bryan S. "The Enclave Society: Towards a Sociology of Immobility." *European Journal of Social Theory* 10.2 (2007): 287–303. Print.

Tusting, Karin, Rosalind Ivanic, and Anita Wilson. "New Literacy Studies at the Interchange." In *Situated Literacies: Reading and Writing in Context*. Edited by David Barton, Mary Hamilton, and Rosalind Ivanic. London: Routledge, 2000. 210–18. Print.

Tsing, Anna Lowenhaupt. *Friction: An Ethnography of Global Connection*. Princeton, NJ: Princeton University Press, 2005. Print.

United States Census Bureau. *2010 American Community Survey*. www.census.gov/programs-surveys/acs/. Accessed April 2, 2012. Web.

Urry, John. *Mobilities*. Cambridge, MA: Polity Press, 2007. Print.

Valdés, Guadalupe. "Bilingualism, Heritage Language Learners, and SLA Research: Opportunities Lost or Seized?" *Modern Language Journal* 89.3 (2005): 410–26. Print.

Valdés, Guadalupe. "Heritage Language Students: Profiles and Possibilities." In *Heritage Languages in America: Preserving a National Resource*. Edited by Joy K. Peyton, Donald A. Ranard, and Scott McGinnis. McHenry, IL: Center for Applied Linguistics and Delta Systems, 2001. 37–80. Print.

Valenzuela, Angela. *Subtractive Schooling: U.S.-Mexican Youth and the Politics of Caring*. Albany: SUNY Press, 1999. Print.

Vertovec, Steven. "Super-Diversity and Its Implications." *Ethnic and Racial Studies* 30.6 (2007):1024–54. Print.

Vieira, Kate. *American by Paper: How Documents Matter in Immigrant Literacy*. London: University of Minnesota Press, 2016. Print.

Vieira, Kate. "Doing Transnational Writing Studies." *Composition Studies* 44.1 (2016): 138–40. Print.

Vieira, Kate. "On the Social Consequences of Literacy." *Literacy in Composition Studies* 1.1 (2013): 26–32. http://licsjournal.org/OJS/index.php/LiCS/article/view/7/. Accessed June 14, 2014. Web.

Vieira, Kate. "Undocumented in a Documentary Society: Textual Borders and Transnational Religious Literacies." *Written Communication* 28.4 (2011): 436–61. Print.

Villanueva, Victor. *Bootstraps: From an American Academic of Color*. Urbana, IL: National Council of Teachers of English, 1993. Print.

Waldinger, Roger. *The Cross-Border Connection: Immigrants, Emigrants, and Their Homelands*. Cambridge: Harvard University Press, 2015. Print.

Warriner, Doris. "'The Days Now Is Very Hard for My Family': The Negotiation and Construction of Gendered Work Identities among Newly Arrived Women Refugees." *Journal of Language, Identity, and Education* 3.4 (2004): 279–94. Print.

Warriner, Doris. "Multiple Literacies and Identities: The Experiences of Two Women Refugees." *Women's Studies Quarterly* 32.1/2 (2004): 179–95. Print.

Wee, Lionel. "Linguistic Instrumentalism in Singapore." *Journal of Multilingual and Multicultural Development* 24.3 (2003): 211–24. Print.

Wingard, Jen. *Branded Bodies, Rhetoric, and the Neoliberal Nation-State*. New York: Lexington Books, 2012. Print.

Wong Fillmore, Lily. "When Learning a Second Language Means Losing the First." *Early Childhood Research Quarterly* 6.3 (1991): 323–46. Print.

Wuest, Judith. "Feminist Grounded Theory: An Exploration of the Congruency and Tensions between Two Traditions in Knowledge Discovery." *Qualitative Health Research* 5.1 (1995): 125–37. Print.

Yancey, Kathleen, Liane Robertson, and Kara Taczak. *Writing across Contexts: Transfer, Composition, and Sites of Writing*. Logan: Utah State University Press, 2014. Print.

Yenika-Agbaw, Vivan. "Textbooks, Literacy, and Citizenship: The Case of Anglophone Cameroon." *Research in the Teaching of English* 50.4 (2016): 378–99.

Yildiz, Yasemin. *Beyond the Mother Tongue: The Postmonolingual Condition*. New York: Fordham University Press, 2012. Print.

You, Xiaoye. "Ideology, Textbooks, and the Rhetoric of Production in China." *College Composition and Communication* 56.4 (2005): 632–53. Print.
Young, Morris. *Minor Re/Visions: Asian American Literacy Narratives as a Rhetoric of Citizenship.* Carbondale: Southern Illinois University Press, 2004. Print.
Young, Vershawn Ashanti. *Your Average Nigga: Performing Race, Literacy, and Masculinity.* Detroit, MI: Wayne State University Press, 2007. Print.
Zelizer, Viviana. *Economic Lives: How Culture Shapes the Economy.* Princeton, NJ: Princeton University Press, 2013. Print.

INDEX

accent, 8, 49, 55, 76, 83, 117, 126, 131; attitudes toward, 4, 5, 6, 30; in English, 56, 82, 111; -free speech, 94, 116; as a liability, 9, 110, 119, 125, 126; written, 64, 120, 121

accreditation organizations, 106, 107, 120. *See also* credentials

Alandra, 64, 73, 126, 129, 131, 132, 135, 153n14; and literacy relays, 45–46; and multilingual resources, 99; and writing, 103–4

Aldene, 50–51, 74–75, 95, 128, 129, 135, 154n7; in Argentina, 62–63; in Brazil, 71; and English-only assumptions, 72; literacy strategies and, 55; and loss, 77, 83; and school, 95

Algeria, 86, 87, 88, 90, 100, 129, 135

Alicia, 73, 124–27, 130–32, 135, 154n7; and Arabic, 38, 47; in Argentina, 34, 38–41, 47, 52, 64, 72–73; and audience, 40–41, 52, 72–73; and language processes, 51–52; and literacy relays, 45, 47, 51–54, 64; and literate repertoire, 34, 39, 40, 64, 124; and multilingual mess, 44, 61, 62, 76, 95–96; and Spanish, 74–75, 132, 153n14; and TOEFL, 103, 117; and writing conventions, 57, 103–4

American English, 80, 120, 124

Americans: African, 10; Arab, 49; Brazilian, 45; monolingual, 62; Muslim-Jordanian-, 49; in Quran study groups, 63

Andrea, 131, 135

Arabic language, 35–36, 48, 51, 69, 95, 135; Alicia and, 38, 47; Faridah and, 86–88; Haneen and, 49, 63; Ishtar and, 77–78

Arab Spring, 35, 86

Argentina, 135; Aldene and, 62; Alicia and, 34, 38–40, 47, 52, 64, 72–73

audience, awareness of, 40–41, 52, 57, 72–73, 95, 127

Azerbaijan, 34, 59–60, 64, 97, 135

Azerbaijani English Teachers Association (AzETA), 60, 61, 153n11

Azerbaijani language, 36–37, 60, 104, 135

Azeri language, 59, 60

AzETA. See Azerbaijani English Teachers Association (AzETA)

babysitting, 100, 114

Belarus, 66, 68

bilingual education, 38, 50, 52, 55, 96, 115, 130; banned, 155n5

bilingualism, 7, 20, 46, 94, 107, 117, 126, 143n2, 152n1; additive, 96, 115; and multilingualism, 143n2; participants and, 23, 50, 51, 54, 55, 64, 71, 112; Spanish-English, 9, 95–96

bounded: analysis, 28; domains, 75; language, 147n18, 152n4; states, 68

Brazil, 38, 45, 46, 50, 71, 74, 83, 123, 135
British Council, the, 60, 101

China, 47, 97, 105, 106, 107, 120, 121, 135
Chinese language, 9, 47, 56, 105
code-meshing, 37–38, 152n4
code-mixing, 37, 152n3
code-switching, 37–38, 41, 152n1, 152n3, 152n4; models, 69
coding, 27–29, 30, 141–42, 150n18
college courses, 103, 110, 114
Colombia, 32, 54, 56, 57, 129, 136
colonialism, 15, 42, 48, 50, 129, 130; post-, 101, 108, 151n20
credentials, 20, 128; lost, 22, 105, 106, 110, 131

Defne, 25, 47, 81, 94–95, 120, 127, 135; Faridah and, 85, 88, 89–90; literacy history, 79–82; literate repertoire, 35, 37–38, 44; and literate valuation, 95, 99, 131; and multilingualism, 79–83; in Turkey, 90–91, 101; and Turkish, 35, 38, 47, 62, 68–69; writing practices, 62, 68, 69, 73, 80, 132
deportation, 6, 11, 82, 128
de-skilling, 22, 23, 88
dictionary use, 36–37, 61, 77, 98
digital literacy: class blogs, 102; e-mails, 3, 24, 69, 80, 84, 96–97, 139; Facebook, 35, 36, 69. *See also* texting
diglossia, 69–70, 154n4
displacement, 39, 147n14, 151n20, 155n4

ELL. *See* language teaching, ELL
e-mails. *See* digital literacy, e-mails
English language, 47–48, 52, 94, 97, 120; acquisition, 14, 78; education, 22, 42, 52, 129, 95, 153n14; essay writing, 53, 103; learning, 46, 60, 86; literacies, 64, 111; reading, 54, 95; skills, 23, 30, 125; writing, 101, 102, 103, 109
ESL. *See* language teaching, ESL
ESP. *See* language teaching, ESP
essays, 24, 69, 102, 104, 106, 127; ACT, 114; personal, 82; testing, 43
essay writing, 39, 42, 51, 52–53, 57; Alandra and, 103–4; citation practices in, 50; Defne and, 80; English language, 53, 102–3; Faridah and, 87, 132; Nimet and, 78–79, 104; in Urdu, 76. *See also* writing

Facebook. *See* digital literacy, Facebook
Faridah, 25, 59, 87–90, 125, 127, 129, 135; and Arabic, 51, 86; and literate repertoire, 62, 68, 100; literate values, 32, 59, 95; writing in English, 55, 132
feminist analysis, 28–31, 151n22
French, 9, 38, 86, 87, 129, 135

Generation 1.5, 102, 131
Georgia, 66, 68
German language, 79–80, 135, 136
Germany, 80, 135, 136
globalization, 11, 13, 48, 83, 94, 107, 120, 123; definition of the term, 145–46n13; in interview questions, 139; and literacy, 129, 130, 133; and regimes of mobility, 128. *See also* transnationalism
global organizations, 61, 121
grounded theory, 27, 29, 152n24
Guatemala, 74, 129, 136

Haneen, 25, 63, 64, 90, 129, 130, 135; and literate fluidity, 32, 35–36, 49
Harriet, 102, 131, 135
Hebrew language, 34, 38, 135
Hindi language, 3, 36, 41, 42, 108, 111, 136

Index

Hmong language, 35, 56, 112, 113–18, 121, 135, 136
Houa, 100, 102, 126, 131, 132, 135

identity, 15, 33, 46, 50, 100, 111; altered, 61, 62, 63, 68, 83, 85; cultural, 63, 108; Faridah and, 87–89, 91; fluid, 147n14, 147n17; immigrant, 38, 76; L2, 7, 9, 131; languages of, 66, 84, 118, 121–22; literacy and, 8–11, 58, 66, 82, 83, 123; and literacy relays, 45, 49; literate, 8, 16, 89, 90, 92, 132; markers of, 13, 93, 148n23; multilingual, 4, 44, 53, 73, 145n11; national, 130, 146n13; transnational, 58, 63
immigrant, 43, 46, 49, 71, 148n2; and discrimination, 9, 125; and downward mobility, 29, 156n12; and English, 72, 80, 130; identity, 38, 76; life in America, 18, 19; and multilingualism, 20, 23, 39, 144n4
immigration, 21, 24, 82, 128, 146n13, 155n5; after, 29, 38, 41, 43, 49, 121; debates, 72, 139; and loss of credentials, 22, 105, 106, 110, 131; lottery, 86, 88; process, 3–4, 6, 132; reasons for, 34, 43, 86, 105, 112
India, 47–48, 126, 130, 136; Tashi and, 3, 41–43, 49, 50, 108–9
Indonesia, 71, 83, 97, 135
Indonesian language, 81, 97, 135
interpreting, 32, 62, 97, 98, 99; for family and friends, 42, 121; skills, 107, 121, 126; and translation services, 14, 105–6, 111. *See also* translation
interviews, 18, 19, 23, 24–25, 26, 29–30, 105, 149n7
Ishtar, 70, 77–78, 84, 95, 99, 135
Islamic school, 48, 51, 95

Japan, 34, 101, 135
Japanese language, 34, 135
Jewish, 38, 39, 47
Jin, 34–35, 95, 101, 129, 131, 135
Jordan, 49, 63, 130, 135
journal writing, 24, 74, 75, 79, 84, 132

Kannada language, 3, 41, 42, 108, 111, 136
Kashmiri, 70–71, 95, 136
Khadroma, 25, 102, 104–7, 135, 154n7, 155n4; and literacy relays, 32, 62, 129; and literate valuation, 109, 110, 111, 112, 119–20, 126, 131; and multilingualism, 64, 71, 97, 127; and Tibetan language, 47, 71, 83, 121
knowledge transfer, 68, 76, 154n6
Kunthi, 71, 83, 95, 97, 135

language teaching, 5, 51, 60, 126; ELL, 51, 52; ESL, 6, 38–39, 41, 54, 56, 102, 112–13, 130–31, 156n12; ESP, 131; TESOL, 51; TOEFL, 52, 103, 117
Laos, 112, 135
Latin America, 20, 22
literacy, 60, 66, 83, 133; academic, 110, 131, 155n4; and identities, 88–89, 90, 92, 132; relays, 33, 44–61, 92; scholars, 8, 27, 148; strategies, 52, 55, 58. *See also* new literacy studies
literacy practices, 7, 12, 22, 27, 32, 38–45, 69; Alicia and, 53, 75–76; Defne and, 79; Faridah and, 88; Haneen and, 49, 63; and interviews, 141, 149n7; and literacy relays, 44, 49–50; and mobility, 23, 25, 33, 61, 68, 89–90; multilingual, 38, 39, 133; Paj and, 112, 120; Sabohi and, 85; Tashi and, 42, 43, 108, 110; and valuation, 14, 92, 144n6; Yolanda, 54
literate repertoire, 33, 35, 64, 67, 85,

89–90, 93, 116; Alicia and, 34, 39, 40; Defne and, 38; devalued, 120, 121; explanation of the term, 6, 7; Faridah and, 86; fluid, 42, 44, 51, 61; Tashi and, 42, 108. *See also* literacy, relays
literate resources, 5–8, 89, 92, 97–101, 105–12, 127, 148n23; Defne and, 81; Khadroma and, 107–8; Nimet and, 98; Paj and, 114–15, 118; Tashi's, 109; valuation of, 10, 12–16, 93, 116, 124
literate valuation, 12–16, 61–64, 93, 118–19; definition of, 6, 148n21
loan words, 36, 61

Mandarin language, 105, 106–7, 108, 121, 135
memo writing, 28, 29, 142. *See also* writing
metalinguistic awareness, 127, 130–31
Middle East, 20, 86
migration studies, 11, 19, 22, 156n12
monolingualism, 5, 6, 36, 44; Alicia and, 74–75; and communication, 34, 58, 64, 119; English, 45, 50, 62, 95, 96, 125, 126, 144n6; myths of, 126, 130; Paj and, 116–17, 118; Russian, 66; and social pressures, 68, 71, 84, 133–34, 151n21; Spanish, 96; teachers, 111, 115, 117; and writing, 73–74, 132
multilingualism, 5–6, 20, 30, 34, 51, 94–95, 108, 118; as contradiction, 125–27; definition of, 143n2; Defne and, 79–83; and identity, 9, 53, 107; Khadroma and, 105, 107; and literacies, 50, 117, 122, 124–25, 126; messy, 44; and repertoires, 41, 51, 63–64, 91, 111; and resources, 97–99, 106, 121; scholars and, 145n8
Muslims, 49, 63, 86

new literacy studies, 27, 89, 150n10
newspapers, 42, 54, 84, 88, 105–6
NGOs. *See* nongovernmental organizations (NGOs)
Nimet, 25, 45, 59–61, 84, 98, 125, 126, 131, 135; in Azerbaijan, 34, 59–60, 64, 97; and dictionary, 36–37; and NGOs, 60, 64; and writing, 78–79, 103, 104
Nina, 69, 70, 129, 131, 136
nongovernmental organizations (NGOs), 59, 101, 105, 106, 151n19; Nimet and, 60, 64
nursing school, 104–5, 106, 109, 110, 117

Paj, 35, 73, 112–21, 125, 126, 127, 136; and family, 100, 104–5; schooling, 112–16; and writing, 102, 103
Pakistan, 36, 47–48, 70, 95, 136
Palestine, 35, 135
Portuguese language, 38, 45, 46, 80, 74, 77, 135

Quran, the, 49, 63

Raani, 95, 103, 129, 136
Renan, 25, 100, 136
Riya, 136
Rosalia, 74, 129, 131–32, 136
Russian language, 36, 69–70, 126, 135, 136; Sofia and, 35, 37, 66, 69, 102–3, 128

Sabohi, 25, 36, 47–48, 126, 129–30, 136, 152n3; and multilingualism, 62, 64, 76–77; in Pakistan, 36, 70–71, 95; and writing, 73, 84–85
sentences, 35, 30–40, 76, 84, 102–3, 115, 127, 130; building, 42, 79, 86; length of, 51, 52, 53, 57, 58, 77, 104
Shirin, 25, 70, 73, 76, 129, 136

Sofia, 29, 66, 68–69, 76, 83, 136; and Russian, 35, 37, 102–3, 128
Spanish language, 45–46, 51–58, 61, 63, 69, 71–75, 135, 136; Aldene and, 77; Alicia and, 34, 39–41, 51–52, 74–75, 132; and English, 9, 38, 39–40, 73; and identity, 83–84; Ishtar and, 78; Khadroma and, 106; and Mandarin or Tibetan, 108; Nimet and, 97–99; rare in interviews, 149n7; in school 95, 96; speakers, 56, 96, 153n14; Yolanda and, 53, 56, 57, 69, 98, 129
Syria and Syrians, 77–78, 123, 135

Tashi, 25, 101, 108–11, 113, 119–21, 129, 136, 154n7; and discrimination, 125–27, 131; and English writing, 3–4, 55, 64, 103, 132; in India, 3–4; and literate repertoire, 90, 99; and literate values, 100, 104, 105, 107; and multilingual messiness, 38, 41–44, 47–50, 99; and Tibetan, 41, 48–49, 50–51, 128
teaching hospitals, 119, 121
TESOL. *See* language teaching, TESOL
textbooks, 24, 62, 69, 96, 116, 129, 130; curricula and, 96, 155n9; language-teaching, 60, 97, 101
texting, 24, 61, 64, 69, 115
texts, 8, 32, 41, 52, 69, 85, 97, 112, 133; interaction with, 26, 42–43; and literacy, 6, 15, 24, 44; multilingualism in, 26, 127; and participants, 25, 149n8; segments of, 141
Tibet, 135, 136
Tibetan language, 3, 47–51, 71, 83, 105–11, 128, 135, 136; Khadroma and, 47, 71, 83, 105, 106–7, 121; refugees, 41–42, 108; Tashi and, 41, 48–49, 50–51, 128
TOEFL. *See* language teaching, TOEFL

translation, 6, 14, 20, 45; into English, 56, 98–99, 103; literary, 79, 86, 88, 126; and multilingualism, 34, 35, 36, 40; into Spanish, 57, 97–98, 129; services, 90, 100, 105–6, 107, 114. *See also* interpreting, and translation services
transnationalism, 146n13, 146n14, 147n15, 151n20; and feminist analysis, 28–31; and globalization, 11, 59; and identity, 58, 63, 83; and literacy studies, 6, 150n11, 151n21; and multilingualism, 66, 67
Turkey, 90, 100, 135, 136
Turkish language, 34, 37, 38, 47, 79–82, 135, 136; Defne and, 35, 62, 69

Ukraine, 35, 37, 66, 68, 129, 136
Ukrainian language, 37, 66, 69, 136
Urdu language, 36, 48, 70–71, 76, 136

Vietnam and Vietnamese, 9, 46
visas, 6, 14, 16, 82, 90, 125, 148n2; and immigration lottery, 86, 90; U.S. work, 23, 128, 143n1

writing, 24, 85, 100, 114, 115; academic, 80–81, 82, 103–4, 109, 119; activities, 43, 99, 130; assessment, 131–32, 156n9; assignments, 102, 111; blocked, 83–84; as contradiction, 132–34; instruction, 59, 102, 103, 116, 144n6; and literacy, 123–24; models of, 147n17; monolingual, 73–74, 132; strategies, 50, 51, 57; transfer, 76, 127. *See also* essay writing; memo writing
writing practices, 42, 52, 68, 73, 85, 96; in interview questions, 137, 139; in motion, 17, 76, 124; multilingualism and, 6, 9, 30, 86, 132; and social values, 88, 90–91, 96

Yolanda, 54–58, 90, 95, 98–100, 103, 128, 131–32, 136, 154n7; in Colombia, 32, 54, 56, 57, 129, 136; and interviews, 25; and literacy relays, 44–45, 51, 71; and multilingualism, 61, 63, 64, 69, 126, 127, 153n14; and Spanish, 63, 69, 83; and writing, 73–74, 75, 85, 96–97, 132; and writing English, 104, 124, 125